MONEY LAUNDERING REPORTING OFFICER'S HANDBOOK

A guide for solicitors

*Frank Maher and Sue Mawdsley
of Legal Risk*

LP

LEGALEASE
PUBLISHING

ISBN: 1-903927-44-7

Published by Legalease Publishing, Kensington Square House, 12-14 Ansdell Street, London W8 5BN

All rights reserved. No part of this book may be reproduced or transmitted in any form or by any means, electronic or mechanical, including photocopying, recording, or any information storage or retrieval system without prior permission from the publisher.

The publisher and authors are not responsible for the results of any actions (or lack thereof) taken on the basis of information in this book. Readers should obtain advice from a qualified professional when dealing with specific situations.

Crown copyright material is reproduced with the permission of the Controller of HMSO and the Queen's Printer for Scotland.

Extracts from Law Society publications are reproduced with the permission of the Law Society. This material is Copyright © The Law Society. All rights reserved.

Printed and bound in Great Britain by Latimer Trend, Plymouth.

© Legalease Ltd 2004 unless otherwise indicated.

www.legalease.co.uk

Preface

Jailed solicitors have already brought home to the profession that money laundering compliance is not optional.

Compliance is not about achieving a bare minimum standard. The largest fines in the financial services sector, running into millions of pounds, have been imposed on institutions which had not been involved in money laundering at all but which were unable to demonstrate that they had proper systems of control to prevent money laundering. This should serve as a warning to law firms.

The authors' objectives in this book are to help solicitors achieve higher standards of compliance. That way, if mistakes are made, they have far more chance of escaping with their liberty and their livelihood.

The legal profession is ten years behind the financial services industry in this field. The authors have therefore drawn on the experience of those in that sector to help identify how law firms can identify and achieve practical solutions which will work for their particular practices.

Real life issues, such as the professional indemnity implications which flow from notifications, are discussed in terms which will help practitioners know what they are supposed to do next. These are combined with practical tips to make everyday life easier, such as how to fill in the official forms on screen and save them without expensive software.

The authors are practising solicitors, each with over 20 years' experience 'at the coal face'. They advise other law firms, from the largest international practices to high street firms, on compliance systems and practical solutions to the problems which have to be managed when making a report – such as privilege issues and dealing with the client to whom they cannot explain the reason for the hold up for fear of tipping off.

The book's aims are to provide workable solutions in a risk-based framework while ensuring that compliance does not prevent solicitors from running their practices for profit.

Frank Maher, October 2004

About the Authors

Frank Maher is a practising solicitor and partner in Legal Risk. He has over 20 years' experience, gained in a national law firm, of acting for insurers and solicitors in the investigation of major fraud cases and other professional indemnity matters. In 2003 with Sue Mawdsley, he set up Legal Risk, a niche firm of solicitors, specialising in advising professional firms on risk management issues including money laundering compliance. The firm's clients include many top 100 UK law firms and other major professional practices.

Sue Mawdsley is also a practising solicitor with wide commercial litigation experience and a former licensed insolvency practitioner. She practised in major law firms before becoming a partner in Legal Risk. She advises a number of top firms on risk management issues, with a particular emphasis on money laundering compliance.

In 2003, Legal Risk was awarded the Law Society's *Gazette* Centenary Award for Excellence in Risk Management.

Contents

Preface	iii
Table of cases	x
Table of statutes	x
Table of statutory instruments	xii

1. Introduction — 1
1.1 The new legislation — 1
1.2 The role of the money laundering reporting officer — 1
1.3 Anti-money laundering in context — 2
1.4 The climate of change — 3

2. Definitions and the phases of money laundering — 7
2.1 What is money laundering? — 7
2.2 The size of the problem — 7
2.3 International definitions — 8
2.4 How is money laundered? — 9

3. The development of the UK anti-money laundering framework – backdrop to the current regime — 11
3.1 Introduction — 11
3.2 The UK's international role — 11
3.3 Financial Action Task Force and the 40 recommendations — 12
3.4 The European Directives — 13
3.5 Legislation — 14
3.6 Guidance — 14
3.7 Investigation and enforcement — 15
3.8 The future — 15

4. The legislation and regulatory framework — 17
4.1 The money laundering regime, 1993 to February 2003 — 17
4.2 The money laundering regime, 24 February 2003 to 29 February 2004 — 20
4.3 The current money laundering regime — 22
4.4 The substantive law — 24
4.5 Proceeds of Crime Act 2002 — 25
4.6 The penalties – Proceeds of Crime Act 2002, s334 — 28
4.7 Defences — 28
4.8 Knowledge — 32
4.9 'All crimes' — 32

5. Relevant business and the regulated sector	**35**
5.1 Definition	35
5.2 Legal services which involve participation in a financial transaction	33
6. Making a disclosure	**41**
6.1 The role of the National Criminal Intelligence Service	41
6.2 The Economic Crime Branch	42
6.3 The importance of disclosures	43
6.4 The money laundering reporting officer and disclosure	44
6.5 Proceeds of Crime Act 2002, s331 – reporting offence disclosures	45
6.6 Proceeds of Crime Act 2002, s331 – failure to disclose: nominated officers in the regulated sector	46
6.7 Proceeds of Crime Act 2002, s339 – form and manner of disclosure	47
6.8 The reporting forms	46
6.9 Completing the report	48
6.10 Sending a report to National Criminal Intelligence Service	49
7. What practical steps must the firm take? – a framework for regulatory compliance	**51**
7.1 The requirements of the Money Laundering Regulations 2003	51
7.2 Systems and procedures	51
7.3 The Law Society's 'Money Laundering Guidance (Pilot – January 2004)'	52
7.4 The Law Society's 'golden rules'	53
7.5 Some general considerations	53
7.6 A risk-based approach to money laundering compliance	53
7.7 Do you know your client?	54
7.8 New clients	56
7.9 The client engagement process	56
7.10 Record keeping	58
7.11 Internal reporting procedures	58
7.12 Training	58
7.13 Monitor for compliance	59
7.14 Annual report to partners	61
8. Client identification procedures	**63**
8.1 Money Laundering Regulations 2003, reg 4	63
8.2 The definition of 'new clients'	64
8.3 One-off transactions and the €15,000 limit	64
8.4 Agents and nominees	66
8.5 At what stage must identification evidence be obtained?	66
8.6 What evidence is required?	66
8.7 Documentary evidence of identification	67
8.8 Identification documents: individual clients	68
8.9 Exceptions: instructions and referrals from the regulated sector	75
8.10 Exceptions: transitional provisions for existing clients	77
8.11 Disadvantaged clients	78
8.12 Where personal attendance is not possible	78
8.13 Commercial providers of client identification	79

9. The money laundering reporting officer	**81**
9.1 Appointment of a nominated officer – the money laundering reporting officer	81
9.2 The choice of person	81
9.3 Sole practitioners	82
9.4 Large firms	82
9.5 Disclosures to the money laundering reporting officer	82
9.6 Framework for internal reporting	83
9.7 Data Protection Act 1998	85
10. Record-keeping procedures	**87**
10.1 Money Laundering Regulations 2003, reg 6	87
10.2 What records should be kept?	88
11. Training	**91**
11.1 The requirement	91
11.2 Relevant employees	92
11.3 The method of training	94
11.4 Proof of training	94
11.5 Systems	95
12. Should you be suspicious?	**97**
12.1 Guidance	97
12.2 Examples of areas of suspicion	98
12.3 Case studies	100
13. P v P and other cases	**107**
13.1 *P v P*	107
13.2 *C v S (Money Laundering: Discovery of Documents)*	111
13.3 *Governor and Company of the Bank of Scotland v A Ltd & ors*	113
13.4 *Tayeb v HSBC Bank Plc & anr*	115
14. Concerns for particular departments	**117**
14.1 Property	117
14.2 Matrimonial	118
14.3 Criminal work	119
14.4 Personal injury and other litigation	120
15. Privilege and confidentiality	**121**
15.1 Introduction	121
15.2 The rules of privilege	122
15.3 Protection for the solicitor who makes a disclosure	125
15.4 Protection for the solicitor who does not make a disclosure	126
15.5 Dangers to avoid in practice	128
15.6 Case study	130
16. International aspects	**137**
16.1 Relevance to domestic firms	137
16.2 Case study	137
16.3 Overseas clients	138
16.4 Instructions from foreign lawyers	139

16.5 Identification checks	139
16.6 Firms with overseas offices	142
16.7 United States of America: the PATRIOT Act	142
16.8 Corporate offences	143
16.9 419s	143
17. Changes in the firm's practice	**145**
18. Solicitors employed outside private practice	**147**
18.1 Application	147
18.2 The regulated sector	147
18.3 Guidance for solicitors whose employers are in the regulated sector	149
18.4 Solicitors whose organisations have a money laundering reporting officer	149
18.5 Confidentiality	149
19. Liability and professional indemnity	**151**
19.1 Key areas of potential liability	151
19.2 Constructive trusts	151
19.3 Negligence claims	154
19.4 Claims for the return of money by clients	155
19.5 Managing these risks	156
19.6 Limiting liability through terms of engagement	156
19.7 Insurance implications	161
20. Conclusion: a risk-based approach	**171**
20.1 Introduction	171
20.2 Assessing the risk	172
20.3 Systems and policies	173
20.4 Documentation	175
20.5 Do you apply the systems across all the practice?	177
20.6 Transactions	178
20.7 Disclosures	181
20.8 Training	181
20.9 Communication	181
20.10 The money laundering reporting officer	182
20.11 Enforcement	182
20.12 Auditing for compliance	183
20.13 Record keeping	184
20.14 The 'reasonable excuse' defence	184
20.15 Privilege	185
20.16 Involvement of insurers	186
20.17 Other reporting obligations	186
20.18 Decision-making	187
20.19 And finally…	188
Appendix 1: Proceeds of Crime Act 2002, Part 7 and Part 8, chapter 1	**189**
Appendix 2: The Money Laundering Regulations 2003	**198**
Appendix 3: Terrorism Act 2000, ss15-18 and 21A	**217**

Appendix 4: NCIS Source Registration Document	220
Appendix 5: NCIS Standard Report form	221
Appendix 6: NCIS Limited Intelligence Value Report form	227
Appendix 7: Guidance Notes for the NCIS Regulated Sector Disclosure Report, Proceeds of Crime Act 2002 & Terrorism Act 2000 – Standard Report	228
Appendix 8: Guidance Notes for the NCIS Regulated Sector Disclosure Report, Proceeds of Crime Act 2002 – Limited Intelligence Value Report	237
Appendix 9: NCIS guidance in relation to disclosures by the legal profession	244
Appendix 10: *P v P* – Law Society Guidance	246
Appendix 11: Law Society Green Card warning on property fraud	250
Appendix 12: Law Society Yellow Card – banking instrument fraud	252
Appendix 13: Law Society Money Laundering Warning Card	255
Appendix 14: The UK's Anti-Money Laundering Legislation and the Data Protection Act 1998 – Guidance Notes for the Financial Sector	258
Index	259

Table of Cases

A Ltd v Governor and Company of the Bank of Scotland [2002] 1 WLR 751 151
Bank of Credit & Commerce International (Overseas) Ltd & ors v Akindele
  [2000] 3 WLR 1423, [2000] 4 All ER 221 152
Bristol and West Building Society v Mothew [1997] 2 WLR 436, [1996] 4 All ER 698 152
C v S & ors [1999] 1 WLR 1551, [1999] 2 All ER 343 111
Finers v Miro [1991] 1 WLR 35, [1991] 1ALL ER 182 136
Governor and Company of the Bank of Scotland v A Ltd [2000] All ER (D) 864 153
Governor and Company of the Bank of Scotland v A Ltd [2001] EWCA Civ 52 113
Lillicrap v Nalder & Son [1993] 1 WLR 94, [1993] 1 All ER 724 167
Nationwide Building Society v Balmer Radmore & ors [1999] PNLR 606 23
Nationwide Building Society v Lewis & anr [1998] 2 WLR 915, [1998] 3 All ER 143 168
Nationwide Building Society v various solicitors [1999] PNLR 53 124
Norwich Pharmacal Co v Commissioners of Customs & Excise [1974] AC 133,
  [1973] 2 All ER 943 111
O'Rourke v Darbishire [1920] AC 581, [1920] All ER Rep 1 136
P v P [2003] EWCA Civ 2260 (Fam), [2003] WTLR 1449 .... 26, 37, 107, 108, 109, 110, 111,
                                                                118, 120, 128, 159, 161
Parry v News Group Newspapers Ltd (1990) 140 NLJ 1719 .... 125, 136
R v Central Criminal Court, ex parte Francis & Francis [1988] 3 WLR 989 122
R v Inner London Crown Court, ex parte Baines & Baines [1988] 1 QB 579 124
R v Manchester Crown Court, ex parte Rogers [1999] 1 WLR 832 125
R v Looseley [2001] 1 WLR 2060, [2001] UKHL 53 29
St Albans City & District Council v International Computers Ltd [1996] 4 All ER 481 157
South West Water Services Ltd v. International Computers Ltd [1999] BLR 420 157
Tayeb v HSBC Bank Plc & anr [2004] EWHC 1529 (Comm) 115, 153
Three Rivers District Council & ors v Governor and Company of the Bank of England
  [2004] EWCA Civ 218 .... 4, 123, 124, 135
Three Rivers District Council & ors v Governor and Company of the Bank of England
  (unreported, 29 July 2004) 4, 124, 133
Twinsectra Ltd v Yardley [2002] 2 AC 164, [2002] WTLR 423 153
Waugh v British Railways Board [1979] 3 WLR 150, [1980] AC 521 .... 124, 136

Table of Statutes

Anti-terrorism, Crime and Security Act 2001 c24. 24
Banking and Financial Dealings Act 1971 c80 29
Companies Act 1985 c6
  s151 131
  ss156-158 131-132
Criminal Justice Act 1988 c33. .... 13, 18
  s93D 112, 113
Criminal Justice Act 1993 .... 13, 18
Criminal Justice (International Co-operation) Act 1990 c5 18
Customs and Excise Management Act 1979 c2
  s167(3) 33
Data Protection Act 1988 c29 85
  s29 85
Drug Trafficking Act 1994 c37 115
  s55 18

Drug Trafficking Offences Act 1986 c32 11
Financial Services Act 1986 c60 19
Financial Services and Markets Act 2000 c8 76
Income and Corporation Taxes Act 1988 c1
  ss765-766 143
Limited Liability Partnerships Act 2000 c12
  s2(1)(a) 78
  s4(4) 78
Northern Ireland (Emergency Provisions) Act 1991 c24 18
Police and Criminal Evidence Act 1984 c60 123
  s10 122-124
  Sch 1 112
Prevention of Terrorism (Temporary Provisions) Act 1989 c4. 18
Proceeds of Crime Act 1995 c11. 18
Proceeds of Crime Act 2002 c29 . . . . 1, 2, 14, 15, 17, 20, 21, 22, 25, 29, 35, 43,
                                                        46, 83, 85, 93, 103, 110, 111, 113, 115, 118,
                                                        138-139, 144, 147, 149, 151, 153, 160, 173, 177
  Pt 7 . . . . 24, 26, 91
  ss327-329 . . . . 25, 43, 102, 117, 118, 133-134
  ss327-334 7
  ss327-340 . . . . 24, 30
  s327 . . . . 28, 32, 39, 43, 48, 125, 128, 129, 161
    (1) 25
    (2) 129
      (a) 43
      (b) 30
  s328 . . . . 28, 30, 32, 38, 48, 107, 108, 109, 111, 120, 125, 128, 161
    (1) 25
    (2)(a) 43
      (b) 30
  s329 . . . . 27, 28, 30, 31, 32, 48, 125, 128
    (1) 25
    (2)(a) 43
      (b) 30
      (c) 31
  ss330-332 25
  s330 . . . . 25, 30, 110, 126, 131, 149, 161
    (2) 32
    (4) 43, 84
    (6) 32, 126, 129, 135
    (10) 126-127
    (11) 127
  s331 . . . . 30, 39, 45, 83, 149
    (2) 32
    (4) 43
  s332 . . . . 26, 30, 39, 83
  s333 . . . . 26, 67, 108, 109, 118, 129, 158-159
    (1) 107, 159
    (2) 32
    (3) 159
  s334 28
  s336(7)-(8) 85
  s337 125
    (4) 125
    (5) 182
  s338 . . . . 28, 44, 125
  s340(2) 27, 31, 139
    (3) 27, 28, 31
    (4) 27
    (5) 27

(11)	7
Pt 8	24, 26
s342	24, 26, 108, 109, 118, 129, 158-159
(2)	107
(3)	32, 159
(4)	159
Solicitors Act 1974 c47	
s60(5)	58, 157-158
Terrorism Act 2000 c11	2, 22, 46, 147, 149
ss15-18	22, 24
s18	7, 91
s21A	24, 91
Unfair Contract Terms Act 1978 c50	58, 157

TABLE OF STATUTORY INSTRUMENTS

Money Laundering Regulations 1993 SI 1993/1933	13, 14, 18, 19
reg 4(1)	19
Sch	19
Money Laundering Regulations 2003 SI 2003/3075	1, 14, 17, 19, 21, 22, 26, 37, 51, 54, 65, 66, 78, 89, 91, 99, 110, 117, 118, 120, 172, 188
reg 2	7, 64, 147-148
(2)	2, 35
(a)-(c)	77
(a)-(e)	75, 76, 77
(f)-(n)	26, 77
(l)	24, 35, 118
(5)	66
(6)	66
reg 3	51, 52, 58, 65, 172, 175-176
(1)	51
(c)	31, 38, 91
(3)	23
(5)	23, 53
reg 4	63
(3)(c)	67
(d)	67
reg 5	75
(3)	76
reg 6	87
(2)	160
reg 7	44, 58, 83
(1)(a)	1, 81
(c)	44, 83
(d)	44
(6)	30, 127, 135
Pt III	149
Sch 1	148-149
Proceeds of Crime Act 2002 (Business in the Regulated Sector and Supervisory Authorities) Order 2003 SI 2003/3074	
reg 4	26

1. Introduction

1.1 The new legislation

The last 18 months have seen far-reaching changes in relation to UK law as it applies to money laundering and in particular how it affects the day-to-day work of the solicitors' practice. Practices conducting investment business under regulation by the Financial Services Authority (FSA) have had to implement effective anti-money laundering procedures for some time. Other practices have now been compelled to review and revise their anti-money laundering policies to comply with the requirements of the Proceeds of Crime Act 2002 (POCA 2002) and, for those in the regulated sector, the Money Laundering Regulations 2003[1] (MLR 2003). This process of change has not stopped with the implementation of the legislation.

The aim of this book is to draw together the relevant legislation and the small amount of case law that has so far arisen as they are likely to affect solicitors and to offer practical guidance to the 'nominated officer',[2] referred to in this book as the money laundering reporting officer (MLRO), within the legal practice upon how best to fulfil their role and steer the firm through to compliance with the legislation.

The use of the word 'practices' rather than 'firms' in the opening paragraph is deliberate – this book is also intended to help solicitors who are not in private practice but are working in commerce and industry, local government or are otherwise employed.

1.2 The role of the money laundering reporting officer

All firms in the regulated sector are required to appoint an MLRO. The only exceptions are sole practitioners who have no staff and who do not work in association with any other person.

---

1. SI 2003/3075.
2 MLR 2003, reg 7(1)(a).

1. Introduction

The book is aimed predominantly at practices that came into the regulated sector on 1 March 2004 due to the widening of the scope of 'relevant business'[3] under the MLR 2003.

On 24 February 2003, the POCA 2002 came into force consolidating and updating the various money laundering offences. The Terrorism Act 2000 (TA 2000) contains additional money laundering offences. The MLR 2003 became effective from 1 March 2004 in relation to the widening of the regulated sector for a number of professions, including relevant business conducted by the legal profession.

This legislation is already in force and the legal profession is now finding itself in the position of having to navigate its way through it in order to avoid potential criminal offences which can result in substantial fines and prison sentences.

The role of the MLRO has become a crucial one within a solicitors' practice, carrying with it serious responsibilities. All solicitors need to be alert to changes in the environment in which they practise and the regulations affecting it.

Legal practices which conduct business which is not in the regulated sector are relieved of many of the requirements for record-keeping, reporting and training but are nonetheless subject to the general law on money laundering. The provisions which affect them are also described in this book. Many practices whose business is not in the regulated sector are nonetheless taking steps to follow the requirements of the regulated sector to safeguard themselves against the risk of non-compliance with the general law.

1.3 Anti-money laundering in context

Much of what is required of practitioners falls within the general ambit of 'know your client'. Knowing the client's business or private affairs is largely good practice in understanding their needs, which form the basis of their request for legal advice.

Solicitors also need to be aware of changes affecting their clients. A recent example encountered by the authors involved a solicitor taking initial instructions from his company client. Three months later, he completed the transaction in accordance with those instructions. Some months after that, it became apparent that during those first three months, the client

---

3 MLR 2003, reg 2(2).

1. Introduction

company's group had undergone restructuring and name changes. The name of the client company had been allocated to a completely different company within the group and the client company now had a completely different name. This had devastating and costly implications on the matter in question as the solicitor had implemented the instructions on behalf of the wrong company. A check on the company number, easily undertaken on the Companies House website,[4] and an ongoing awareness and knowledge of the client would both have prevented this happening.

Although the case had no money laundering implications, it underlines the need to be constantly updating knowledge of the client's affairs.

1.4 The climate of change

The profession is undergoing many changes. Examples include incorporation, in most cases as limited liability partnerships (LLPs) and the possibility of requiring authorisation by the FSA.

Many firms are considering converting to LLP status and will need to consider whether they need to recheck identity. This issue is discussed at **8.10**.

The legal profession is becoming more mobile: increasingly, partners will move on to join a rival practice, taking their clients with them. The new practice will now need to be satisfied that its engagement of the new clients introduced with the new partner complies with its own procedures.

More may soon find themselves regulated by the FSA due to the impending regulation of insurance mediation activities from 14 January 2005. As well as introducing further regulation to the practice as a whole, this may also add to the requirements for money laundering compliance with additional regulation. The additional requirements for firms regulated by the FSA are outside the scope of this work at present.

Solicitors need to be alert to change in the field of fraud which outsiders may try to visit on their practice. The Fraud Advisory Panel, along with the National Criminal Intelligence Service (NCIS) and others, has drawn attention to the increase in identity theft.[5] Its report, 'Identity Theft: Do you know the signs?' highlights some alarming examples, with even high

---

4 www.companies-house.gov.uk/info.
5 See www.fraudadvisorypanel.org/pdf/Identity Theft Final Proof 11-7-03.pdf.

street banks noted as victims of bogus or copycat websites which have been set up as part of a fraud by organised West African criminal gangs.

Increasingly firms are finding that others are carrying out checks on them, perhaps as they change banks or accountants and instruct other advisers. They may also be subject to checks for compliance overseas, for example when setting up their own captive insurer.

Increased numbers of people working abroad mean that even the smallest high street practice can find itself with overseas clients and the increased obligations in satisfying itself as to client identity.

Entering new markets, for example bulk remortgage work or personal injury, could expose the firm to increased risk, or at least changes in risk, which in turn will make it necessary to implement new procedures and more training.

The areas of practice regulated by the legislation are constantly evolving and firms will therefore need to involve their MLRO in all the changes which take place. The law is also changing in other related areas and this can in turn impact on money laundering compliance. A prime example of this was the erosion of legal professional privilege by the decision of the Court of Appeal in *Three Rivers District Council & ors v Governor and Company of the Bank of England*.[6] Although an appeal to the House of Lords resulted in that decision being overturned,[7] the judgments were still awaited at the time of going to press and the full impact of the appeal cannot yet be assessed. Whatever the basis of the decision, however, the message is that the money laundering legislation cannot be viewed in a vacuum.

There are therefore numerous case studies – all bar one are based on real cases in which one of the writers has been involved on behalf of insurers, but some details have been changed to protect identities.

References in this book to the Law Society are to the Law Society of England and Wales. References to the LS Guidance are to the guidance published under the title 'Money Laundering Guidance (Pilot – January 2004)', copies of which were sent to all firms and which is available on the Internet.[8] The Law Societies of Scotland and Northern Ireland have each issued their own guidance for solicitors qualified and practising in those jurisdictions.

---

6 [2004] EWCA Civ 218.
7 Unreported, 29 July 2004, HL.
8 See www.lawsociety.org.uk/professional/conduct/guideonline/view=page.law?POLICYID=161546.

Understanding of the legislation is also developing at a rapid pace as lawyers begin to understand its ramifications.

This book endeavours to set out, in a practical format, the authors' understanding of the law in practice as at 7 October 2004. Readers should however note that this is an area of law undergoing constant change and must ensure that they keep abreast of any developments by taking account of guidance from the Law Society, the NCIS and any reported cases.

2. Definitions and the phases of money laundering

2.1 What is money laundering?

2.1.1 General

Money laundering is the process by which the proceeds of crime are converted into assets which appear to have a legitimate origin, so that they can be retained permanently or recycled into further criminal enterprises. As will be seen, the definition now covers the proceeds of all crime and not just drug trafficking and terrorism.

2.1.2 The legislative definition

Regulation 2 of the Money Laundering Regulations 2003 defines money laundering as an act which falls within s340(11) of the Proceeds of Crime Act 2002 (POCA 2002), ie committing one of the offences under ss327-334 of that Act, or an offence under s18 of the Terrorism Act 2000.

Money laundering is the washing of dirty money and changing it into apparently clean money. A person deriving money from criminal activity typically ends up with large sums of potentially traceable moneys. In order to use that money with less fear of detection, perhaps to further a lavish lifestyle or to purchase further supplies of drugs or pay off accomplices, it is of great assistance to the criminal to be able to disguise its true origins. The criminal can do this by putting the money through the clean financial systems once, twice or a number of times in order to cloud the audit trail so that, if anybody investigates, it is far harder to detect and identify it as the proceeds of criminal conduct. In other words, cash from crime is fed into the financial system to disguise the audit trail, giving criminal proceeds the appearance of normality.

2.2 The size of the problem

2.2.1 National Criminal Intelligence Service assessment

The National Criminal Intelligence Service (NCIS) is the United Kingdom agency charged with analysing and collating the intelligence available on

2. Definitions and the phases of money laundering

money laundering. NCIS has published a report entitled the 'United Kingdom Threat Assessment of Serious and Organised Crime 2003'.[1] This provides information not only on the most favoured methods employed by money launderers but also some information on the estimated size of the problem.[2] It states:

> 6.5 The overall size of criminal proceeds in the UK is not known, nor is the amount that is laundered. However, HM Customs and Excise recently estimated the annual proceeds from crime in the UK at anywhere between £19 billion and £48 billion, with £25 billion possibly being a realistic figure for the amount actually laundered. Based on the January 2000 International Monetary Fund estimate of undeclared economic activity in the UK representing around 13 percent of Gross Domestic Product, £25 billion would equate to roughly one fifth of all undeclared economic activity.

The size of the industry in the UK alone is therefore enormous, but the problem is on a global scale and is mind-numbingly large. The NCIS report, using the example of cash being taken out of the UK, provides a further indication of scale:[3]

> 6.4 … The total amount of criminal cash seized en route out of the UK has risen year on year since 2001. However, additional provisions aimed at tackling the flow were introduced in the Proceeds of Crime Act 2002. By May 2003, approximately £21 million cash had been seized, some 80 percent of which could be attributed to the new PoCA provisions.

2.3 International definitions

The potential effect of such a massive industry was internationally recognised some years ago:

> In response to mounting concern over money laundering, the Financial Action Task Force on money laundering (FATF) was established by the G-7 summit in Paris in 1989 to develop a co-ordinated international response…
>
> Members of the FATF include [29] countries and jurisdictions – including the major financial centre countries of Europe, North and South America and Asia – as well as the European Commission and the Gulf Co-operation Council.
>
> The FATF works closely with other international bodies involved in combating money laundering. While its secretariat is housed by the OECD, the FATF is not part of the Organisation. However, where the efforts of the OECD and FATF complement each other, such as on bribery and corruption or the functioning of the international financial system, the two secretariats consult with each other and exchange information.[4]

The FATF maintains a list of non-co-operating countries which it updates from time to time.

The FATF's website describes money laundering in the following terms:

---

1 See www.ncis.co.uk/ukta.asp.
2 See ch 6 of the NCIS report, entitled 'Money Laundering'.
3 *Ibid*.
4 *OECD Policy Brief*, July 1999. Copyright © FATF.

The goal of a large number of criminal acts is to generate a profit for the individual or group that carries out the act. Money laundering is the processing of these criminal proceeds to disguise their illegal origin. This process is of critical importance, as it enables the criminal to enjoy these profits without jeopardising their source.

Illegal arms sales, smuggling, and the activities of organised crime, including for example drug trafficking and prostitution rings, can generate huge sums. Embezzlement, insider trading, bribery and computer fraud schemes can also produce large profits and create the incentive to 'legitimise' the ill-gotten gains through money laundering.

When a criminal activity generates substantial profits, the individual or group involved must find a way to control the funds without attracting attention to the underlying activity or the persons involved. Criminals do this by disguising the sources, changing the form, or moving the funds to a place where they are less likely to attract attention.[5]

2.4 How is money laundered?

2.4.1 The phases of money laundering

In summary, the aims of the money launderer are to:

1. Place money derived from criminal activity into the financial system, without arousing suspicion. This is known as placement.

2. Move the money around, often in a series of complex transactions crossing multiple jurisdictions, so it becomes difficult to identify its original source – in other words, separating criminal proceeds from their source. This is known as layering.

3. Move the money back into the financial and business system, so that it appears as legitimate funds or assets. This is known as integration.

Figure 1 illustrates the process.

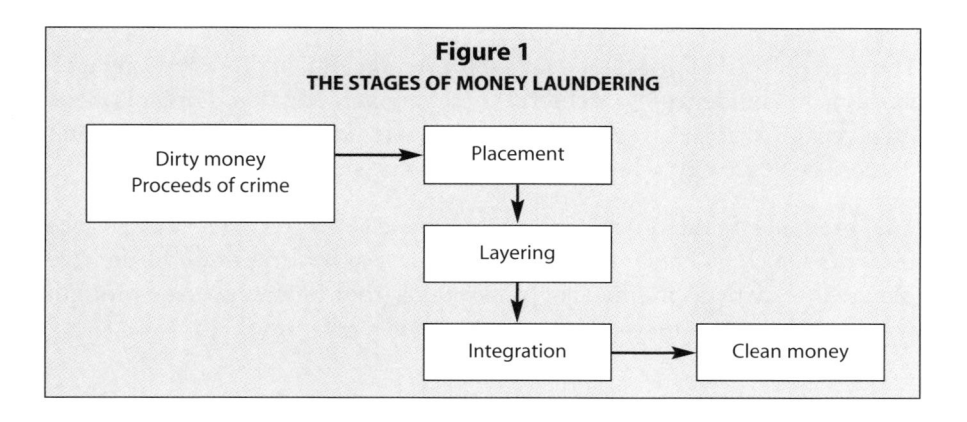

Figure 1
THE STAGES OF MONEY LAUNDERING

Dirty money / Proceeds of crime → Placement → Layering → Integration → Clean money

---

[5] See www1.oecd.org/fatf. Extract Copyright © FATF.

2.4.2 Examples

Placement

This could be delivering cash to a solicitor's office to fund the completion of a property purchase, paying in cash directly to the solicitor's client account over the counter at their bank in readiness for a purchase. The proceeds of crime could be mixed with moneys from a legitimate source, for example a cash business such as a car park, taxi service, hairdresser or licensed premises.

Layering

This could involve any amount of transactions conducted once the proceeds of crime are in the financial system. It is likely to be more difficult for a solicitor assisting with such transactions to detect that criminal proceeds are involved, but suspicions may be aroused if, for example, the transaction has a lack of economic purpose.

Integration

Again, this could be potentially difficult for a solicitor to spot, but it could involve any type of transaction, from purchasing a property or business to the setting up of a trust for the benefit of the money launderer or their family.

The Law Society's 'Money Laundering Guidance (Pilot – January 2004)' at para 1.13 gives an idea of how a solicitor may be used in each of these phases.

2.4.3 Aim of the legislation

The current legislation is aimed at making it more difficult for those engaged in money laundering to achieve these aims by making organisations involved in financial transactions gatekeepers, with duties to report and disclose such activity, where it is or ought to be suspected.

The previous regulations applied to financial institutions and service providers such as banks and building societies. Bearing in mind the role played by law firms in financial transactions, they have now been brought within this same framework of detection and prevention.

3. The development of the UK anti-money laundering framework – backdrop to the current regime

3.1 Introduction

The United Kingdom has a comprehensive and highly developed anti-money laundering framework which has been evolving for more than 15 years. This development has taken place in line with the UK's pro-active position in international affairs and against the backdrop of its position as part of the European Union.

This sophisticated system encompasses primary and secondary legislation, which in itself has been updated and amended in line with EU Directives, together with supervisory and regulatory bodies and guidance and advice from trade associations. Voluntary principles and best practice guides have also evolved and been adopted.

Ongoing participation in assessment and evaluation of the framework enhances its effectiveness still further. (See **Figure 2** on p12.)

3.2 The UK's international role

The UK has always played a pro-active role in addressing money laundering. As a leading global financial centre, its reputation and integrity have been regarded as paramount and strenuous efforts have been made to maintain that reputation. The Drug Trafficking Offences Act 1986 was implemented before more international action was taken, with the UK leading the way.

The late 1980s saw the advent of an international initiative to address the problem of drug trafficking. A 1988 United Nations Convention meeting in Vienna led to the signing of the Vienna Convention. G7 and EU countries agreed to join together to combat the laundering of the proceeds of drug trafficking. The measures included the criminalisation of money laundering and enhanced international cooperation, together with the commitment by participating countries to procure that the laws of their jurisdictions should be amended. A definition of money laundering, based

3. The development of the UK anti-money laundering framework

on drug trafficking, was provided and most subsequent legislation has been based on it.

To oversee the implementation of these principles, the Financial Action Task Force (FATF) was established by the G7 summit in Paris where it is based, as mentioned at **2.3**.

3.3 Financial Action Task Force and the 40 recommendations

The FATF developed 40 recommendations setting out the measures governments should take to implement effective anti-money laundering programmes and upon which our legislation is based. They were updated in 2003.[1]

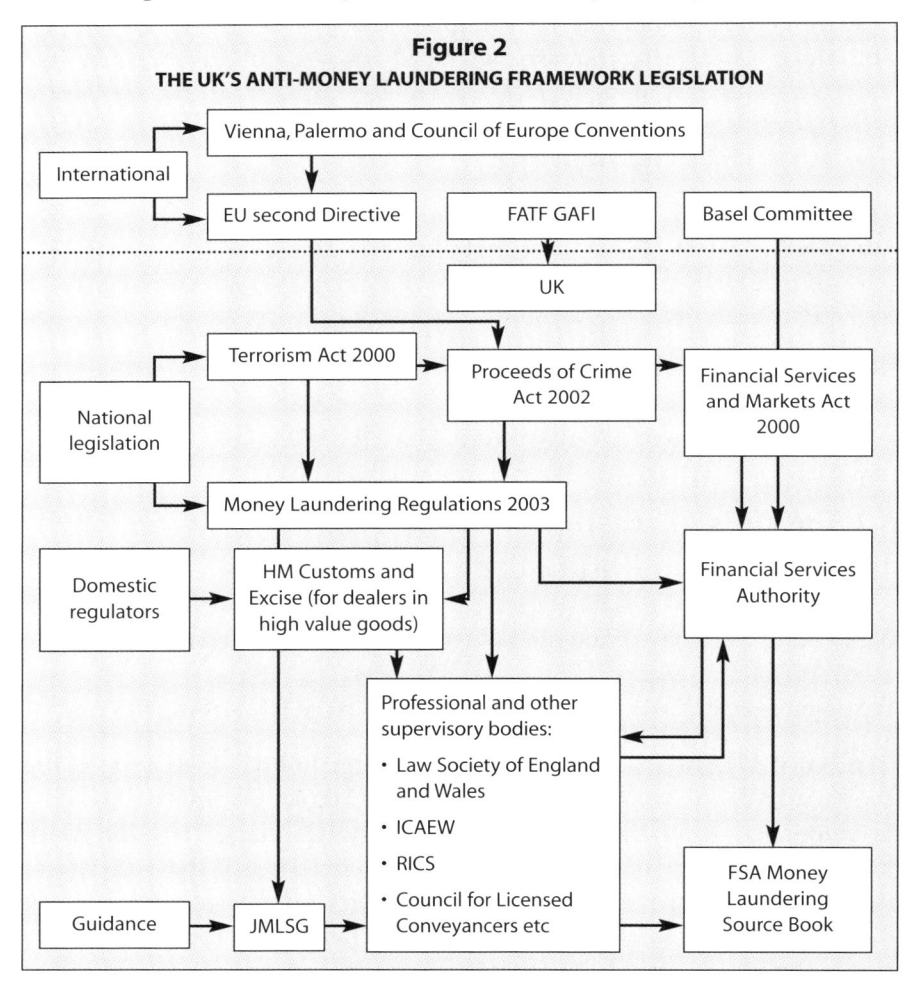

Figure 2
THE UK'S ANTI-MONEY LAUNDERING FRAMEWORK LEGISLATION

International
- Vienna, Palermo and Council of Europe Conventions
- EU second Directive
- FATF GAFI
- Basel Committee
- UK

National legislation
- Terrorism Act 2000
- Proceeds of Crime Act 2002
- Financial Services and Markets Act 2000
- Money Laundering Regulations 2003

Domestic regulators
- HM Customs and Excise (for dealers in high value goods)
- Financial Services Authority
- Professional and other supervisory bodies:
  - Law Society of England and Wales
  - ICAEW
  - RICS
  - Council for Licensed Conveyancers etc

Guidance
- JMLSG
- FSA Money Laundering Source Book

---

[1] See www1.oecd.org/fatf/pdf/40Recs-2003_en.pdf for the full text.

Essentially, FATF member countries monitor and evaluate compliance by each other with the recommendations. Membership can be suspended in the event of failure to rectify breaches.

3.4 The European Directives

The European Parliament and Council adopted a first money laundering Directive[2] in 1991. This resulted in changes to the UK law through the Criminal Justice Act 1993 and the Money Laundering Regulations 1993 (MLR 1993).[3] The Directive was designed to give legal force in the EC to the FATF's 40 recommendations.

The Directive was confined to drug trafficking, although member states were encouraged to extend the scope to other serious crimes.

In July 1998, the European Commission noted that although implementation was generally satisfactory, the long-term and evolving nature of the threat from money laundering meant that the legislation needed to be updated and its coverage extended. A consultation period then followed.

The second Directive[4] was enacted in December 2001 and the principal features were that the scope of businesses brought within the money laundering framework and the scope of crime covered were widely expanded.

Although several European countries have yet to comply with the second Directive,[5] a third Directive is currently under discussion.[6] The European Commission was required by Article 2 of the second Directive to propose a new Directive before 15 December 2004. A draft proposal for a third Directive was issued on 22 March 2004, and the Commission issued the formal proposal on 30 June 2004 with some changes. The draft contains a new definition of 'serious offences' but, as UK legislation applies to the proceeds of all crime, not just serious crime, it will not have any significant impact in the UK, as in most areas UK law already complies. There are increased requirements on customer due diligence in Article 7 but they are largely covered by current good practice requirements, at least in the financial sector.

---

2 Directive 91/308/EEC of 10 June 1991.
3 SI 1993/1933.
4 Directive 2001/97/EC of 4 December 2001.
5 In February 2003 the European Commission sent formal requests to Italy, Portugal, Greece, Sweden, Luxembourg and France to implement the Second Directive. Italy, Portugal and France have now complied.
6 See europa.eu.int/comm/internal_market/en/company/financialcrime/docs/com-2004-448_en.pdf.

3.5 Legislation

By December 2001, the scene was therefore set for UK legislation to be updated in line with the second Directive's requirements. The FATF's 40 recommendations had been updated. In the UK, the Financial Services Authority (FSA) had developed the 'FSA Handbook of rules and guidance' (FSA Handbook) applicable to all FSA-regulated businesses.[7]

In terms of primary legislation, the Terrorism Act 2000 was already in place. With the passing of the Proceeds of Crime Act 2002 (POCA 2002) the scope of money laundering offences which could be committed was widened to reflect the EU Directive and the FATF recommendations, and in some instances, went further, for example the 'all crimes' definition, rather than all serious crimes.

This legislation is backed up by the secondary legislation, the Money Laundering Regulations 2003 (MLR 2003) and the FSA Handbook,[8] with which FSA-regulated businesses are statutorily obliged to comply.

3.6 Guidance

The MLR 2003 have widened the scope of the regulated sector. The various supervisory authorities and trade associations have provided guidance upon their interpretation of the legislation as it affects organisations within their own sector.

The businesses already within the sector prior to the MLR 2003 were already required to follow the FSA Handbook, which has regulatory status. In addition, members of those sectors had formed the Joint Money Laundering Steering Group (JMLSG). The JMLSG had provided 'Prevention of Money Laundering Guidance Notes for the UK Financial Sector' (JMLSG Guidance Notes) for businesses in the financial sector and regulated by the FSA. The MLR 1993, and subsequently the MLR 2003 provide that in determining whether the regulations have been complied with, a court may take account of any relevant guidance issued or approved by a supervisory or regulatory body and must take account of it where Treasury approval has been given. In the absence of guidance issued by the regulators, relevant guidance may be provided by a trade association or other representative body.

---

7 See www.fsa.gov.uk/handbook.
8 See www.fsa.gov.uk/vhb/html/ml/mltoc.html.

The FSA did not issue regulatory guidance in support of the regulations. The JMLSG Guidance Notes were intended for this purpose, being within the category of those issued by a trade association or representative body. The JMLSG Guidance Notes were approved by the Treasury.

Of those businesses new to the regulated sector, their supervisory bodies (who are designated by the FSA) have each provided guidance, in pilot or interim form. As yet, none has been approved by the Treasury. The Law Society's 'Money Laundering Guidance (Pilot – January 2004)' (LS Guidance) refers to the JMLSG Guidance Notes as being 'helpful to consult' if the LS Guidance is silent on a matter.[9]

3.7 Investigation and enforcement

The implementation of such a far-reaching system requires a suitable body to collate and evaluate intelligence provided by the various organisations making reports. The National Criminal Intelligence Service (NCIS) fulfils this role. NCIS was set up by the government to 'provide leadership and excellence in criminal intelligence to combat serious and organised crime'.

NCIS's Economic Crime Branch analyses suspicious transaction reports and sends approximately a fifth of those received out for further investigation. Such investigation is undertaken by the appropriate law enforcement bodies, such as HM Customs and Excise, the Inland Revenue, and the various police forces. NCIS publishes a 'United Kingdom Threat Assessment of Serious and Organised Crime', providing figures, methods and example typologies.

3.8 The future

The UK now has an effective international mechanism for ongoing review and evaluation of its anti-money laundering structure. The definition of crime for the purposes of the principal money laundering offences could hardly be wider. Procedures of control to forestall and prevent money laundering, including the training of all relevant employees in recognition of money laundering, are now required in not only all financial services businesses, but also many professional practices. Intelligence from this vast array of businesses is collated centrally at NCIS. Funding for NCIS appears to be increasing, in fact some of the laundered assets seized under the POCA 2002

---

[9] LS Guidance, para 1.16.

3. The development of the UK anti-money laundering framework

have been deployed for the purpose. Trade and professional bodies are investing in guidance to assist their members. All these factors mean that the UK anti-money laundering framework is developed, virtually all-embracing and increasingly effective.

4. THE LEGISLATION AND REGULATORY FRAMEWORK

4.1 The money laundering regime, 1993 to February 2003

4.1.1 Introduction

For many law firms, the advent of the Proceeds of Crime Act 2002 (POCA 2002) and the Money Laundering Regulations 2003 (MLR 2003) have had a dramatic impact on their anti-money laundering strategy. Nevertheless, it should be remembered that regulations and guidance from the Law Society on the subject have been in place since 1993. It is helpful to be aware of the main areas of that legislation and guidance and to know how to access it should the need arise.

4.1.2 Investigations

Frequently, by their very nature, the investigation of money laundering offences relates to transactions which have already taken place and involve following the audit trail to identify what has been paid to whom and from whom. Such investigations by the various law enforcement bodies can in some instances relate back to matters handled a number of years ago.

For example, if requested by the police to produce a file from, say, five years ago, concerning a matter now under investigation, the money laundering reporting officer (MLRO) will want a clear idea of the duties and obligations which existed at the relevant time.

4.1.3 Keeping a record of the legislation and guidance

In fact, in this developing area, it is useful for an MLRO to retain physical copies of any past and current money laundering legislation and guidance with changes that are made to it duly dated as a historical record. That way, if an enquiry is ever made into a potential money laundering situation, the appropriate legislation and guidance will be easily identified.

4. The legislation and regulatory framework

4.1.4 The legislation

The previous legislation, implementing Directive 91/308/EEC was focused on the proceeds of crimes deriving from drug trafficking and terrorist funding offences. This was later widened to include all serious crime.

The law relating to money laundering in England and Wales was contained in several different statutes:

1. Criminal Justice Act 1988;
2. Prevention of Terrorism (Temporary Provisions) Act 1989;
3. Criminal Justice (International Co-operation) Act 1990;
4. Northern Ireland (Emergency Provisions) Act 1991;
5. Criminal Justice Act 1993 (amending parts of a number of these Acts);
6. Drug Trafficking Act 1994; and
7. Proceeds of Crime Act 1995 (amending the Criminal Justice Act 1988).

The principal money laundering offences applied to all firms. Further provisions, applying only to firms carrying on investment business, were contained in the Money Laundering Regulations 1993[1] (MLR 1993).

The offences were summarised in the Law Society's 'Money Laundering Legislation: Guidance for Solicitors'[2] (the 1993 Guidance). In outline, the principal offences were as follows:

1. *Assistance* – it was an offence for any person to provide assistance to a money launderer to retain the benefit of funds if that person knew or suspected or, in the case of terrorist activities, should have known or suspected, that those funds were the proceeds of drug trafficking, terrorism or serious criminal conduct. The offence was punishable on conviction by up to 14 years' imprisonment and/or a fine.

2. *Tipping off* – this offence related to anyone prejudicing an investigation by informing the person who was the subject of a suspicion, or any third party, that a disclosure had been made either internally, or externally to the relevant authorities, or that the authorities were acting or proposing to act in connection with an investigation into money laundering. The offence was punishable on conviction by up to five years' imprisonment and/or a fine.

---

1 SI 1993/1933.
2 2nd ed, 1999, p5.

3. *Failure to report* – this related to drug trafficking and terrorist offences. It was an offence for any person who acquired knowledge or suspicion of money laundering in the course of a trade, profession, business or employment not to report the knowledge or suspicion of money laundering as soon as reasonably practicable after the information came to their attention.

4.1.5 Regulations

The MLR 1993 applied to solicitors conducting investment business. The Schedule to the MLR 1993 set out the type of work which fell within the provisions.[3] The MLR 1993 were the forerunner to the current MLR 2003 and introduced a regulatory framework requiring client identification procedures, record keeping, training and reporting for organisations conducting investment business and subsequently regulated by the Financial Services Authority (FSA). This included banks, building societies and solicitors who engaged in investment business within the meaning of the Financial Services Act 1986.

4.1.6 The Law Society's 1993 Guidance

The 1993 Guidance was provided by the Law Society following the implementation of the MLR 1993. A second edition was distributed in December 1999, following the revision of the Joint Money Laundering Steering Group's (JMLSG) Guidance Notes in April 1999.[4]

Although the MLR 1993 only applied to solicitors conducting investment business, the 1993 Guidance was relevant to those outside the then regulated sector, as all firms were subject to the provisions created by the substantive law.

In addition, the Law Society issued warning cards on property fraud (the 'Green Card') in March 1991, reissued in updated form in July 2002, and on banking instrument fraud in September 1997, revised in July 2001.

4.1.7 The money laundering reporting officer

Annex G to the 1993 Guidance confirmed that it was then mandatory only for solicitors conducting investment business to appoint an MLRO, this being a regulatory requirement of the MLR 1993. Firms were generally

---

[3] MLR 1993, Sch and reg 4(1).
[4] 2nd ed, 1999.

4. The legislation and regulatory framework

encouraged to appoint an MLRO however, as all firms, regardless of whether or not they conducted investment business, could be caught by the assistance offences.

4.1.8 Powers of investigation and orders for production

At some point, the MLRO in any law firm could be asked to produce a file in connection with a money laundering investigation. Where the matter was conducted prior to the existing legislation, MLROs should refer to the relevant substantive law applicable at the time, such as the Drug Trafficking Act 1994, s55 for the powers of investigation into money laundering offences relating to drug trafficking proceeds.[5]

The 1993 Guidance explains[6] the relevant procedure regarding the order for production of a file or papers. Solicitors, bound as they are by the laws governing their retainer, had, and still do have, to exercise caution in abiding by their professional obligations to maintain confidentiality. The 1993 Guidance referred to three important exceptions to these professional obligations:

1. where they have the client's consent;
2. where compelled by a court order; or
3. where there is strong *prima facie* evidence that they are or were being used by the client for a fraudulent or criminal purpose.

Where an appropriate order is granted, it will normally relate to non-privileged material and its terms should be complied with as the duty of confidentiality is then overridden.

Reference should first be made under such circumstances to the specific terms and breadth of the order, the 1993 Guidance and if appropriate, specialist legal advice should be sought. Issues of privilege and confidentiality are discussed in **Chapter 15**.

4.2 The money laundering regime, 24 February 2003 to 29 February 2004

4.2.1 The Proceeds of Crime Act 2002

The POCA 2002[7] received Royal Assent on 24 July 2002 and came into force on 24 February 2003.

---

5 See www.hmso.gov.uk/acts/acts1994/Ukpga_19940037_en_5.htm#mdiv55.
6 See Section D, at p13.
7 See www.legislation.hmso.gov.uk/acts/acts2002/20020029.htm.

It consolidated, updated, expanded and reformed the criminal law in the UK with regard to money laundering not only by updating the principal money laundering offences but also by creating and widening the scope of reporting offences, resulting in potential custodial sentences and fines for those working in the 'regulated sector'. During this period, the scope of the regulated sector remained as defined by the 1993 Guidance. The scope of relevant business was not widened to include other legal services until 1 March 2004.

The POCA 2002 vastly broadened the scope of money laundering offences by adopting an 'all crimes' framework (see **4.5.5**). Apart from those firms regulated by the FSA, solicitors remained outside the regulated sector and so only needed to be aware of the changes in the offences under the POCA 2002. However, the MLR 2003 became available in draft on 15 November 2003, and firms knew that within a short timeframe they would be brought within the regulated sector and needed to prepare for compliance. The provisions of the POCA 2002 are examined in greater detail at **4.4.1**.

4.2.2 Law Society Guidance

The 1993 Guidance was still current, supplemented by two letters containing guidance from the chief executive of the Law Society, in February and September 2002 as well as the Law Society's 'Money Laundering Warning Card' produced in September 2002, all of which were circulated to solicitors warning of the implications of the POCA 2002 and the forthcoming regulations. The warning cards on property fraud and bank instrument fraud referred to in **4.1.6** above continued to apply.

4.2.3 The position of the legal profession

As a profession handling financial and real property transactions on a daily basis, the low number of suspicious transactions reported was criticised by the Home Office. Considering that two of the most prevalent means of laundering money are thought to be the purchase of property and the use of trusts, both of which usually involve the services of the legal profession, the number of reports as a percentage of the whole appeared to be very low.

This is illustrated by a number of quotes appearing in the legal press during that period:

> The number of suspicious transactions [notified by] the legal profession is very low indeed. It simply cannot be a reflection of the genuine occasions that exist. We do expect to see that there will be a substantial increase in suspicious transaction reports from the legal profession. (Bob Ainsworth, Home Office Minister)[8]

---

8 Law Society *Gazette*, 13 March 2003, p1.

4. The legislation and regulatory framework

> Lawyers need to be more 'hard-nosed' ... reporting suspicious transactions is not inconsistent with the lawyer's ethics – 'in such cases, the greater duty is to Society'. (Lord Goldsmith QC, Attorney-General)[9]

4.3 The current money laundering regime

4.3.1 *The relevant legislation*

The substantive law on money laundering offences can now be found in the POCA 2002 and the Terrorism Act 2000[10] (TA 2000). The TA 2000, ss15-18, create offences relating to terrorist fundraising, using moneys for terrorist purposes and involvement in arrangements which facilitate money being made available for purposes of terrorism, of which solicitors' practices need to be aware.

4.3.2 *The Regulations*

The MLR 2003[11] were published at the end of 2003 and came into force in relation to a wide number of additional areas of business on 1 March 2004. These extended the scope of the regulated sector by widening the definition of 'relevant business' – they apply to the work of most solicitors' practices, accountancy firms, estate agents and auctioneers in England and Wales.

What this means for practices is that whereas before, regulation related only to financial crime linked to drug trafficking or terrorism, the duty of disclosure now applies to money laundering relating to all crime. It also means that firms must have in place systems of internal control and communication to forestall and prevent their practices being used for money laundering. This involves putting in place training for all relevant staff, identification procedures for clients, record keeping and internal reporting procedures and reporting money laundering activity, to ensure compliance with the regulations.

4.3.3 *Guidance from the Law Society*

The Law Society had warned the profession to prepare for these changes for a considerable period preceding the advent of the MLR 2003, but in the absence of the final version was unable to produce anything more than outline guidance on the form that such preparation should take. Detailed guidance ('Money Laundering Guidance (Pilot –

---

[9] Law Society *Gazette*, 25 September 2003, p1.
[10] See www.hmso.gov.uk/acts/acts2000/20000011.htm.
[11] See www.legislation.hmso.gov.uk/si/si2003/20033075.htm.

4. The legislation and regulatory framework

January 2004) (LS Guidance)) was produced in January 2004 in pilot form. It is available on the Law Society's website[12] or directly from them.[13]

The importance of following the LS Guidance when implementing procedures within a firm cannot be overstated. Regulation 3(3) and (5) of the MLR 2003 indicate what a court must consider when considering whether an organisation has complied with its regulatory obligations or not:

(3) In deciding whether a person has committed an offence under this regulation, the court must consider whether he followed any relevant guidance which was at the time concerned –

   (a) issued by a supervisory authority or any other appropriate body;

   (b) approved by the Treasury; and

   (c) published in a manner approved by the Treasury as appropriate in their opinion to bring the guidance to the attention of persons likely to be affected by it...

(5) In proceedings against any person for an offence under this regulation, it is a defence for that person to show that he took all reasonable steps and exercised all due diligence to avoid committing the offence.

The Law Society is the appropriate supervisory authority for these purposes. As yet, in its pilot format, the Law Society has not sought Treasury approval for its Guidance.[14] Nevertheless, once feedback on the pilot Guidance is received, the Law Society will consider whether to seek Treasury approval and, in any event, the courts may take account of the LS Guidance.[15] In showing that all reasonable steps have been exercised in accordance with reg 3(5), it would be helpful to show that the LS Guidance has been followed.

With the MLR 2003 now in force, firms have the practical difficulty of putting effective systems in place which follow the guidance of their supervisory body and which comply with the regulatory requirements.

It will not surprise anybody to see high-profile prosecutions being taken if a firm gets it wrong. The writers suspect, however, that in practice a firm which is able to show that it had appropriate systems in place including training and audit for compliance, but whose system has not

---

12 See www.lawsociety.org.uk/professional/conduct/guideonline/view=page.law?POLICYID=161546.

13 The Law Society, 113 Chancery Lane, London WC2A 1PL.

14 LS Guidance, paras 1.5–1.7.

15 See *Nationwide Building Society v Balmer Radmore* [1999] PNLR 606, in which the court took account of the Law Society's 'Green Card' on property fraud.

detected one isolated transaction, will have some prospect of avoiding prosecution, in contrast to the position of those who have made no attempt at all. At the time of writing, a solicitor has already been imprisoned under the previous legislative regime and several more await trial or have been interviewed under caution.

4.4 The substantive law

4.4.1 Proceeds of Crime Act 2002

Part 7 of the POCA 2002 draws together and consolidates the various former money laundering offences. The main sections covering these issues are ss327 to 340. It applies to everybody regardless of their business or whether they are within or outside the regulated sector. Section 342 is in Pt 8 of the POCA 2002 but is also highly relevant to legal practice and is referred to in more detail below.[16]

The POCA 2002 requires action to be taken where there is knowledge or suspicion of the proceeds of criminal conduct.

4.4.2 Terrorism Act 2000 and the Anti-terrorism, Crime and Security Act 2001

Sections 15 to 18 of the TA 2000 contain additional money laundering offences of which firms need to be aware relating to terrorist fundraising. The Anti-terrorism, Crime and Security Act 2001 inserted s21A in the TA 2000, which provided that it is a criminal offence for those in the regulated sector not to report where there are reasonable grounds for suspecting terrorist funding.

4.4.3 Money Laundering Regulations 2003

By widening the scope of 'relevant business', the MLR 2003, reg 2(2)(l), effectively brings most, if not all, solicitors' practices into the legislation from 1 March 2004 in relation to the need for anti-money laundering procedures, systems and training as well as the reporting offences.

The definition of relevant business found within the MLR 2003 includes at reg 2(2)(l):

> ... the provision by way of business of legal services by a body corporate or unincorporate or, in the case of a sole practitioner, by an individual and which involves participation in a financial or real property transaction (whether by assisting in the planning or

---

16 See 4.5.4.

4. The legislation and regulatory framework

execution of any such transaction or otherwise by acting for, or on behalf of, a client in any such transaction;...

4.5 Proceeds of Crime Act 2002

4.5.1 *The offences*

The LS Guidance, para 2.12 divides the offences into three sections:

1. principal money laundering offences;
2. failing to report; and
3. tipping off.

4.5.2 *Principal money laundering offences: Proceeds of Crime Act 2002, ss327-329*

These offences relate to the laundering of the proceeds of crime or assisting in that process if a person:

1. conceals, disguises, converts, transfers or removes criminal property from England and Wales, Scotland or Northern Ireland (POCA 2002, s327(1));
2. enters or becomes concerned in an arrangement which he knows or suspects facilitates the acquisition, retention, use or control of criminal property by or on behalf of another person (POCA 2002, s328(1)); or
3. acquires (without consideration), uses or possesses criminal property (POCA 2002, s329(1)).

These offences are punishable on conviction by a maximum of 14 years' imprisonment and/or a fine.

4.5.3 *Failing to report: Proceeds of Crime Act 2002, ss330-332*

These offences occur where there is knowledge or suspicion (or reasonable grounds to suspect) money laundering, which came to a person on or after 24 February 2003 and a report is not made:

1. if a person knows or has reasonable grounds to suspect money laundering, that knowledge or suspicion came to them during the course of their business in the regulated sector and they fail to make a disclosure as soon as practicable (POCA 2002, s330);
2. if a person is a nominated officer in the regulated sector, knows or has reasonable grounds to suspect money laundering, and they fail to make disclosure as soon as practicable to NCIS (POCA 2002, s330); or

4. The legislation and regulatory framework

3. if a person is a nominated officer within an organisation outside the regulated sector, knows or suspects money laundering, that knowledge or suspicion came to them in consequence of a disclosure to them as nominated officer, and they fail to make a disclosure as soon as practicable to NCIS (POCA 2002, s332).

Offences are punishable by up to five years' imprisonment and/or a fine.

Note that reg 4 of the Proceeds of Crime Act 2002 (Business in the Regulated Sector and Supervisory Authorities) Order 2003[17] provides that ss330-331 of POCA 2002 shall not have effect in relation to a person who engages in any of the activities mentioned in those sectors listed in the MLR 2003, reg 2(2)(f)-(n) where the information or other matter on which knowledge or suspicion that another person is engaged in money laundering is based, or which gives reasonable grounds for such knowledge or suspicion, came to that person before 1 March 2004. Those do not include bureaux de change and banking services, which were already in the regulated sector prior to that date.

4.5.4 Tipping off – Proceeds of Crime Act 2002, ss333 and 342

These offences occur when a disclosure has been made in accordance with the requirements of the reporting offences and a person makes a disclosure which is likely to prejudice any investigation which may be conducted. There are two offences. In passing, it should be noted that the second of these is in Pt 8 of the POCA 2002 – oddly the MLR 2003 only require firms to train staff in the provisions of Pt 7 which covers the other principal provisions outlined above, perhaps saying more about the quality of the drafting than the intention of the legislature.

The offence under the POCA 2002, s333 is committed if a person knows or suspects there has been a report of laundering and that person makes a disclosure which is likely to prejudice any investigation which might be conducted following the disclosure. Guidance on dealing with the client, given in the case of *P v P*,[18] is discussed in **Chapter 13**.

The offence under s342 relates to confiscation investigations under Pt 8 of the POCA 2002, and the work of the Asset Recovery Agency. It is an offence if a person makes a disclosure which is likely to prejudice the investigation, or falsify, conceal, destroy or otherwise dispose of or cause or permit the falsification, concealment, destruction or disposal of documents which are relevant to the investigation.

---

17 SI 2003/3074, see www.bailii.org.uk/uk/legis/num_reg/2003/20033074.html.
18 [2003] EWHC 2260 Fam.

These offences are punishable on conviction by a maximum of five years imprisonment and/or a fine.

4.5.5 Definitions within the legislation

For the purposes of the money laundering offences, the definition of 'criminal conduct' and 'criminal property' are very wide indeed.

Criminal conduct – POCA 2002, s340(2):

> Criminal conduct is conduct which—
>
> (a) constitutes an offence in any part of the United Kingdom, or
> (b) would constitute an offence in any part of the United Kingdom if it occurred there.

Criminal property – POCA 2002, s340(3):

> Property is criminal property if—
>
> (a) it constitutes a person's benefit from criminal conduct or it represents such a benefit (in whole or part and whether directly or indirectly), and
> (b) the alleged offender knows or suspects that it constitutes or represents such a benefit.

In addition, it is immaterial who carried out the criminal conduct of which the proceeds are being laundered, who benefited from the conduct, or whether the conduct occurred before or after the passing of the POCA 2002.[19] A person benefits from conduct if they obtain property as a result of or in connection with the conduct.[20] It would therefore be possible for a solicitor or any other person to commit a principal money laundering offence without being involved in the original criminal conduct from which the proceeds arose, by virtue of dealing with those proceeds, where they know or suspect money laundering.

Potentially, a person committing any offence which:

1. gives rise to profit; or
2. saves on expense,

may also be guilty of a money laundering offence. For example, the person who steals something is then in possession of the proceeds of crime and could be guilty of an offence of possession under POCA 2002, s329.

---

[19] POCA 2002, s340(4).
[20] *Ibid*, s340(5).

4. The legislation and regulatory framework

An example of an offence which saves on expense would be a business which fails to implement requisite health and safety measures such as safety equipment – the money it saves by this failure would represent the proceeds of crime.

4.6 The penalties – Proceeds of Crime Act 2002, s334

The penalties for money laundering offences are stated in the POCA 2002, s334 as follows:

(1) A person guilty of an offence under section 327, 328 or 329 is liable –

   (a) on summary conviction, to imprisonment for a term not exceeding six months or to a fine not exceeding the statutory maximum or to both, or

   (b) on conviction on indictment, to imprisonment for a term not exceeding 14 years or to a fine or to both.

(2) A person guilty of an offence under section 330, 331, 332 or 333 is liable –

   (a) on summary conviction, to imprisonment for a term not exceeding six months or to a fine not exceeding the statutory maximum or to both, or

   (b) on conviction on indictment, to imprisonment for a term not exceeding five years or to a fine or to both.

4.7 Defences

4.7.1 Lack of knowledge or suspicion

No offence is committed if it is neither known nor suspected that the property constitutes or represents a benefit from criminal conduct.[21] However, there is an important caveat to this – constructive knowledge may suffice for the disclosure offences which apply in the regulated sector, as discussed in **4.8**.

4.7.2 Consent – Proceeds of Crime Act 2002, s338

It is a defence to do what would otherwise be a prohibited act under the principal offences of concealment (POCA 2002, s327), arrangements (POCA 2002, s328) or acquisition, use or possession (POCA 2002, s329), if a person has appropriate consent. In practice, consent is appropriate if it is given by the MLRO to whom it was reported, but it is an offence for the MLRO to give that consent unless they have obtained consent from NCIS first. (Where disclosure has been made to a constable or customs officer, consent is required from that person.)

---

[21] POCA 2002, s340(3).

Deemed consent may arise where disclosure is made to NCIS and either:

1. NCIS does not serve notice within seven working days ('the notice period') that consent is refused; or
2. NCIS refuses consent within the seven working day period but does not further refuse consent during the period of 31 days ('the moratorium period') starting on the day on which the person received the first notice.

Note that the first period mentioned above is seven working days, defined as excluding Saturday, Sunday, Christmas Day, Good Friday or a day which is a bank holiday[22] in the part of the United Kingdom in which the person is when making a disclosure. All days count towards the 31-day period.

Note more importantly (and this is one of the few areas where the writers depart from the advice in the LS Guidance) that it is submitted that it would be imprudent to proceed on the basis of deemed consent alone. Many, if not most, practitioners will have had experience at some time of a letter out not having reached its destination, or an incoming letter being mistakenly placed on the desk of an absent colleague or otherwise going astray in the internal post. It is submitted that the prudent solicitor would already have telephoned NCIS to check the position and would also be well advised to send a fax when the time limit has expired mentioning the apparent lack of response and the intention to proceed in, say, two hours' time.

The final note of caution here is that consent from NCIS is only a defence to the principal offences under the POCA 2002 and does not in itself provide a defence to offences under any other provision or at common law, or to a civil claim for constructive trust or damages. The anticipated defence to charges under any other provision would be that it may be an abuse of process for a prosecution to proceed.[23] So far as liability under a constructive trust is concerned, the Law Society's view is that the fact of disclosure makes it less likely that a claimant could establish the dishonesty which is a prerequisite to liability for dishonest assistance claims, though liability cannot be ruled out.[24]

Practitioners should exercise considerable caution before proceeding, the more so when relying on deemed consent. Questions will doubtless arise at some point in the future as to whether a particular disclosure contained all the material which should have been disclosed.

---

[22] Under the Banking and Financial Dealings Act 1971.
[23] See, for example, *R v Looseley* [2001] UKHL 53.
[24] LS Guidance, para 5.17. See also **13.4**.

4. The legislation and regulatory framework

4.7.3 Reasonable excuse

Each of the principal offences in the POCA 2002 – s327 (concealing), s328 (arrangements) and s329 (acquisition, use and possession), contain an identical 'reasonable excuse' defence.

A different 'reasonable excuse' defence appears in s330 (failure to disclose: regulated sector), s331 (failure to disclose: nominated officers in the regulated sector) and s332 (failure to disclose: other nominated officers).

First, dealing with the principal offences, the reasonable excuse defence appears in subsection (2)(b) of the respective ss327, 328 and 329:

> But a person does not commit such an offence if –
>
> (b) he intended to make such a disclosure but had a reasonable excuse for not doing so...

This may be narrower than at first appears. The key to the problem is that the person must first have intended to make a disclosure. Persons who are threatened with violence if they report a matter may strictly never reach the stage of forming an intention, although they may well in practice manage to persuade either the prosecuting authorities or the court that they had done.

Where the provision might apply in practice would be where, for example, the MLRO intended to fax the report to NCIS but due to a fault with the fax machine or a mistake by the operator, the MLRO had a printout showing the right number of pages had been sent to the right number but nothing other than blank pages had appeared in NCIS's office. It may be that less strenuous attempts at compliance would also come within the provision but in the absence of any authority it is not possible to give any categorical assurance.

Turning to the 'failure to notify' provisions in ss330, 331 and 332, the defence does not require a prior intention to make a disclosure, merely that the person concerned had 'a reasonable excuse for not notifying the information or matter'.

A wide variety of circumstances may bring this into play. The LS Guidance cites the example of a non-lawyer expert who may nevertheless be within the professional legal adviser[25] exception but may report the matter to their MLRO who is outside that definition. *Prima facie* they may have to report the matter but, it is said, could rely on the 'other reasonable excuse' defence.

---

25 See definition in the MLR 2003, reg 7(6) and the LS Guidance, para 4.36.

4.7.4 Adequate consideration – Proceeds of Crime Act 2002, s329

Section 329(2)(c) of the POCA 2002 provides that there is a defence to a charge under the principal provisions of that section (acquisition, use or possession) if a person 'acquired or used or had possession of the property for adequate consideration'.

This defence applies unless the person knows or suspects that services (or goods) may help another person carry out criminal conduct. This may apply where the services are legal services supplied by a solicitor. Crown Prosecution Service guidance advises that this may apply where, for example, solicitors or accountants receive money for, or on account of, costs. The fee must however be reasonable. Note that this does not apply if the work is worth substantially less than the amount paid. This provision will probably be of particular assistance to criminal lawyers if the availability of legal aid is restricted in future. However, the LS Guidance[26] warns that a credit balance at the end of a matter may present a problem if the lawyer knows or suspects that it is criminal property – in those circumstances the practice will need consent from NCIS before making a repayment.

4.7.5 No training – Proceeds of Crime Act 2002, s330(7)

It is a defence to the regulated sector 'failure to disclose' offence in the POCA 2002, s330(7) (but not the principal offences) if a person:

(a) does not know or suspect that another person is engaged in money laundering, and

(b) has not been provided by their employer with the required training.

The defence in this subsection only applies to employees. It may therefore, in rare circumstances, aid salaried partners, but will not apply to fixed-share or equity partners, however junior.

The inevitable consequence of the defence is that the employer – rather than the MLRO – may be guilty of an offence of failing to provide the training in the first place.[27]

4.7.6 No offence in the United Kingdom

The definition of criminal property in the POCA 2002, s340(3) requires that it constitutes a benefit from criminal conduct. Section 340(2) provides that

---

[26] See para 2.31.
[27] MLR 2003, reg 3(1)(c).

criminal conduct is conduct which constitutes an offence in any part of the United Kingdom, or would constitute an offence if it occurred there. So however reprehensible the matters giving rise to the property, and however severely the conduct may be regarded in a foreign jurisdiction, it is the criminal law of the United Kingdom which is the test.

4.7.7 Professional legal adviser

There is a defence for professional legal advisers – broadly a legal professional privilege defence – in relation to the offences of failure to disclose (POCA 2002, s330(6)), tipping off (s333(2)) and prejudicing an investigation (s342(3)). This issue is discussed in more detail in **Chapter 15**.

4.8 Knowledge

The principal offences under the POCA 2002, s327 (concealing), s328 (arrangements) and s329 (acquisition, use and possession) require actual knowledge or suspicion that the property constitutes a person's benefit from criminal conduct, or represents such a benefit, and that the alleged offender knows or suspects that it constitutes or represents such a benefit. Similarly, the failure to disclose offence for nominated officers who are not in the regulated sector (s332) requires actual knowledge.

This is why, despite their apparent wording, the principal offences are not strict liability: there has to be knowledge or suspicion.

In marked contrast, however, in relation to the regulated sector failure to report offences (s330(2) and, for MLROs, s331(2)), knowledge can be actual or constructive. Constructive knowledge is an objective test – knowledge of facts which would put a reasonable person on enquiry.

4.9 'All crimes'

It is important to note that there is no minimum value of crime for the purposes of the money laundering legislation. In this respect, the UK went beyond its international treaty obligations. The issue has been the subject of much critical comment. There are two reasons why the government adopted the stance it did on the point. First, many terrorist atrocities are committed with minimal funds. To illustrate this, it has been reported that the Bishopsgate bomb in London in 1993 cost only about £3,000 yet caused about £1bn worth of damage.

The second reason for the adoption of an all crimes policy is that several small sums can collectively amount to a large sum. NCIS claims a number of successes arising from reports of small amounts.

Concerns have also been raised that solicitors and others might be required to report matters such as a client who derives part of his income from bullfighting in Spain, where the activity is legal, whereas it is not here.

Some assistance on the point can be found in the NCIS guidance note on the use of 'Limited Intelligence Value Reports'.[28] This is a shorter form of report than the standard one and is discussed in more detail in **6.8.1**.

One particular area where the NCIS guidance assists is in the case of errors on VAT or Customs returns. Under the Customs and Excise Management Act 1979, s167(3), the submission of an incorrect return, however innocent, is a criminal offence. In the guidance notes, NCIS state that a disclosure is not required for innocent error in these circumstances. There is no statutory authority for this, but the assurance should be sufficient in practice. Where the person knows of the omission and does not rectify the situation there will be a duty to report, and in those circumstances a Limited Intelligence Value Report is appropriate.

---

28 Available on www.ncis.co.uk.

5. Relevant business and the regulated sector

5.1 Definition

Regulation 2(2) of the Money Laundering Regulations 2003 (MLR 2003) defines 'relevant business'. Firms which undertake relevant business are in the regulated sector for the purposes of the Proceeds of Crime Act 2002 (POCA 2002).

So far as law firms are concerned, the following are the provisions of the MLR 2003, reg 2(2) which will be of principal concern, in varying degrees depending on the nature of the practice:

(f) estate agency work;...

(h) the activities of a person appointed to act as an insolvency practitioner within the meaning of section 388 of the Insolvency Act 1986 or Article 3 of the Insolvency (Northern Ireland) Order 1989;

(i) the provision by way of business of advice about the tax affairs of another person by a body corporate or unincorporate or, in the case of a sole practitioner, by an individual;

(j) the provision by way of business of accountancy services by a body corporate or unincorporate or, in the case of a sole practitioner, by an individual;...

(l) the provision by way of business of legal services by a body corporate or unincorporate or, in the case of a sole practitioner, by an individual and which involves participation in a financial or real property transaction (whether by assisting in the planning or execution of any such transaction or otherwise by acting for, or on behalf of, a client in any such transaction);

(m) the provision by way of business of services in relation to the formation, operation or management of a company or a trust;...

5.2 Legal services which involve participation in a financial transaction

Most of the definitions above are self-explanatory. The greatest difficulties arise from parts of sub-para (l) above, ie 'the provision by way of business of legal services... which involves participation in a financial... transaction'. Particular problems arise in the case of personal injury work which merits separate mention and is discussed further below.

5. Relevant business and the regulated sector

This provision in the MLR 2003 vastly widened the scope of the regulated sector from 1 March 2004. In contrast to the position of accountants and estate agents, all of whose work is clearly in the regulated sector, legal practices find that it is only some of the work which the profession undertakes which brings them within the regulated sector. The distinction depends on what type of work the lawyer is doing at any given moment. The Law Society's 'Money Laundering Guidance (Pilot – January 2004)' (LS Guidance) makes clear that not all the work of a solicitor's practice is necessarily relevant business:

> 1.31 It is important to note that the ML Regulations 2003 apply when 'relevant business' is undertaken rather than to a particular organisation as a whole. Firms must first establish which areas of work are subject to the ML Regulations 2003 and then set up systems to ensure compliance in those areas.[1]

The section advises that a risk-based approach may suggest that a wider approach to compliance with the MLR 2003 may be appropriate:

> As a matter of risk assessment and management, firms should consider whether their internal AML [anti-money laundering] systems should require compliance with the regulations more widely than required by a strict interpretation of what is 'relevant business' under the ML Regulations 2003. For example, firms may see less risk in requiring that all clients' identity be checked rather than having different procedures in different areas.[2]

In practice, in the absence of clear written guidance on the point, most firms have been attempting to adopt this wider approach and have sought to make no distinction between work types for MLR 2003 and 'relevant business' purposes. The exception to this has been firms conducting more or less exclusively personal injury work.

Firms initially tried to follow the requirements in earnest, but it proved unduly cumbersome for certain work types and a number started reviewing whether some very limited and closely monitored exceptions could be made.

Many personal injury practitioners have been taking the view that in principle, their work generally falls outside the definition of relevant business. The point turns on what is meant by a financial transaction.

The LS Guidance[3] points to the second EU Directive[4] requiring the member states to implement appropriate provisions for guidance upon the type of work which forms part of relevant business:

---

1 LS Guidance, para 1.31.
2 *Ibid.*.
3 *Ibid,* Para 3.10. Extracts Copyright © The Law Society.
4 Directive 2001/97/EC of 4 December 2001.

5. Relevant business and the regulated sector

3.10 ... The text of the Directive should help in understanding the type of financial transactions which are included within the definition of Regulation 2(2)(l). The Directive provides that the following should be included:

'Independent legal professionals, when they participate, whether:

(1) by assisting in the planning or execution of transactions for their client concerning the:

- buying and selling of real property or business entities;
- managing of client money, securities or other assets;
- opening or management of bank, savings or securities accounts;
- organisation of contributions necessary for the creation, operation or management of companies; or
- creation, operation or management of trusts, companies or similar structures; or

(2) by acting on behalf of and for their client in any financial or real estate transaction.'

Paragraph 3.12 then goes on to indicate the Treasury view, which confirms that certain types of work will not generally be regarded as 'participation in financial transactions':

1. payment on account of costs to a solicitor or payment of a solicitor's bill (because the solicitor is not participating in a financial transaction *on behalf of* the client);
2. legal advice;
3. participation in litigation;
4. will writing; and
5. publicly funded work.

In spite of this, the Law Society then goes on to recommend a 'cautious approach',[5] a risk-based approach[6] to the question of whether the MLR 2003 should be applied to a strictly interpreted category of relevant business – it advises that a wider approach may involve less risk.[7]

The difficulties with categorising 'relevant business' and having in place different systems are:

1. In what circumstances does litigation fall within the money laundering legislation? *P v P*[8] clearly showed that litigation, in that instance for

---

5 LS Guidance, para 3.14.
6 *Ibid*, para 1.17.
7 *Ibid*, para 1.31.
8 [2003] EWHC 2260 (Fam).

ancillary relief, could lead solicitors into involvement in a principal money laundering offence, in that case, under the POCA 2002, s328, an arrangement.

2. New clients for relevant business being accepted by a back door method once they have been introduced as a client for non-relevant business.

3. The Treasury view and/or LS Guidance may change. Firms taking the split approach or conducting solely personal injury work would have to keep abreast of developments and keep the position closely monitored.

4. Those conducting personal injury work need to appreciate that, although they may not necessarily have to follow the strict identification requirements of the MLR 2003, they must be cautious about considering themselves outside the money laundering legislation. Plainly the POCA 2002 applies to them, so there is the necessity for relevant training and awareness within otherwise non-relevant business departments. The MLR 2003, reg 3(1)(c) states that persons involved in relevant business must:

> ... take appropriate measures so that relevant employees are –
>
> (i) made aware of the provisions of these Regulations, Part 7 of the Proceeds of Crime Act 2002 (money laundering) and sections 18 and 21A of the Terrorism Act 2000; and
>
> (ii) given training in how to recognise and deal with transactions which may be related to money laundering.

The perception needs to be re-emphasised from time to time to ensure that they do not consider that they are outside the legislation.

Examples of circumstances where a personal injury solicitor may be involved in a 'financial transaction' include:

1. Exaggerated or fraudulent claims. If an accident has not really taken place, any damages would arise from the proceeds of a crime (obtaining a pecuniary advantage by deception).

2. Clients who pretend that damage was caused in an accident when it was caused previously.

3. Claims for fictitious expenses.

4. Using false invoices to support claims for repairs and other losses.

Personal injury lawyers need therefore to be aware of the following when assessing the risks and considering what procedures to implement:

1. settlement of a fraudulent claim could arguably amount to a financial transaction within the regulated sector, notwithstanding the Treasury advice on litigation generally being excluded;

2. a money laundering reporting officer who is notified of matters giving him knowledge or suspicion of money laundering is obliged to report it, whether or not in the regulated sector;[9] and

3. lawyers may become aware that a client is holding the proceeds of crime, such as tax evasion, and themselves become party to a concealment offence under s327 of the POCA 2002.

It is understood that the Law Society is considering whether it is able to provide guidance to the effect that personal injury work is not ordinarily considered relevant business and that the strict identification requirements of the MLR 2003 do not ordinarily apply. If it does so, it is likely to make it clear that training and awareness of money laundering and the legislation within that field are still required. It will also emphasise that the position could change and that firms should review the position regularly.

---

[9] POCA 2002, s331 (regulated sector) and s332 (others).

6. Making a disclosure

6.1 The role of the National Criminal Intelligence Service

The National Criminal Intelligence Service (NCIS), is the organisation which deals with disclosures made by money laundering reporting officers (MLROs). It deals with suspicious transaction reports not only from law firms but also all other organisations conducting relevant business within the regulated sector, eg banks, building societies, accountants, and estate agents. Accordingly, it is in a position to collate a potentially massive amount of information relating to money laundering.

NCIS was set up to 'provide leadership and excellence in criminal intelligence to combat serious and organised crime'.[1] Its website contains much useful information for MLROs, some of which is essential, such as the financial reporting forms which organisations are encouraged to use to make reports, and guidance on their completion. It also contains, crucially, guidance on disclosures by the legal profession.[2]

> NCIS provides strategic and tactical intelligence on serious and organised crime, nationally and internationally. It is the gateway for UK law enforcement enquiries overseas via Interpol, Europol and the overseas liaison officers networks. It is also the coordinating authority on behalf of police forces in the UK for the tasking of the Security Service, in accordance with the Security Service Act 1996.[3]

NCIS headquarters are in London, housing national-level strategic and tactical units which provide assessments and advice to HM government and law enforcement agencies.

NCIS has published its report 'United Kingdom Threat Assessment of Serious and Organised Crime 2003' which provides interesting and informative detail about the fight against serious and organised crime including identified methods of money laundering, such as the purchase of property in the UK and the estimated value of the proceeds of crime laundered in the UK.[4]

---

1 See www.ncis.co.uk.
2 See www.ncis.co.uk/legaldisclosures.asp.
3 See www.ncis.co.uk.
4 See www.ncis.co.uk/ukta.asp. at ch 6, entitled 'Money Laundering'.

6. Making a disclosure

6.2 The Economic Crime Branch

NCIS is divided into five divisions, including the Economic Crime Branch. This is the unit which deals with suspicious transaction reports and analyses those reports. Reports come into NCIS from all over the financial sector, they are analysed for intelligence value and then, where appropriate, are sent out to the various law enforcement agencies such as HM Customs and Excise, the Inland Revenue, and the police forces. NCIS is therefore much in the nature of a clearing house:

> These disclosures – also known as suspicious activity reports – can contribute to existing law enforcement operations, identify the proceeds of crime, and prompt investigation into previously unknown criminal activities.[5]

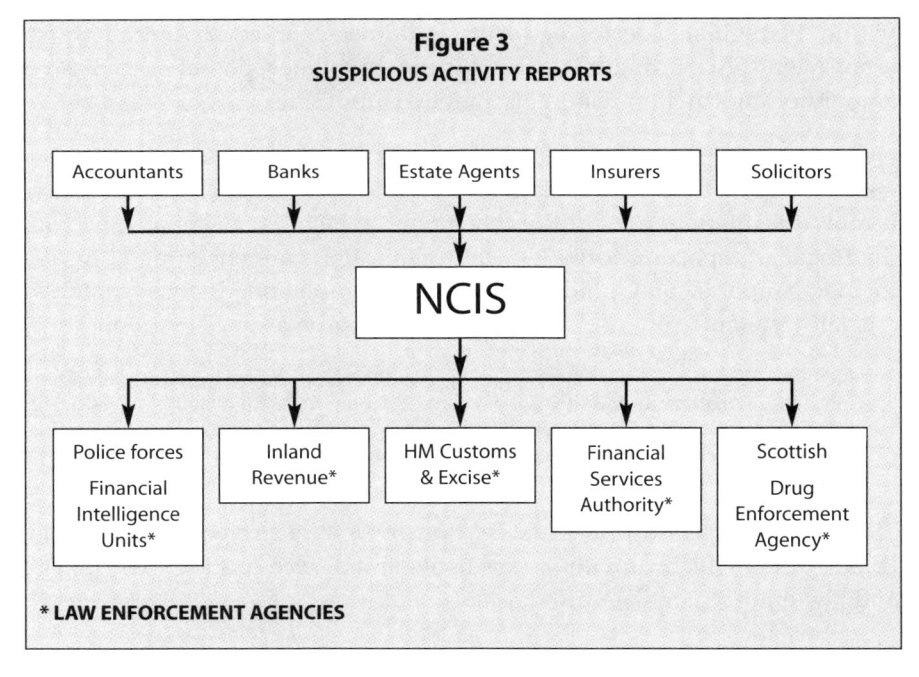

Figure 3
SUSPICIOUS ACTIVITY REPORTS

Accountants, Banks, Estate Agents, Insurers, Solicitors → NCIS → Police forces Financial Intelligence Units*, Inland Revenue*, HM Customs & Excise*, Financial Services Authority*, Scottish Drug Enforcement Agency*

* LAW ENFORCEMENT AGENCIES

In 2003, NCIS received around 100,000 disclosures – an increase of nearly 60% on 2002, itself nearly double the figures recorded in 2001, and expected to rise to 150,000 in 2004. NCIS prioritises disclosures on the basis of risk for development and direct dissemination to partner agencies. Of these, currently about 1,000 per month are from solicitors, compared with 150 a year ago. Two thousand law firms have made reports over the past year. The single highest number from one firm was 42, whereas most sent in five or fewer. Solicitors are expected to make about 8% of the

---

5 See www.ncis.co.uk/financialintelligence.asp.

reports that the NCIS estimates it will receive during this year, with the vast majority coming from ten banks.[6] The NCIS website states:

> On some disclosures, consent to act may be required under the Proceeds of Crime Act 2002 (POCA 2002). The number of such disclosures has increased by a factor of ten, and NCIS's partner agencies now prioritise the handling of consent referrals. As at March 2004, £25m had been protected (ie restrained, seized or returned to the victim) as a result of the consent process.[7]

Solicitors are responsible for 82% of the consent requests, which are running at between 1,200 and 1,500 a month after rising by 400% between September 2003 and February 2004.[8]

A central element of the MLRO's role and perhaps the most obvious, but at times the most challenging, is the responsibility to pass on suspicious activity reports to NCIS (sometimes referred to as suspicious transaction reports, but the reporting obligation is not limited to transactions). MLROs need to understand how the reporting system works and to have a practical system in place to enable them to do so.

6.3 The importance of disclosures

It is a defence to the principal money laundering offences under the POCA 2002, ss327-329 that a person:

> ... makes an authorised disclosure under s338 and (if the disclosure is made before he does the act mentioned... [ie leading to the offence]) he has the appropriate consent.[9]

In relation to the offences which can be committed by virtue of being part of the regulated sector – the 'failure to disclose' offences under ss330 and 331 – again, an offence is only committed if:

> ... he does not make the required disclosure as soon as is practicable after the information or other matter comes to him.[10]

Consequently, the importance of understanding the reporting procedures cannot be overstated. It would be possible for an MLRO to purport to make a disclosure and to find that they cannot benefit from the defence because it simply does not properly reflect the known facts of the matter. When consent is given to proceed, the consent may then have been given in ignorance of vital facts rendering the consent useless. Similarly, the

---

6 *The Times*, 20 July 2004.
7 See www.ncis.co.uk/financialintelligence.asp.
8 Source: www.ncis.co.uk.
9 See POCA 2002, ss327(2)(a), 328(2)(a), 329(2)(a).
10 See POCA 2002, ss330(4) and 331(4).

phrasing of the disclosure itself may lead to difficulties if it falls outside the confidentiality cover by divulging unnecessary information. A client subsequently learning of this may allege a breach of confidentiality.

6.4 The money laundering reporting officer and disclosure

The Money Laundering Regulations 2003 (MLR 2003), reg 7 provides for organisations to have internal reporting procedures in order that relevant information comes to the MLRO to enable them to make appropriate disclosures to NCIS (see **9.6**). In the event that information is received by the MLRO via this internal reporting system, reg 7(1)(c) and (d) provide:

> (c) where a disclosure is made to the nominated officer, he must consider it in the light of any relevant information which is available to A [the organisation carrying on relevant business] and determine whether it gives rise to such knowledge or suspicion or such reasonable grounds for knowledge or suspicion; and
>
> (d) where the nominated officer does so determine, the information or other matter must be disclosed to a person authorised for the purposes of these Regulations by the Director General of the National Criminal Intelligence Service.

The authorised disclosure defence to the POCA 2002, ss327–329 offences is defined under the POCA 2002, s338:

> (1) For the purposes of this Part a disclosure is authorised if –
>
> > (a) it is a disclosure to a constable, a customs officer or a nominated officer by the alleged offender that property is criminal property,
> >
> > (b) it is made in the form and manner (if any) prescribed for the purposes of this subsection by order under section 339, and
> >
> > (c) the first or second condition set out below is satisfied.
>
> (2) The first condition is that the disclosure is made before the alleged offender does the prohibited act.
>
> (3) The second condition is that –
>
> > (a) the disclosure is made after the alleged offender does the prohibited act,
> >
> > (b) there is a good reason for his failure to make the disclosure before he did the act, and
> >
> > (c) the disclosure is made on his own initiative and as soon as it is practicable for him to make it.
>
> (4) An authorised disclosure is not to be taken to breach any restriction on the disclosure of information (however imposed).
>
> (5) A disclosure to a nominated officer is a disclosure which—
>
> > (a) is made to a person nominated by the alleged offender's employer to receive authorised disclosures, and
> >
> > (b) is made in the course of the alleged offender's employment and in accordance with the procedure established by the employer for the purpose.

6. Making a disclosure

(6) References to the prohibited act are to an act mentioned in section 327(1), 328(1) or 329(1) (as the case may be).

6.5 Proceeds of Crime Act 2002, s331 – reporting offence disclosures

When conducting relevant business, solicitors are in the regulated sector. As such, the additional 'failure to report' offences apply (see **4.5.3**). Dealing for the time being only with the position of the MLRO and assuming that a member of staff has brought some information amounting to a suspicion that money laundering may have come to his attention, the MLRO needs to make a disclosure. This disclosure is defined under s331, as set out below.

6.6 Proceeds of Crime Act 2002, s331 – failure to disclose: nominated officers in the regulated sector

The POCA 2002, s331(5) states:

(5) The required disclosure is a disclosure of the information or other matter —

(a) to a person authorised for the purposes of this Part by the Director General of the National Criminal Intelligence Service;

(b) in the form and manner (if any) prescribed for the purposes of this subsection by order under section 339.

In practice, disclosures of both sorts are sent to NCIS.

6.7 Proceeds of Crime Act 2002, s339 – form and manner of disclosure

Section 339(1) of the POCA 2002 indicates that the Secretary of State may by order prescribe the form and manner of disclosures for POCA 2002 purposes. So far (as at October 2004), this has not been done:

The Form has not been prescribed by the Secretary of State under s339 of the Proceeds of Crime Act 2002 and, therefore, use of the form as a method for reporting money laundering is not mandatory.[11]

Organisations are encouraged to use the standard forms which appear on the NCIS website. They were updated at the end of February 2004 in anticipation of the widening of the regulated sector. Further minor amendments were made in September 2004. Although these forms are not mandatory, they are the preferred means of passing on information to NCIS. The previous stan-

---

11 NCIS – 'Guidance Notes for the NCIS Regulated Sector Disclosure Report'.

6. Making a disclosure

dard forms were rather unsuited to the work of a solicitor. They were more suited to the financial work of the then regulated sector: banks, building societies and financial services providers.

The forms can be completed on the screen and printed off from a computer but cannot be submitted online to NCIS. The completed forms must be printed off and sent by fax or post to NCIS. If an MLRO does not have ready access to the NCIS website, copy forms and guidance can be obtained from ECBDutyDesk@ncis.co.uk.

The forms on the NCIS website are not to be used for filling in by hand: NCIS requests that people do not complete the version of the form downloaded from the Internet for this purpose. Those wishing to complete a report by hand, therefore, need to request a special version of the form by telephoning 020 7238 8282. The report forms are only advisory at present, so in theory a letter would suffice if it contained the required information, but a compulsory reporting form may be prescribed in due course by the Home Office and will be available on both the NCIS and Law Society websites.

6.8 The reporting forms

There are two types of reporting forms:

1. Standard Disclosure Report form; and
2. Limited Intelligence Value Report form.

NCIS guidance in respect of both types of report is set out in **Appendices 7 and 8**.

Whichever type of report is to be made, upon making their first report to NCIS, the MLRO must complete a Source Registration Document (Module 1).[12] This need only be done if the organisation has *never* previously reported to NCIS. The form is also to be used to update relevant contact information.

6.8.1 *Limited Intelligence Value Report form*

This is a one page form which requires only:

1. the details of the organisation reporting;
2. the name and date of birth of the suspect; and
3. the reason for disclosure.

---

12 See www.ncis.co.uk.

It can only be used where the discloser has a suspicion of POCA 2002 offences and not in relation to offences under the Terrorism Act 2000. It is intended for use where the information will be of limited intelligence value to law enforcement, although wider analysis of such reports may provide useful data. NCIS reserves the right to come back to a discloser and seek a full report on the circumstances.

A list of examples is given in the NCIS guidance notes.

The guidance advises that a Limited Intelligence Value Report can be used where the suspicious activity takes place outside the UK and is not a criminal offence in the jurisdiction where it is committed and relates either to local differences in regulation or social and cultural practices.

The Limited Intelligence Value Report can also be used where there are minor accounting irregularities such as balance discrepancies and small credit balances not returned because of the administrative costs involved, or other minor discrepancies which are judged to have resulted from a mistake rather than dishonest behaviour. Where there is nothing to suggest dishonesty and no criminal property is involved, it may be that no report is needed at all.

Similarly, it can be used where the discloser is aware that a report from another organisation in the regulated sector has already been made or prosecution or government agencies are already aware of the offence and there is no additional information to add. This applies particularly in relation to health and safety offences, environmental offences and failure to file annual returns with the Companies Registrar. It is important however that the firm has no additional information. Serious tax evasion cases, including those covered by the Hansard procedure, require a Standard Disclosure Report.

6.8.2 Standard Disclosure Report form

The new form consists of six pages not including the Source Registration Document. These are as follows:

1. disclosure report details;
2. subject details;
3. additional details;
4. transaction details;
5. reason for disclosure; and
6. reason for disclosure continuation.

6. Making a disclosure

Obviously, when completing these forms, MLROs have to think carefully how to complete the 'reasons for disclosure' and at the same time ensure that they do not go outside what would be considered necessary to pass concerns onto NCIS without breaching client confidentiality.

The guidance on the regulations prepared for accountants by the Consultative Committee of Accountancy Bodies recommends that, in order to help preserve anonymity, the name of the person passing on their concerns should not be included in the report itself; they also advise that as a matter of good practice that the name of the client should generally be referred to in the heading and not in the text of the report to help minimise the risk of inadvertent disclosure to others.[13]

Note that further changes may be made to the forms from time to time. It is expected that these will appear on the NCIS website. Note also that it is anticipated that the forms will in due course become compulsory.

6.9 Completing the report

First, it is important to identify the statutory reason for making the report, because it may be necessary in due course to establish that the disclosure was both: (1) complete; and (2) properly made.

The MLRO should be clear whether the report is of one of the principal offences in the POCA 2002: s327 (concealing); s328 (arrangements); or s329 (acquisition, use and possession), or alternatively, a failure to disclose offence.

Second, the report should be clear on whether or not consent is being sought. An NCIS spokesman was reported as saying that many solicitors' reports end with the words 'We look forward to hearing from you',[14] words which are as redundant almost as often as they are used, but which leave it unclear as to whether consent is sought or the sender is merely 'rounding off' the report.

Typing reports can help with legibility, and therefore speed of response. The forms can be filled in on screen and printed off, but cannot be saved without software for creation of Portable Document Format (pdf) files.[15]

---

13 Anti-Money Laundering (Proceeds of Crime And Terrorism), Second Interim Guidance for Accountants, February 2004, para 20.3.
14 *The Times,* 20 July 2004.
15 Eg Adobe Acrobat or there are various free alternatives on the Web, see for example www.pdf995.com or www.primopdf.com.

6. Making a disclosure

Firms submitting their first report should also complete the Source Registration Document which is also available in any of the above ways. This is not required for subsequent notifications.

The LS Guidance advises[16] that reports should include as much information as possible about the suspected person or organisation, eg full name, address, telephone numbers, passport details, and date of birth. The National Insurance number may also assist (and will generally be available on personal injury claims because of the requirements of the Compensation Recovery Unit).

Reports should also include contact details. As a matter of good practice, it is recommended that this be the details of the MLRO rather than the individual involved in the matter.

It is said that NCIS has been known to reject reports in which a reason for suspicion has not been provided; although the statutory basis for a rejection is less than clear, this is not territory which the average MLRO will wish to explore. The LS Guidance[17] advises that in explaining the reasons for suspicion the person reporting may include an explanation of the background to the retainer, making clear the identity of the suspected person or organisation and why there are suspicions surrounding them. Taking time to set out clear reasons should help NCIS respond more quickly.

6.10 Sending a report to the National Criminal Intelligence Service

Reports must be made to the Financial Intelligence Division of NCIS in writing. They cannot be made by telephone. Reports can be posted or faxed to the Financial Intelligence Division: The National Criminal Intelligence Service, Economic Crime Unit, PO Box 8000, London SE11 5EN, fax 020 7238 8286.

The LS Guidance suggests[18] that it is helpful to telephone the NCIS duty desk to confirm that a disclosure is about to be made, and the basis for the disclosure. This can be particularly helpful where solicitors are seeking 'appropriate consent'. The duty desk is manned between 9.00am–5.00pm Monday to Friday, tel: 020 7238 8282.

The time limits for NCIS to respond (seven working days and 31 days respectively) are discussed at **4.7.2**.

---

16 At para 7.7.
17 *Ibid.*
18 *Ibid.*

6. Making a disclosure

Where consent is being sought, there may be time constraints – for example, completion of a purchase. The MLRO must not allow urgency to take precedence over other considerations, such as whether the transaction should be completed at all, with or without consent, given the potential for civil (and theoretically at least, criminal) liability even if consent is obtained.

NCIS has a hotline and fast track system in order to progress such matters. Those who have had cause to use these systems report a fast turnaround by NCIS. Where there is urgency, the MLRO should contact the duty desk on 020 7238 8262 or 020 7238 8607.

The Law Society Professional Ethics Line also runs a confidential helpline which provides guidance for solicitors. It does not provide legal advice but it is available and open Monday-Friday between 11.00-1.00 and 2.00-4.00.

7. What practical steps must the firm take? – a framework for regulatory compliance

7.1 The requirements of the Money Laundering Regulations 2003

At all times, those working in a solicitors' practice must be aware of and avoid becoming involved in any of the principal money laundering offences. Where they are conducting any relevant business[1] at all, they must also comply with the requirements of the Money Laundering Regulations 2003 (MLR 2003). Regulation 3 sets out the necessary systems that a practice needs to have in place to achieve compliance:

> **Systems and training etc to prevent money laundering**
>
> 3(1) Every person must in the course of relevant business carried on by him in the United Kingdom –
>
>   (a) comply with the requirements of regulations 4 (identification procedures), 6 (record-keeping procedures) and 7 (internal reporting procedures);
>
>   (b) establish such other procedures of internal control and communication as may be appropriate for the purposes of forestalling and preventing money laundering; and
>
>   (c) take appropriate measures so that relevant employees are –
>
>   (i) made aware of the provisions of these Regulations, Part 7 of the Proceeds of Crime Act 2002 (money laundering) and sections 18 and 21A of the Terrorism Act 2000; and
>
>   (ii) given training in how to recognise and deal with transactions which may be related to money laundering.

7.2 Systems and procedures

Put simply, the following systems and procedures are required:

1. client identification procedures;
2. record keeping procedures;
3. internal reporting procedures, which includes the appointment of a nominated officer, the money laundering reporting officer (MLRO);

---

[1] The definition of 'relevant business' and its application are considered in **Chapter 5**.

7. What practical steps must the firm take?

4. training for all relevant staff; and
5. such other procedures of internal control and communication as appropriate to forestall and prevent money laundering.

The key words are 'procedures of internal control'. The responsibility is on the firm, not the MLRO. All the partners must be satisfied that the firm has procedures, that they are documented, communicated to all, and applied in practice. That inevitably requires an audit to ensure compliance. The partners will also, if they are wise, require an annual report from the MLRO on the systems in place and how they are working. This is the basic requirement for firms regulated by the Financial Services Authority (FSA) and partners facing criminal sanctions for non-compliance with the legislation should demand no less.

7.3 The Law Society's 'Money Laundering Guidance (Pilot – January 2004)'

Implementing the advice in the Law Society's 'Money Laundering Guidance (Pilot – January 2004)' (LS Guidance) is of crucial importance to firms and their MLROs trying to achieve regulatory compliance and establish procedures of internal control and communication as may be appropriate for the purposes of forestalling and preventing money laundering. The guidance was initially published on-line in January 2004 and has now been distributed in hard copy format to solicitors throughout the country. Copies can be obtained directly from the Law Society.[2] For firms with an intranet, it may be useful to provide a dedicated money laundering section with a direct link to the LS Guidance.[3] For other firms, it should be ensured that everybody within the firm is aware of it and knows how to access it.

Failure to comply with the requirements set out in reg 3 of the MLR 2003 by those conducting 'relevant business' is an offence punishable on conviction by up to two years' imprisonment and/or a fine. Crucially, in deciding whether an offence has been committed, the court must consider whether any relevant guidance, issued by a supervisory authority and approved by the Treasury, was followed. The Law Society is a supervisory authority. The status of the LS Guidance, which has been issued without seeking Treasury approval, is explained in **4.3.3**.

---

[2] The Law Society, 113 Chancery Lane, London WC2A 1PL.
[3] See www.lawsociety.org.uk/professional/conduct/guideonline/view=page.law?POLICYID=161546.

Moreover, reg 3(5) provides, additionally, that 'it is a defence for a person to show that they took all reasonable steps and exercised all due diligence to avoid committing an offence under the regulations. If a practice is able to demonstrate that it has put in place procedures and training in accordance with the LS Guidance, this should go a long way towards establishing this defence.

7.4 The Law Society's 'golden rules'

The LS Guidance provides 'golden rules' in relation to anti-money laundering for practices to follow. They are as follows:[4]

1. know the legislation;
2. know the professional guidelines;
3. know the practice's client;
4. know the practice's business;
5. train the practice's staff; and
6. monitor compliance.

The LS Guidance will be considered in more detail in relation to each of the individual regulatory requirements in **Chapters 8–11**.

7.5 Some general considerations

Before turning to a detailed look at each of the requirements, it is important for a firm to view its anti-money laundering strategy in context and to be aware of some general considerations which it should apply to compliance. The following sections are an overview.

7.6 A risk-based approach to money laundering compliance

The LS Guidance identifies risk management as a key to effective compliance.[5] See also Chapter 6, Part 2 of the LS Guidance:

> Risk based means judging the risk and devising procedures proportionate to it. The success of any AML procedures will in part depend upon whether they are sufficient to identify situations which pose a high or low risk of money laundering, and yet are flexible enough to adapt where appropriate.[6]

This is discussed further in **Chapter 20**.

---

4 LS Guidance, para 1.4.
5 *Ibid*, para 1.17.
6 *Ibid*, para 6.4. Extract Copyright © The Law Society.

7. What practical steps must the firm take?

7.7 Do you know your client?

Underpinning the requirements of the MLR 2003 and integral to their effective implementation is the concept of 'know your client'. Knowing who your client is, understanding their business and understanding the economic framework of what they are trying to achieve will assist lawyers greatly in putting information in context and making an assessment of whether something is suspicious or not. 'Know your client' is one of the Law Society's golden rules. 'KYC' (know your client) is recognised terminology in the financial services industry and businesses regulated by the FSA, and implementing KYC is recognised best practice within the industry. Put another way, it constitutes customer due diligence.

KYC is a valuable risk management tool anyway, and failure to address it is the cause of many claims. An example of this is the firm which acted on the purchase of a house, only to discover later that the clients wanted to run a restaurant from it which would be a breach of covenant and require planning consent which would not be forthcoming. Had the solicitor enquired, he would have found this out and advised the clients that it was unsuitable for their intended purpose.

If the firm does know the client, is there anything adverse about its previous experience? Have other people in the firm acted for the same client? Perhaps the client has been involved in past transactions which have made colleagues uncomfortable.

Practitioners should not forget that if they are dealing with an established client who is instructing them in a representative capacity – husband and wife, company director, or a partner in a firm – they should be asking if they in fact know that circumstances have not changed since the last instruction. Examples of such problems which in the past have given rise only to civil liability include:

1. Company dissolution or restructuring, resulting in the solicitor purporting to act for a company which no longer exists, or is under different control, or where the name has been reallocated to a different company in the same group – the only safe procedure is to search against the company number, which can easily be done on the Companies House website. This problem is mentioned at **1.3** in a case where the company's parent group was restructured between the solicitor's initial instruction and commencement of proceedings a few months later. As a result, the proceedings were issued in the name of the wrong company and by the time it was discovered the limitation period had expired.

2. A husband selling a jointly owned matrimonial home, forging his wife's signature to effect the sale without her knowledge.
3. A director of a small company purporting to instruct a solicitor when he is in dispute with his co-directors and shareholders.

Client identification helps in other aspects of risk management too. Practices are required to undertake conflict checks when taking on a new client. They should be identifying who their client is effectively so that they understand with whom, and the extent to which, they are contracting to provide legal services. They need to understand the economics of a matter upon which they are advising in case it necessitates specialist advice on particular issues, such as tax. In addition, consideration of whether a client is going to be able to pay the firm's costs would ordinarily form part of the due diligence exercise.

From a money laundering compliance point of view, the intended use of property which clients are buying is highly material – the clients may intend using the property for rental but may not have disclosed to their lenders that the purchase is for anything other than use as their main residence. There may be a material misrepresentation on the mortgage application and the client may be embarking on a criminal act.

The Joint Money Laundering Steering Group provides the following guidance:

> 4. Know your customer and identification evidence
>
> **Introduction**
>
> 4.1. Having sufficient information about your customer and making use of that information underpins all other anti-money laundering procedures and is the most effective weapon against being used to launder the proceeds of crime. In addition to minimising the risk of being used for illicit activities, it provides protection against fraud, enables suspicious activity to be recognised, and protects individual firms from reputational and financial risks.
>
> 4.2. Generally a firm should never establish a business relationship until all relevant parties to the relationship have been identified (see paragraphs 4.15 onwards) and the nature of the business they expect to conduct has been established. Once an ongoing business relationship has been established, any regular business undertaken for that customer should be assessed against the expected pattern of activity of the customer. Any unexplained activity can then be examined to determine whether there is a suspicion of money laundering (see Section 5).[7]

---

[7] This extract from the 'Prevention of Money Laundering Guidance Notes for the UK Financial Sector', 2003 Edition is reproduced with the permission of BBA Enterprises Ltd. Copyright of this material remains with BBA Enterprises Ltd. All rights reserved.
© BBA Enterprises Ltd 2004.

7.8 New clients

If the client is completely new, why has this firm been selected? Be wary of clients who sing the firm's praises too highly when they cannot even know the firm. Is it a type of work the practice normally undertakes? One small general practice found its partner with a judgment against himself for around $200 million in the Supreme Court of California because he had been duped into becoming involved in prime bank instrument frauds – he had thought that the world of 'international finance' was more enticing than his staple diet of conveyancing and publicly funded matrimonial work.

It is highly material whether the lawyer has met the client. The risk inherent in accepting instructions from clients they have not met is inevitably higher. Firms will have to decide what they will accept by way of identification in these circumstances. Clearly the checking of individual identity is going to have to be done by someone else ideally in the regulated sector (or, if foreign, of equivalent status) and the firm will have to have confidence in the identity of the person doing the check as well. Firms should therefore consider drawing up a policy in advance and will need to consider how far this goes. If they are prepared to accept the signature of a bank manager, is it going to be any bank or only UK clearing banks for example?

Who has authority to accept new clients? If procedures are to be enforced, the partners will doubtless wish to have some control. Who will certify the process under which new matters are opened? Whatever process is put in place, there needs to be an audit trail to show how the requirements were satisfied, and by whom.

Firms whose practice involves them in work where one client's instructions result in them acting for another client as well will wish to consider their processes. This might happen where a lender introduces the borrower as a client. It will be an issue for insurance practices, where insurers instruct firms to act for their insureds. Once on the court record, the firm has a new client. This may be particularly relevant, for example, if the firm is then instructed on a counter-claim, or in the course of investigating a professional negligence claim, the solicitor comes across evidence of mortgage fraud.

7.9 The client engagement process

The advice to accountants from the Consultative Committee of Accountancy Bodies (CCAB) is worth reading. It comments as follows:

7. What practical steps must the firm take?

Nothing prevents a business from making normal commercial enquiries to learn more about a transaction or to determine whether a concern amounts to a suspicion. This cannot amount to tipping off if it is done before an internal report is made, and the individual has no knowledge or suspicion that a report has been filed with NCIS. Once a report has been made, businesses and individuals should take care in making any further enquiries and should consider only doing so under the MLRO's direction. In addition, caution is required where circumstances exist, such that the offence of prejudicing an investigation may be committed.

Clients and potential clients may seek to ask direct questions as to the intentions of businesses and individuals as regards reporting to NCIS or whether any such reports have been made. Responses need to be considered in the light of the dangers of tipping off and prejudicing an investigation, and businesses may wish to consider taking a standard position of refusing to comment or to respond in any way to all such enquiries, and make clear that this is a standard response.

It is unlikely to be regarded as tipping off if a business places a notice in its reception area or includes a standard paragraph in every engagement letter to the effect that it is obliged to report any knowledge, suspicion or reasonable grounds to suspect money laundering to NCIS. Clearly, there are circumstances where tipping off could occur, for example where a firm sends such an engagement letter immediately after they have been informed of a potential crime. In considering whether to include such a notice in reception, or standard paragraph, firms may wish to take into account that it is not necessary to do so and may not be desirable.[8]

It is submitted that the last sentence may be unduly cautious.

Firms will also wish to consider their terms of engagement carefully. It would seem reasonable to assume, though case law may yet establish otherwise, that there would be no liability for notifying the authorities of a money launderer's activities. Where the biggest exposure to potential liability may yet arise, however, is for breach of confidentiality in notifying a matter which results in delay – perhaps losing a contract race or at the very least incurring an interest penalty – when it appears with hindsight that there was in fact no cause for suspicion.

Consider, too, the scenario where there were initial grounds for suspicion but further enquiry which it might have been reasonable to make would have discharged those suspicions.

Firms will also wish to consider what limits they may impose on clients contractually as to the source of funds which may be used to complete a transaction. This issue is discussed further below.

---

[8] Anti-Money Laundering (Proceeds of Crime And Terrorism), Second Interim Guidance for Accountants, March 2004, appendix 3. Treasury approval has not been sought for this guidance and no formal legal advice was obtained on it. The CCAB intends to provide revised guidance for its members as soon as possible.

7. What practical steps must the firm take?

A policy decision needs to be made – and recorded in the terms of engagement – as to whether the firm will accept any cash payments and, if it will, what limits apply and whether any discretion can be exercised.

Terms of engagement may help here, though there can be no certainty of their efficacy and they will be subject to the provisions of:

1. the Unfair Contract Terms Act 1978; and
2. the Law Society's prohibition on excluding liability below the statutory minimum cover (broadly £1m in most cases); and
3. the restriction for contentious business in s60(5) of the Solicitors Act 1974.

7.10 Record keeping

There are two aspects of record keeping. First, there are the statutory requirements on firms in the regulated sector to keep records of identity and records of transactions. Second, there are the records which it is prudent to keep in order to prove, if called upon to do so at some time in the future, that firms have implemented the other systems required by law and what the systems in place were – particularly training, internal reporting procedures and 'such other procedures of internal control and communication as may be appropriate for the purposes of forestalling and preventing money laundering' as required by the MLR 2003, reg 3. These requirements are discussed further in **Chapter 10**.

7.11 Internal reporting procedures

Regulation 7 of the MLR 2003 requires firms to implement systems of internal reporting which require the appointment of the MLRO, a procedure for members of the firm to report knowledge or suspicion of money laundering to the MLRO and for the MLRO to report to NCIS where necessary. This is discussed further in **9.6**.

7.12 Training

Regulation 3 of the MLR 2003 requires training of relevant employees in the statutory provisions and in awareness of money laundering to enable them to recognise it. Firms should also consider training all staff whether or not they are working in the regulated sector and whether or not they are fee-earners. It is important that firms communicate their policies and procedures to staff if they are to have any effect. This is discussed in **Chapter 11**.

7.13 Monitor for compliance

Those firms who have audited for compliance in the early stages have found substantial breaches. Those who have not yet audited for compliance would be well advised to do so, otherwise, how can they be sure that they are complying? It is better for the firm to discover any breaches itself so it can improve on training and compliance, than to have the police discover them when the errors have been replicated many times over and it is too late to implement any improvements. Inevitably pressures of time are an issue, but if it cannot be given the priority it deserves, firms should consider seeking outside help from solicitors with appropriate experience, or accountants. The price for non-compliance is too high.

As with any audit process, the basis of file selection will be critical. Self-evidently, there is little point in selecting files only from the case handler who handles minor motoring offences in the magistrates court when the firm also has a volume Internet-based conveyancing service where the risks are far higher.

The selection of files, like so many other aspects of compliance, therefore needs a risk-based approach. The focus will be more on those carrying out work in the regulated sector, but not to the exclusion of other areas where there are also risks in relation to the principal money laundering offences. All departments should be audited in varying degrees and ideally all fee-earners will be checked at some point, though the frequency will depend on the type of work they are doing.

MLROs will also wish to form an overview of the firm's performance as a whole. For example, if there are two offices each doing volume conveyancing and one has made 20 reports, the other none, the MLRO is on enquiry that something may be amiss. The explanation for the disparity needs to be found.

The objective will be to:

1. establish that the firm's policies and procedures are being applied in practice;
2. identify remedial action to ensure compliance with the policies and procedures, such as rechecking clients' identification and, where necessary, implementing further training; and
3. identify whether the existing policies and procedures are adequate.

7. What practical steps must the firm take?

The tests must be appropriate to establish compliance with the relevant provisions, and the size of the sample should be large enough, in relation to the population, for a conclusion to be drawn.

Accountancy practices adopt differing approaches to sampling and the selection of sample sizes, for both monetary and non-monetary sampling. One approach would be to have a predetermined structure of sample sizes that is based on an assessment of risk, eg, low, medium and high risk. Determining which category the client falls into should be established from the number of high-risk answers from a checklist that includes:

1. work type;
2. whether work is in the regulated sector or not;
3. sources of referral, if any;
4. geographical location of the client;
5. type of client (so, for example, an offshore trust may be higher risk than a publicly listed company);
6. whether client money will pass through the firm's account;
7. whether the firm receives cash payment;
8. experience of the fee-earner generally and with the firm;
9. whether the fee-earner is supervised;
10. whether identification checks have been done;
11. systems and controls applied to the category of work;
12. historical knowledge of clients;
13. previous non-compliances for the department or individual; and
14. any other business information.

Any sample size should be representative of the firm for the whole of the period of the review, covering all the fee-earners and the various specialist areas of work undertaken within the practice. In attempting to identify an ideal sample size, all relevant information should be considered, ensuring that the work to be performed is particularly targeted to high-risk areas where sample sizes may need to be increased.

Where non-compliance is found, even if apparently trivial, consideration should be given to auditing further files for the same fee-earner.

7.14 Annual report to partners

Although this is not a statutory requirement for firms (unless they are regulated by the FSA), it is good practice for a number of reasons.

First, the overall responsibility for compliance is that of the partners in the firm, rather than the MLRO, though the MLRO has specific appointed functions in relation to notifications to NCIS. Second, it ensures that money laundering compliance is on the senior management agenda. Third, if the MLRO has need of further resources or funding to achieve the objective of compliance, it is the opportunity to raise it.

It is submitted that good practice would involve a report at least once in each calendar year covering the following areas:

1. assessment of the firm's compliance with the relevant legislation and the LS Guidance;
2. the number of internal reports by staff from each department and each office, and the proportion which have resulted in notification to NCIS;
3. changes made or forthcoming in the legislation and guidance;
4. particulars of any serious compliance failings in policies or procedures, action taken and recommendations for change;
5. a risk assessment of any changes proposed in the firm – for example new areas of work, new offices or lateral hires of teams from other firms;
6. MLROs in firms with any international aspects to their client base (and this may affect many firms, as explained in **Chapter 16**) should address national and international findings on countries with inadequacies in their approach to money laundering prevention;
7. the extent of internal audit and the results of it;
8. any deficiencies identified in the reporting procedures with recommendations for improvement;
9. details of staff training which has taken place, the method used and any key issues arising out of it;
10. additional information concerning communications to staff; and
11. recommendations regarding the resources and funding needed to ensure effective compliance.

8. CLIENT IDENTIFICATION PROCEDURES

8.1 Money Laundering Regulations 2003, reg 4

The Money Laundering Regulations 2003 (MLR 2003) sets out the identification procedures practices must follow in order to fulfil the regulatory requirement:

Identification procedures

4 (1) In this regulation and in regulations 5 to 7 –
  (a) 'A' means a person who carries on relevant business in the United Kingdom; and
  (b) 'B' means an applicant for business.
(2) This regulation applies if –
  (a) A and B form, or agree to form, a business relationship;
  (b) in respect of any one-off transaction –
    (i) A knows or suspects that the transaction involves money laundering; or
    (ii) payment of 15,000 euro or more is to be made by or to B; or
  (c) in respect of two or more one-off transactions, it appears to A (whether at the outset or subsequently) that the transactions are linked and involve, in total, the payment of 15,000 euro or more by or to B.
(3) A must maintain identification procedures which –
  (a) require that as soon as is reasonably practicable after contact is first made between A and B –
    (i) B must produce satisfactory evidence of his identity; or
    (ii) such measures specified in the procedures must be taken in order to produce satisfactory evidence of B's identity;
  (b) take into account the greater potential for money laundering which arises when B is not physically present when being identified;
  (c) require that where satisfactory evidence of identity is not obtained, the business relationship or one-off transaction must not proceed any further; and
  (d) require that where B acts or appears to act for another person, reasonable measures must be taken for the purpose of establishing the identity of that person.

This is required in respect of all new clients for whom the firm is doing relevant business in the regulated sector. Having made a risk-based assessment, firms may decide that they are going to implement these checks and requirements for all new clients, regardless of the type of business. This is a decision which needs to be taken one way or the other.

8.2 The definition of 'new clients'

Firms then need to consider what is meant by 'new clients'. Some existing clients may need checking where, for example, they only instructed the firm on the purchase of property five years previously and have not been seen since. Are they an existing or a new client? The firm might decide that existing clients for these purposes are restricted to those with whom it has had either a long standing relationship or with whom it has dealt within the last two years. Whatever the approach, it needs to be documented, communicated to those concerned and applied in practice.

It is fundamental to a risk-based approach to compliance to put it into the context of what the firm knows about the client. The Law Society's Money Laundering Warning Card advises:

> The better you know your client and the full details of and reasons for the transaction before accepting the retainer, and particularly before accepting funds, the less likely you are to become involved in money laundering.[1]

The crucial questions a legal representative typically needs to consider are:

1. Is the client who they say they are?
2. Do they live where they say they live?
3. Do I know enough about their background?
4. Do I understand the reasons for the transaction?
5. What am I taking on trust?
6. Does the whole picture 'stack up'?

The requirement for identification procedures applies where a business relationship is formed with a client, since 'applicant for business' is defined under the MLR 2003, reg 2 as meaning:

> ... a person seeking to form a business relationship, or carry out a one-off transaction with another person acting in the course of relevant business carried on by that other person in the United Kingdom.

8.3 One-off transactions and the €15,000 limit

As can be seen, identification is also required for a one-off transaction where there is knowledge or suspicion of money laundering, or where the transaction is going to involve payment of €15,000 or more to be made by or to the client. In respect of two or more one-off transactions, it is also

---

[1] Law Society 'Money Laundering Guidance (Pilot – January 2004)' (LS Guidance), Annex 5. Extract © Copyright The Law Society 2004.

required if it appears that the transactions are linked and involve in total a payment of €15,000 or more by or to 'B'.

In effect, therefore, where a business relationship is formed with a client for which the value of business is unknown, identification procedures are required where the work undertaken comprises relevant business. Where a one-off transaction is undertaken, unless the matter can be identified as being of a value lower than the appropriate exchange rate for €15,000 and it can be guaranteed that no potentially linked transactions will be handled for the same client, identification is not required even where the matter would otherwise be relevant business unless the firm has knowledge or suspicion of money laundering. Note that the MLR 2003 do not state the date at which the euro exchange rate is to be determined, which is a matter for the courts.

In practice, where firms are conducting relevant business, because of the practical difficulties of ensuring that subsequent matters are not missed and linked transactions are then inadvertently handled for unidentified clients, firms are putting in place identification procedures which identify all clients conducting relevant business. Looking at the larger picture in relation to a firm's role in the regulated sector, the MLR 2003, reg 3 provides for systems and training to prevent money laundering to be implemented and requires such other procedures of internal control and communication as may be appropriate for the purpose of forestalling and preventing money laundering. The foundation to such procedures of internal control and communication is knowing the clients.

Firms are encouraged by the Law Society to take a risk-based assessment of the opportunities that work they are conducting might present to money launderers. Developing and encouraging a full understanding by all members of the firm in relation to knowing the firm's clients and understanding their business is of great assistance in relation to this. The LS Guidance suggests[2] that for some firms the most appropriate and practical course may be to treat all new matters as they arise in the course of a business relationship, notwithstanding the strict position under the MLR 2003. It goes on to say that others may wish to consider each new matter on a case-by-case basis. It suggests that if a one-off transaction with a client which is below the €15,000 threshold has the potential to develop into a business relationship, firms should ask for identification evidence early on. The Guidance further notes that this will have the advantage of ensuring the firm is compliant when the nature of the retainer changes.

---

2 LS Guidance, para 3.34.

8. Client identification procedures

8.4 Agents and nominees

Where a client acts, or appears to act, for another person (eg if the client is acting as agent or nominee), the MLR 2003 require that 'reasonable measures' must also be taken to establish the identity of the other person. The LS Guidance comments[3] that the requirement to establish evidence in relation to underlying principals is less onerous than the evidential requirement for an 'applicant for business'. Solicitors may however feel uncomfortable, as a matter of policy, in settling for less.

8.5 At what stage must identification evidence be obtained?

The identification evidence must be obtained as soon as reasonably practicable after contact is first made between the solicitor and prospective client. At that point, the client must produce satisfactory evidence of their identity or the business relationship or one-off transaction must not proceed any further.[4]

8.6 What evidence is required?

Regulation 2(5) and (6) of the MLR 2003 defines the meaning of 'satisfactory evidence of identity', though this raises as many questions as it answers. The provisions are as follows:

> (5) For the purposes of these Regulations, and subject to paragraph (6), 'satisfactory evidence of identity' is evidence which is reasonably capable of establishing (and does in fact establish to the satisfaction of the person who obtains it) that the applicant for business is the person he claims to be.
>
> (6) Where the person who obtains the evidence mentioned in paragraph (5) knows or has reasonable grounds for believing that the applicant for business is a money service operator, satisfactory evidence of identity must also include the applicant's registered number (if any).

Therefore, the person obtaining the evidence from the person being identified must satisfy himself that the evidence produced is reasonably capable of establishing and does establish to his satisfaction that the person is who he claims to be. The LS Guidance[5] describes this as requiring the passing of two tests:

- an objective test in that the evidence must be 'reasonably capable' of establishing that the client is the person he or she claims to be; and
- a subjective test in that the person who obtains the evidence must be satisfied that it does in fact establish that the client is the person he or she claims to be.

---

3 LS Guidance, para 3.36.
4 See *ibid*, para 3.37.
5 *Ibid*, para 3.28. Extract Copyright © The Law Society.

8. Client identification procedures

Therefore, from a practical point of view, firms need to obtain this evidence at the outset of the matter and where their procedures allow for the file to be opened without it, they should have a very careful system in place to ensure that the identification evidence is followed up and the matter not allowed to progress, and in particular that no money is handled prior to the evidence being put in place and no transactional advice is given.

Firms who have the opportunity to correspond with a client prior to them visiting their office to provide full instructions should put some appropriate wording in their initial letter explaining the necessity for the production of identification evidence. The Law Society has produced a single sheet of guidance for clients as to why such procedures are necessary.[6]

The MLR 2003, reg 4(3)(c) requires that practitioners must take into account the greater potential for money laundering which arises when the client is not physically present when being identified. It is also clear from reg 4(3)(d) that when a client appears to act or for another person, reasonable measures must be taken for the purpose of establishing the identity of that person.

The LS Guidance[7] gives an example of difficulties a firm can face if it allows moneys to be handled prior to the evidence being obtained. If a solicitor accepts money from a client before establishing identity, and then cannot proceed because identity is not established, care must then be taken before returning the money to the client. If, by reason of the failure to produce evidence or for any other reason, the solicitor has formed a suspicion that the client or another may be involved in money laundering, it may be necessary to make a report and obtain NCIS consent before even being able to return that money to the client or otherwise progressing the matter. Solicitors may then need to take steps to ensure they do not inadvertently tip off the client in breach of s333 of the Proceeds of Crime Act 2002. For further information on tipping off, see **4.5.4**.

8.7 Documentary evidence of identification

The firm will wish to lay down its policy on what constitutes suitable evidence of identification. This will generally comprise two pieces of evidence, one proving clients are who they say they are and the other proving their address. Note that institutional clients may also have their own requirements, such as those set out in the Council of Mortgage Lenders' *Handbook*,[8] and the

---

6 See www.lawsociety.org.uk/newsandevents/news/view=newsarticle.law?NEWSID=171777.
7 LS Guidance, para 3.37.
8 See www.cml.org.uk/servlet/dycon/zt-cml/cml/live/en/cml/ms_handbook_england.

8. Client identification procedures

firm must ensure that the evidence it accepts satisfies both the money laundering requirements and the clients' requirements.

Ideally, the proof of identity for individuals will include a photograph. The same document should not be used for proof of both identity and address. The LS Guidance states that lawyers should be satisfied that any documents offered are originals to guard against forged or counterfeit documents and that photographs, if any, provide a likeness to the client.[9]

The person obtaining the documentary evidence should keep a copy and certify that it is a true copy of the original produced to them. They should date the copy. They should ensure that the copy of any photographic evidence is sufficiently clear and should certify that it is a true likeness of the client. Copies can be kept electronically.

The writers recommend that the identification evidence is then kept centrally, otherwise it will probably not be replicated on a subsequent file and may be lost if a file is destroyed in some years time – note that the requirement is to keep records for five years from conclusion of the last transaction. The record-keeping may be tied in to the accounts opening procedure to ensure compliance. It can be a powerful incentive if lawyers are unable to record their chargeable time in the meantime.

8.8 Identification documents: individual clients

Table 1 below lists the documentation advised in the LS Guidance.[10] It is important to ensure that documents are originals to guard against forged or counterfeit documents, and that photographs, if any, provide a likeness to the client. Documents which have been used as evidence of name should not also be used as proof of address.

Note however the inclusion of the words 'cheque drawn on an account in the name of the client with a bank in the UK or EEA' at para 3.84 of the LS Guidance: it is submitted that this should be avoided as it is highly prone to abuse. Even as a last resort it is undesirable, as that may be an avenue used by a criminal for exploitation. Not only are chequebooks stolen daily, but the adequacy of the checks carried out by banks, or lack of it, has come under the spotlight with millions of pounds being levied by the Financial Services Authority (FSA). In none of these cases so far has there been any suggestion of the bank's complicity in actual money laundering – the fines have been levied either for inadequate checks being made or lack

---

9 LS Guidance, para 3.84.
10 *Ibid*.

8. Client identification procedures

of a sufficient audit trail to show that the required checks have in fact been made. Solicitors need to consider the broader picture here – rather than simply ticking a box to indicate that they have made and can prove that the requisite checks have been carried out – they need to be on the lookout for exposure to the wider risk of money laundering offences, both on the notification side and the risk of being involved in an arrangement.

The writers have considerable doubts about the adequacy of this evidence. There can be no real grounds for confidence in the identity checks which may – or may not - have been carried out by a bank decades ago, and it would seem highly imprudent to accept this without other evidence.

Table 2 below contains various alternatives which the LS Guidance suggests for categories of private client who may be unable to produce standard documents for specific reasons. These should only be considered when standard documentation is unavailable. It also sets out the recommendations for trusts and estates. Particular care should be taken in dealing with companies and trusts because, although the majority are no doubt legitimate, these are common vehicles for fraud.

Table 3 contains the LS Guidance recommendations for companies. Company structures can be high risk. For subsidiaries of companies, a copy of the latest annual return or comparable evidence such as an extract from a reputable online information provider showing the parent/subsidiary relationship should be obtained. When using electronic checks, such as databases kept by Companies House[11] or the FSA,[12] copies should be printed for the firm's records.

In all cases a risk assessment is required and further evidence may be appropriate.

---

11 See www.companies-house.gov.uk/info.
12 See www.fsa.gov.uk.

8. Client identification procedures

TABLE 1 – LS Guidance: Individual identification documentation – one document from 'Proof of identity' and one document from 'Proof of address' is required.

Proof of identity (see LS Guidance para 3.84)	Proof of address (see LS Guidance para 3.85)
Note: Ensure documents are originals to guard against forged or counterfeit documents and photographs, if any, provide a likeness to the client	Note: Do not use any of these documents if you have already used them as evidence of name
Current signed passport	Confirmation from an electoral register search that a person of that name lives at that address
EEA member state identity card (which can also be used as evidence of address if it gives this)	A recent utility bill or statement, or a certificate from a utilities supplier confirming an arrangement to pay for services on pre-payment terms (do not accept mobile telephone bills which can be sent to different addresses)
Cheque drawn on an account in the name of the client with a bank in the UK or EEA[13]	Local council tax bill for current year
Residence permit issued by Home Office to EEA nationals on sight of own country passport	Current full UK driving licence – old-style provisional driving licences should not be accepted
Current UK or EEA photo-card driving licence	Bank, building society or credit union statement or passbook containing current address
Current full UK driving licence – old-style provisional driving licences should not be accepted	A recent original mortgage statement from a recognised lender
Benefit book or original notification letter from the Benefits Agency confirming the right to benefits	Solicitor's letter confirming recent house purchase or land registry confirmation of address
Photographic registration cards for self-employed individuals and partnerships in the construction industry C1S4 (the card does not contain an issue or expiry date and is renewed only if the individual's appearance changes dramatically)	Local council or housing association rent card or tenancy agreement
Firearms or shotgun certificate	Benefit book or original notification letter from the benefits agency confirming the right to benefits
National identity card containing a photograph of the client	EAA member state identity card
An entry in a local or national telephone directory confirming name and address	Inland Revenue self-assessment statement or tax demand
	House or motor insurance certificate
	Record of any home visit made
	An entry confirming name and address in a local or national telephone directory

---

13 Note the comments at the introduction to **8.8**.

8. Client identification procedures

TABLE 2 – LS Guidance: Other individual clients – identification documentation

Other individual clients	Law Society recommended identification evidence Important notes: 1 Standard documentation is preferred in all cases, otherwise follow the alternatives below 2 In all cases a risk assessment is required and further evidence may be appropriate	LS Guidance paragraph
Asylum seekers	Applicant's registration card with other evidence. Details should, if possible, be verified by passport, identity card or birth certificate. Note: The registration card does not contain a signature – Home Office relies on a biometric check (fingerprint held on microchip) to confirm identity.	3.99
Disadvantaged clients	Consider letter or statement from eg solicitor, doctor, minister of religion, teacher, hostel manager, social worker who knows the client and, if applicable, confirms client's permanent address.	3.95
	Evidence of address: • correspondence from a relevant government agency, benefits payment book or giro cheque; • tenancy agreement from a local housing association; • letter from the householder with whom the client is living who is named on a current council tax bill; • letter from nursing or residential care home matron or the client's care worker; • letter from hostel manager confirming temporary residence; • letter from Home Office confirming refugee status and granting permission to work, or Home Office travel document for refugees.	3.96
Employee and pension trusts	Normally low risk – where the client is sponsoring the employer or settlor of a pensions trust or employee benefits trust, only the identity of sponsoring employer or settlor need be verified. Where the client is the trustee of a tax approved pension scheme trust, identification of sponsoring employer is normally sufficient.	3.108
Estates	Identify executors/administrators as individuals – at least two if there is more than one. Obtain grant of probate/letters of administration; where already granted, obtain death certificate. Note: trustees of a will trust may differ and need separate identification.	3.103

8. Client identification procedures

Mentally incapacitated clients[14]	Medical workers, hostel staff, social workers, or Receivers or Guardians appointed by a court, may assist with locating and producing identification documents. Some flexibility is allowed including oral identification evidence from a person who knows the client	3.98
Students and minors	Check: • through the home address of the parents; • once the student is in residence, confirm UK address with registrar of client's higher education institution; • tenancy agreement or student accommodation contract; or • confirmation of a temporary address and documentary evidence from the householder with whom the student is living (eg see the council tax bill in the householder's name).	3.101
	If instructions are given by a family member or guardian, you should check the identity of that adult as well as the minor.	3.102
Trusts	Risk assessment critical: distinguish between long-established family settlement and offshore discretionary trust. Check the identity of two trustees (if more than one) and consider checking the settlor. No need to check the beneficiaries unless acting for them but it may be advisable before making any distribution.	3.104-3.107

---

[14] Refer to Law Society Guide to Professional Conduct, para 24.04 for guidance on mental incapacity.

8. Client identification procedures

TABLE 3 – LS Guidance: Company clients – identification documentation

Corporate clients	Law Society recommended identification evidence	LS Guidance paragraph
	Notes: 1. Company structures can be high-risk 2. In all cases a risk assessment is required and further evidence may be appropriate 3. For subsidiaries, obtain a copy of the latest annual return or comparable evidence such as an extract from a reputable on-line information provider showing the parent/subsidiary relationship 4. When using electronic checks, such as databases kept by Companies House or the FSA, copies should be printed for the firm's records.	
Banks, investment firms and insurance companies carrying on relevant business in the UK	Copy of the relevant dated page from the on-line FSA register[15] showing that the bank, investment firm or company is authorised by the FSA to carry on relevant business.	3.112
London Stock Exchange, other recognised UK investment exchange	Evidence of listing (eg copy of the relevant dated page from the *Financial Times* or the London Stock Exchange's list of companies).[16]	3.110
Other recognised, designated or approved exchange	Evidence of listing – see FSA or JMLSG list of exchanges.[17]	3.111
Overseas corporations (unlisted)	Certificate of incorporation, if available, but see also lists for UK companies. Where no certificate of incorporation exists, other evidence that reasonably satisfies that the corporation is in existence (eg copy of most recent audited accounts). Consider reputable online information provider/directory/information search agency. Where reasonably practicable, obtain evidence of identity in relation to a director or shareholder, usually the person instructing you or apparently active in the management or control of the company. Where not reasonably practicable to obtain additional evidence, consider list of shareholders holding 20% or more of the shares in the company or, if there are none, the principal owners.	3.117-3.118

15 See www.fsa.gov.uk.
16 See www.londonstockexchange.com.
17 A list of these exchanges is published by the FSA: www.fsa.gov.uk and on the Joint Money Laundering Steering Group website: www.jmlsg.org.uk.

8. Client identification procedures

Partnerships, limited partnerships and limited liability partnerships	Evidence of the identity of two partners including the partner instructing you and satisfactory evidence of trading address (consider directories). UK LLPs as other corporate clients. Partnership, limited partnership or a UK LLP of lawyers, chartered or certified accountants or chartered surveyors, consider evidence of: (a) confirmation of existence from reputable directory or professional body (eg printout from Law Society's on-line directory of solicitors); and (b) confirmation of firm's trading address, eg page from reputable directory (eg Chambers, Legal 500 or Martindale Hubble). For these professional partnerships it is not usually necessary to obtain evidence in relation to individual partners or members of the limited partnership or LLP.	3.120-3.121
Subsidiaries and sister companies – UK or abroad	Where new client is subsidiary of existing client, and existing client identification check recent, evidence of subsidiary or other relationship may suffice, provided record of existing client identification kept in relation to both.	3.119
UK companies	Use official, or recognised independent source including an extract from a reputable on-line information provider to verify: • copy certificate of incorporation; • list of directors; • list of shareholders; • registered address. Where reasonably practicable, evidence of identity for a director or shareholder should be obtained, including the person instructing or, apparently, in the management or control of the company. Lists of directors and shareholders should contain details of home addresses for the relevant individuals satisfying the need for evidence of an address. Where it is not reasonably practicable to obtain additional identification evidence, consider the list of shareholders holding 20% or more of the shares in the company or, if there are none, the principal owners. It may be necessary for further checks to be made about beneficial ownership if the initial information obtained is of the identity of nominees. Where the company is a well-established household name there is no need to obtain the additional identification referred to in this subparagraph.	3.116

8.9 Exceptions: instructions and referrals from the regulated sector

Regulation 5 of the MLR 2003 provides for various exceptions where identification procedures are not required. Such exceptions are narrow and as the LS Guidance explains,[18] solicitors in most cases will need to obtain satisfactory evidence of identity.

The first exception, reg 5(2)(a), is where the client carries on relevant business in the UK within reg 2(2)(a)-(e).

> **'Exceptions**
>
> 5(1) Except in circumstances falling within regulation 4(2)(b)(i), identification procedures under regulation 4 do not require A to take steps to obtain evidence of any person's identity in any of the following circumstances.
>
> (2) Where A has reasonable grounds for believing that B–
>
> (a) carries on in the United Kingdom relevant business falling within any of sub-paragraphs (a) to (e) of regulation 2(2), is not a money service operator and, if carrying on an activity falling within regulation 2(2)(a), is an authorised person with permission under the 2000 Act to carry on that activity;
>
> (b) does not carry on relevant business in the United Kingdom but does carry on comparable activities to those falling within sub-paragraph (a) and is covered by the Money Laundering Directive; or
>
> (c) is regulated by an overseas regulatory authority (within the meaning given by section 82 of the Companies Act 1989) and is based or incorporated in a country (other than an EEA State) whose law contains comparable provisions to those contained in the Money Laundering Directive.
>
> (3) Where –
>
> (a) A carries out a one-off transaction with or for a third party pursuant to an introduction effected by a person who has provided a written assurance that evidence of the identity of all third parties introduced by him will have been obtained and recorded under procedures maintained by him;
>
> (b) that person identifies the third party; and
>
> (c) A has reasonable grounds for believing that that person falls within any of sub-paragraphs (a) to (c) of paragraph (2).
>
> (4) In relation to a contract of long-term insurance –
>
> (a) in connection with a pension scheme taken out by virtue of a person's contract of employment or occupation where the contract of long-term insurance –
>
>   (i) contains no surrender clause; and
>
>   (ii) may not be used as collateral for a loan; or
>
> (b) in respect of which a premium is payable –

---

18 LS Guidance, para 3.41.

8. Client identification procedures

          (i)   in one instalment of an amount not exceeding 2,500 euro; or

          (ii)   periodically and where the total payable in respect of any calendar year does not exceed 1,000 euro.

  (5)   Where the proceeds of a one-off transaction are payable to B but are instead directly reinvested on his behalf in another transaction –

      (a)   of which a record is kept; and

      (b)   which can result only in another reinvestment made on B's behalf or in a payment made directly to B.

As can be seen, the first exception applies where clients carry on relevant business themselves, or are authorised to do so under the Financial Services and Markets Act 2000 and are not a money service operator. Examples of those who would fall within these categories are United Kingdom clearing banks and building societies (which may provide some comfort to those engaged in volume remortgage work). The list is set out below. It is not a list of all those carrying out regulated business such as solicitors or accountants.

  (2)   For the purposes of these Regulations, 'relevant business' means –

      (a)   the regulated activity of –

          (i)   accepting deposits;

          (ii)   effecting or carrying out contracts of long-term insurance when carried on by a person who has received official authorisation pursuant to Article 4 or 51 of the Life Assurance Consolidation Directive;

          (iii) dealing in investments as principal or as agent;

          (iv) arranging deals in investments;

          (v)   managing investments;

          (vi) safeguarding and administering investments;

          (vii) sending dematerialised instructions;

          (viii) establishing (and taking other steps in relation to) collective investment schemes;

          (ix) advising on investments; or

          (x)   issuing electronic money;

      (b)   the activities of the National Savings Bank;

      (c)   any activity carried on for the purpose of raising money authorised to be raised under the National Loans Act 1968 under the auspices of the Director of Savings;

      (d)   the business of operating a bureau de change, transmitting money (or any representation of monetary value) by any means or cashing cheques which are made payable to customers;

      (e)   any of the activities in points 1 to 12 or 14 of Annex 1 to the Banking Consolidation Directive (which activities are, for convenience, set out in Schedule 1 to these Regulations) when carried on by way of business, ignoring an activity falling within any of sub-paragraphs (a) to (d);…

8. Client identification procedures

In addition, under reg 5(3), evidence of identity is not required where a solicitor carries out a one-off transaction with or for a client pursuant to an introduction of one person who provides a written assurance that evidence of identity of all third parties introduced by them will have been obtained in accordance under procedures maintained by them and:

1. the introducer identifies the client; and
2. the lawyer has reasonable grounds for believing the introducer falls into any of the categories listed above in reg 2(2)(a)-(c).

A specimen certificate appears at Annex 11 of the LS Guidance. This was produced by the Joint Money Laundering Steering Group.

Referrals from trusted sources may give grounds for confidence, but can they displace the need for the firm to carry out its own checks? Firms will wish to form their own view on whether to accept that evidence as sufficient or not. Acceptance absolves them from breach of the statutory requirement to obtain evidence of identification, but in relying on other organisations who in some cases have themselves been found to be lacking in their procedures (and fined accordingly by the FSA) they assume a number of risks which they should consider:

1. They may deny themselves access to other information which could alert them to risks of other breaches of the legislation such as becoming involved in transactions.
2. They are relying on the adequacy of checks carried out by others over whom they have no control and no monitoring. This may absolve them from liability for breach of the identification requirements but not help them on more substantive issues.
3. They accept the adequacy of the referring body's systems which may subscribe to a lower level of security.

8.10 Exceptions: transitional provisions for existing clients

Firms which carry on relevant business falling within the MLR 2003, reg 2(2)(a)-(e) do not have to verify the identity of clients with whom they had formed a business relationship before 1 April 1994. (These are activities such as banking and investment management.) The LS Guidance advises[19] that this transitional provision is likely to apply only to firms which were subject to the Money Laundering Regulations 1993.

---

19 LS Guidance, para 3.49.

8. Client identification procedures

Firms which carry out relevant business falling within any of reg 2(2)(f)–(n) of the MLR 2003 (those which are relevant to all law firms in the regulated sector) do not have to verify the identity of clients where a business relationship was formed before 1 March 2004.

What of the firm which incorporates? The new practice, be it limited company or limited liability partnership (LLP), did not exist at the time. The status of an LLP is somewhere between a limited company and a partnership, in that although it is a separate legal entity, it is clear that the members are not employees unless they would have been in the case of a traditional partnership[20] and the requirements on formation are that two or more persons are associated for carrying on a lawful business with a view to profit.[21] On that basis it may be that the members are still carrying on business, albeit they contract only through the medium of the LLP, and will (or should) have obtained identification evidence, albeit in their previous capacity as partners. If this is not a solution to the problem, it in turn begs the question of how new partners in a firm can establish compliance where the identity was checked before they were admitted to the partnership. The requirements in the MLR 2003 do not fit comfortably with the concept of a partnership whose constitution will often be fluid.

However, it may still be prudent to use the opportunity to check the identity of clients who have not previously had their identity checked.

8.11 Disadvantaged clients

Sometimes firms who act for socially disadvantaged clients or the elderly will be faced with situations where the client cannot produce photographic identification evidence – they have no passport, and no photo-driving licence. Firms will have to decide what they will regard as acceptable. Refer to **Table 2** above. It is not the intention of the money laundering legislation to exclude socially disadvantaged clients from obtaining legal advice.

8.12 Where personal attendance is not possible

As part of its risk assessment, the firm will wish to consider how far it can go in accepting evidence without personal attendance. The opportunity to check the likeness of photographic evidence is lost and the opportunity to question the client diminished. The Law Society advises against asking for originals of valuable documents, such as passports, to be sent through the post.[22]

---

20 Limited Liability Partnerships Act 2000, s4(4),
21 *Ibid*, s 2(1)(a).
22 LS Guidance, para 3.78.

It may be possible to accept documents which are less valuable but the solicitor will all the time be weighing this against the level of risk associated with the particular instruction. Remortgages where no money passes to the client might, for example, be perceived as less risky than a new purchase.

One option is to ask clients to attend upon either another law firm or another business in the regulated sector and arrange for a copy to be certified by them. In that case the firm will need to check the identity of the organisation certifying the documents, for example by checking a professional directory. The lawyer will also be aware of the increased risk.

Caution should be exercised against accepting copy documents certified by anyone who is not in the regulated sector and will not therefore be familiar with the needs and obligations which the firm has to satisfy. It is suggested in some quarters that a copy of an identity document certified by a minister of religion may suffice.[23] Ministers of religion are not, and never have been, in any sector which was regulated for the purposes of delivering financial transactions. Further, and perhaps more importantly, there is considerable scope for a wide variety of views on what exactly constitutes a minister of religion.

8.13 Commercial providers of client identification

The LS Guidance[24] lists a number of organisations offering client identification information, some rather expensive, and solicitors will wish to consider when to use their services as a matter of policy. It is difficult to give guidance in the abstract – much will turn on the firm's own area of practice and source of clients. It may however form useful additional evidence where the solicitor has not seen the client.

---

[23] See, for example, the Royal Institution of Chartered Surveyors' guidance (www.rics.org/Management/Businessmanagement/Financialmanagement/Accounting/Moneylaundering/money_laundering.htm), though it acknowledges that it is due for review imminently.
[24] LS Guidance, Annex 16.

9. THE MONEY LAUNDERING REPORTING OFFICER

9.1 Appointment of a nominated officer – the money laundering reporting officer

Regulation 7(1)(a) of the Money Laundering Regulations 2003 (MLR 2003) require that 'A person in A's organisation is nominated to receive disclosures under this regulation ("the nominated officer")'. This role now usually forms the greater part of the role of the money laundering reporting officer (MLRO). Note that the term 'money laundering compliance officer' is starting to be used in the financial services sector.

9.2 The choice of person

The Law Society's 'Money Laundering Guidance (Pilot – January 2004)' (LS Guidance) provides guidance about who should be appointed to the role.[1] The seniority of the person appointed is clearly of importance. It is essential from the point of view that the person appointed needs to be able to have access to all of the firm's client files and business information. In addition, bear in mind that information passed to the MLRO may involve suspicions about unusual circumstances or contain allegations regarding somebody within the firm, whether founded or unfounded.

Additionally, the information may concern one of the firm's most important clients. The MLRO needs to be able to deal with either of these issues which could be of the utmost sensitivity. By its very nature, the material coming into their possession will be of a sensitive and confidential nature and needs to be kept so in most cases.

In addition, the officer ought to be somebody who is approachable in order that people do not feel intimidated in taking their concerns to them. Less senior members of staff could feel intimated by the idea of making a report if they are unsure whether it amounts to more than mere speculation and

---

1 LS Guidance, paras 3.56–3.65.

actually could be said to be a suspicion. The MLRO needs to encourage people to feel able to come forward in such instances.

For similar reasons and for continuity, it is also important that the MLRO is somebody who is often in the office. Whilst it is essential that MLROs arrange cover for the times they will be out of the office on business or on holiday, nevertheless, they need to have sufficient time to treat the job seriously. Legal professional privilege issues are likely to arise. Litigation practitioners are often more familiar with the issues in practice. Liaison with the firm's professional indemnity contact partner will also be necessary. In many firms the roles may be combined.

9.3 Sole practitioners

A sole practitioner who does not employ anybody or act in association with anyone else does not need to appoint an officer. A sole practitioner must appoint an MLRO who will generally be themselves.

9.4 Large firms

In larger firms, certain of the duties of the MLRO may be delegated but a firm cannot appoint joint officers, and the MLRO must retain overall responsibility for compliance with the obligations. The LS Guidance advises[2] that in some large firms, one or more permanent deputy officers of suitable seniority may be appointed but at the end of the day, the MLRO is responsible. It would seem sensible for most firms to appoint at least one deputy because the MLRO cannot be there all the time. Firms with multiple offices might consider appointing a deputy in each office.

9.5 Disclosures to the money laundering reporting officer

Once the appointment is made, anybody within the organisation who in the course of relevant business knows or suspects, or has reasonable grounds for knowing or suspecting, that a person is engaged in money laundering must as soon as is practicable after the information or other matter comes to them, disclose it to the nominated officer. Information acquired on client matters is obviously covered, but what about information acquired at a client's social event, or in the taxi going home from client entertaining? There will clearly be borderline cases. It might be harder to argue that this was not in the course of business if the solicitor has claimed the travel expenses for attending the event from the firm.

---

[2] LS Guidance, para 3.62.

When a disclosure is made to the MLRO, the MLR 2003, reg 7(1)(c) requires that the MLRO must consider it in the light of any relevant information which is available to the organisation and determine whether it gives rise to such knowledge or suspicion, or reasonable grounds for knowledge or suspicion. If the MLRO determines that it does, it must be reported to NCIS. The LS Guidance makes clear that the decision to report must not be subject to the consent of anybody else and the nominated officer must liaise with NCIS.[3]

Failure to do so as soon as is practicable after the information or other matter comes to the MLRO constitutes an offence under the Proceeds of Crime Act 2002 (POCA 2002), s331 (in the case of MLROs in the regulated sector) and s332 (for those outside the regulated sector).

This is obviously the key part of the MLRO's role within the firm. The MLR 2003, reg 7 requires internal reporting procedures to enable compliance with the provisions of the POCA 2002, both in relation to the principal and reporting offences within the regulated sector – compliance with the requirements depends heavily on this particular role being effectively undertaken by the MLRO.

The MLRO needs to make any decisions upon reporting based upon all relevant information available from whatever source. It is important to consider, for example, whether any other matters on which the firm may have acted are relevant, or any other information which may have caused grounds for suspicion within the firm – perhaps an earlier report to the MLRO was not considered enough to warrant suspicion in isolation but additional evidence which has subsequently come to light becomes the missing piece in the jigsaw.

9.6 Framework for internal reporting

The MLR 2003, reg 7 also requires the firm to implement internal reporting procedures. There needs to be a framework for collecting the essential information and collating it.

Typically, depending upon the size of the firm, firms should have available a short and clear form to enable straightforward reports to be made quickly and easily to the MLRO. Whilst there is nothing to stop a firm having a preliminary system of speaking directly to either the department head or the MLRO themselves prior to completion of the form, the form would serve as good evidence for the individuals of having complied with

---

3 LS Guidance, para 3.61.

the requirements of the POCA 2002, s330(4) and would also mean that the individuals address the key issues that the MLRO will need to consider. The MLRO should provide the sender with a receipt.

As part of the training given within the firm, staff need to know where to obtain these forms or how to make an internal report to the MLRO. They should also be made aware of how to contact the MLRO, and whom to contact when the MLRO is absent. In addition, staff should be aware of the potential sensitivity of the information contained in their report. They should keep copies of their reports on a private file, not on the client file.

The question of where to keep such information is worthy of proper consideration. Firms do not want such potential confidential information easily accessible. Similarly, material obtained by the MLRO ought to be kept highly confidential.

The issue of confidentiality could arise where upon reflection, the MLRO does not consider that the content of an employee's report constitutes a reasonable suspicion. Bear in mind, however, that when read with later reports, it may do so. There is generally no breach of confidentiality to a client if during the course of their business, they gain a reasonable suspicion and report it. (This issue is discussed in more detail in **Chapter 15**.)

It is worth noting also that if during the course of a matter, a client seeks to transfer instructions to another firm, care should be taken when making a physical transfer of the client file contents. In any event, solicitors should be aware of which documents they are required to transfer over and which they are not.[4] It would be unfortunate to inadvertently transfer papers over, failing to appreciate that they contained confidential reporting information. Where a report had been made to NCIS, this could constitute a tipping off offence. Even if the MLRO decides not to make a report, it would still be highly undesirable.

Again from a practical point of view, once a file is closed, time may elapse and those handling it may forget about the fact that at some point they did actually have a concern regarding potential money laundering. If they are then asked to obtain the file from their archives and pass information to the client, or to someone else, they may have forgotten that reporting documentation appears on the file and pass it over inadvertently.

---

4 See the Law Society's 'Guide to Professional Conduct of Solicitors', 8th ed, Annex 12A for guidance. This is available on-line at www.lawsociety.org.uk.

An additional practical risk might result if, whilst in the process of awaiting clearance from NCIS under the POCA 2002, s336(7) or (8), reference to the report is made on the file. If the client comes into the office and a meeting takes place, the client may accidentally see the documentation on the open file.

If the MLRO decides not to make a report to NCIS, it may be prudent to record the reasons for not doing so. When viewed with hindsight in the light of subsequent events, it may be hard to reconstruct how little the MLRO knew at the time, or what analysis was done at the time in forming the view that there was no ground for suspicion.

9.7 Data Protection Act 1998

Where a person makes a subject access request under the Data Protection Act 1998 (DPA 1988), careful consideration needs to be given on whether or not to disclose a suspicious activity report to NCIS. It could raise concerns that this will amount to a tipping off offence under the POCA 2002. Guidance has been given by the Treasury in consultation with the Information Commissioner and this is reproduced in full as **Appendix 14** of this book.

The DPA 1988, s29 provides that personal data are exempt from the disclosure provisions in any case to the extent to which the application of that provision would be likely to prejudice the prevention or detection of crime or the apprehension or prosecution of offenders.

The firm will need to consider on a case-by-case basis whether, in a particular case, disclosure of the report to NCIS or an internal report would be likely to prejudice the prevention or detection of crime. In determining whether the section 29 exemption applies, it is legitimate to take account of the fact that the detection of money laundering often depends on fitting together a number of separate pieces of information and the fact that one report does not prove criminal conduct on its own is not determinative.

The Treasury guidance note states that where a financial institution is in doubt as to whether disclosure would be likely to prejudice an investigation or potential investigation, it should approach NCIS for guidance. It is submitted that it would be highly imprudent to disclose reports without first seeking guidance from NCIS in any event.

Firms should bear in mind the requirement to respond promptly to a subject access request and in any event within 40 days and ensure that they approach NCIS in good time.

9. The money laundering reporting officer

Where a firm decides to withhold a piece of information in reliance on the section 29 exemption, it is not obliged to tell the individual that any information has been withheld. It can simply leave out that piece of information and make no reference to it when responding to the individual who made the request.

10. Record-keeping procedures

10.1 Money Laundering Regulations 2003, reg 6

In broad terms the Money Laundering Regulations 2003 (MLR 2003), reg 6 requires that firms carrying out relevant business keep records of identity and transactions for five years after the last transaction for the client. The regulation provides:

Record-keeping procedures

6(1) A must maintain procedures which require the retention of the records prescribed in paragraph (2) for the period prescribed in paragraph (3).

(2) The records are –

  (a) where evidence of identity has been obtained under the procedures stipulated by regulation 4 (identification procedures) or pursuant to regulation 8 (casinos) –

   (i) a copy of that evidence;

   (ii) information as to where a copy of that evidence may be obtained; or

   (iii) information enabling the evidence of identity to be re-obtained, but only where it is not reasonably practicable for A to comply with paragraph (i) or (ii); and

  (b) a record containing details relating to all transactions carried out by A in the course of relevant business.

(3) In relation to the records mentioned in paragraph (2)(a), the period is –

  (a) where A and B have formed a business relationship, at least five years commencing with the date on which the relationship ends; or

  (b) in the case of a one-off transaction (or a series of such transactions), at least five years commencing with the date of the completion of all activities taking place in the course of that transaction (or, as the case may be, the last of the transactions).

(4) In relation to the records mentioned in paragraph (2)(b), the period is at least five years commencing with the date on which all activities taking place in the course of the transaction in question were completed.

Failure to comply is an offence punishable on conviction by a maximum of two years' imprisonment and/or a fine, irrespective of whether money laundering has actually taken place.

10.2 What records should be kept?

The regulations require:

1. identification evidence; and
2. records of transactions.

Identification evidence is discussed in **Chapter 8**. Identification evidence should not be kept on the client file. It may easily be handed over by mistake if a client asks for it to be sent to another solicitor. Another risk is that the file will be destroyed after the firm's normal file retention period has expired but where there has been another transaction which restarts the five year 'clock'.

The Law Society's 'Money Laundering Guidance (Pilot – January 2004)' (LS Guidance)[1] advises that in most cases, the requirement to keep records of transactions will be satisfied by keeping a copy of the client file and the accounting records for this period should satisfy this requirement. If a firm is required to keep copy files for the five-year period, it could mean keeping files far longer where the firm has either entered into a business relationship with the client or a series of one-off transactions. This will have practical implications – and potentially costly ones for file storage – and firms may wish to consider whether something less will suffice, perhaps electronic evidence if it sufficiently identifies the detail of the transaction, coupled with the accounting records. If firms are going to retain less than the full file beyond a certain period, they might consider now whether to separate the documents for long-term retention, for example original contracts, into a subfolder. It is an area where more professional guidance would assist.

Firms will need to revise their policies on file retention. If they are not going to retain all files indefinitely, they will have to be astute to watch out for subsequent matters opened for the same client which might either form a series of transactions or an ongoing business relationship, because all records will have to be kept for five years from the conclusion of the last transaction. This in turn means that lawyers and their accounts staff will have to ensure that they do not open up a new client identity on their accounts system when they should instead be opening up a second or subsequent matter for the existing client. Central record-keeping by the accounts department is therefore to be preferred. This may also assist in the general compliance process, ensuring that client identification checks are in fact carried out.

---

[1] LS Guidance, para 3.53.

However, in practice firms will have to keep rather more. If a breach of the MLR 2003 is alleged, it may be necessary for a firm to show that it has complied with the MLR 2003 training requirements and therefore firms should consider keeping training records. They should either ask staff to sign an acknowledgement of the date and nature of the training received, or compile a list showing details of the training given and the persons attending.

Questions may also arise during an investigation as to what procedures a firm had in place at the time of a particular transaction which occurred several years before. Firms will therefore be well advised to ensure that they maintain an audit trail of changes in their policies and procedures – including anything kept on the firm's intranet.

The money laundering reporting officer will also wish to retain copies of all notifications and correspondence with NCIS. These should be kept secure.

11. Training

11.1 The requirement

Careful thought needs to be given to training. It is a statutory requirement to train staff. A firm can have very clear and appropriate reporting procedures but if they are not understood by the staff, or in fact the staff are unaware of who the money laundering reporting officer (MLRO) is, then they will count for little in helping make the firm compliant with the Money Laundering Regulations 2003 (MLR 2003).

The MLR 2003, reg 3(1)(c) requires that appropriate measures must be taken so that relevant employees are:

1. made aware of the provisions of the MLR 2003, the Proceeds of Crime Act 2002 (POCA 2002), Part 7 and the Terrorism Act 2000, ss18 and 21A; and

2. given training in how to recognise transactions which may be related to money laundering.

The Law Society's 'Money Laundering Guidance (Pilot – January 2004)' (LS Guidance) advises[1] that as at the commencement date of 1 March 2004, the Treasury had indicated that the requirements should be interpreted with common sense and did not, for example, require that as at that date all employees must be fully and finally trained. The difficulty with that approach is that while it may provide a defence to a charge of failing to train staff, there is no exemption for breach of the substantive offences. In addition, staff who have not been trained have less reason to be relied upon to notify the MLRO of information which they might have preferred to have been made aware of. All firms should, however, have completed their initial training at this point in time.

It is an ongoing requirement and firms should establish a rolling process. One-off training clearly cannot be good for all time – many circumstances will change – internal procedures, the role of individuals within the firm, statutory regulations and the LS Guidance. Staff should receive refresher

---

1 LS Guidance, paras 3.20 to 3.27.

11. Training

training at least every 24 months, and annual training is probably to be preferred. More frequent training may be appropriate for high-risk areas where awareness of latest trends and issues is important. This might usefully include lessons learned during the year including any adverse experiences (always assuming this can be done without falling foul of the tipping off provisions).

Firms will doubtless wish to include training as part of their induction procedures for new staff and that should include new partners, a point to bear in mind when making lateral hires. Lateral hire partners can bring a whole host of problems. A survey by Legal Risk revealed that even many top-100 law firms do not carry out all the checks they should on the partners they recruit. But what about checking the clients they bring with them? They have probably been recruited on the basis that they will bring the clients, yet the evidence of identity checks, if it has been done at all, will be with the partner's old firm. Clearly the MLRO must be involved in the process. Sometimes partner hires take place very quickly and matters such as this can easily be overlooked in the hype which goes with a major acquisition.

There can be little comfort derived from the fact that new recruits have had training in their previous firms. Different considerations may have applied in a different environment, the systems will have differed, and important controls and checks may even have been in place to protect that firm which are not in place in the new firm. Clearly therefore, training will have to be directed to the particular systems in operation in individual firms.

11.2 Relevant employees

The LS Guidance[2] states that all relevant staff within a firm should receive appropriate training in line with their responsibilities, activities and skills. This all begs the question – which staff should be trained?

Some staff may require only basic training on the relevant legislation, the firm's procedures and more obvious warning signs.[3] A firm may conclude after undertaking its risk assessment that secretarial staff, for example, do not need to be trained. However, while it may be the case that pool typists for example will have no client contact, they should consider whether secretaries may receive information through telephone calls from the client, those representing the other party to a transaction, or other third parties.

---

2 LS Guidance, para 3.21.
3 *Ibid*, para 3.24.

11. Training

Receptionists may even overhear calls on mobile telephones in reception and acquire important information.

A further reason for giving serious thought to training support staff is that they may be the firm's last line of defence if a fee-earner fails to discharge their duty – either because the firm has a rogue individual, or simply because of oversight and failure to appreciate the significance of material facts. In addition, the LS Guidance makes clear that if secretaries or receptionists are involved in obtaining evidence of identification they may require training[4] – indeed it is submitted that it is unlikely that they will not require it.

If any further reasons were needed for training all staff, thought should be given to the principal offences which apply to all firms and are not limited in application to those in the regulated sector under the POCA 2002. More training will be required for case handlers, especially those most at risk such as conveyancers and tax advisers.

The LS Guidance[5] recommends that members of a firm's accounts department who handle funds be trained so they can help in monitoring payments into and out of client accounts. Firms must also consider whether clerical, secretarial and administrative staff should receive training, as they may encounter evidence of money laundering. They are at the front line of detecting potentially suspicious circumstances such as:

1. funds coming in from a previously unidentified third party, when they were expected from a client; or
2. when funds are expected from a UK clearing bank in an account in the name of the client but they are actually received from a bank in a territory on the Financial Action Task Force list of non-participating countries.

The accounts team can be at the forefront in ensuring that procedures of internal control to forestall and prevent money laundering are applied. Some firms involve support staff in file opening procedures and possibly client identification procedures. Similarly, some support staff may be involved in speaking to clients on the telephone, or taking messages concerning transactions or funds. Receptionists may well come across information of potential importance which would, or should, arouse suspicions.

In one case, a small firm's fee-earners were away from the office on a training course. The client came in with a case full of banknotes for a

---

[4] LS Guidance, para 3.24.
[5] Ibid.

11. Training

property purchase. The receptionist had received money laundering training and told him that the firm did not accept cash. So far, so good, their internal procedure worked. However, the client then went round to the firm's own bank and paid the cash into the client account directly. Knowing that they were in funds, but not the nature of the funds, the firm completed the purchase. A firm cannot simply rely upon the bank's procedures working however, as the firm has to have its own procedures in place. A member of the accounts department later picked up that the cash transaction had taken place and was able to alert the MLRO.

Temporary staff – not just secretarial but locums as well – could also pose problems, and their duties must be clearly circumscribed to ensure the firm's compliance overall.

11.3 The method of training

Having decided which staff are to be trained, what form will it take? Beyond introductory training, there is no 'one size fits all'. Clearly the firm will need to do a risk assessment to tailor the training to the work type and the status of individuals within the firm.

The LS Guidance[6] advises that this may be by guidance notes, staff manuals, internal money laundering handbooks, face-to-face training, e-learning or otherwise. A word of caution: any system that depends on staff reading documents without live or other audio-visual forms of training exposes the firm to great risk. Educationalists advise that different people learn in different ways – audio, visual, kinaesthetic (ie by doing practical exercises) or a combination of these. There is an old Chinese proverb with much truth in it:

> I hear, I forget;
> I see, I remember;
> I do, I understand.

Relying solely on handouts seems potentially dangerous – there is little control over whether staff read them or understand them. If the firm has reason to know they are unlikely both to read them and understand them, then it is unlikely to have discharged its duties.

11.4 Proof of training

Having trained staff, it is essential that staff sign for the fact they have received and understood the training and that appropriate records are kept.

---

6 LS Guidance, para 3.21.

This raises the question – should a firm accept this alone, or should the firm test its staff? A decision has to be taken on this, and if staff are to be tested, it is an area where a score of nine out of ten will not suffice. If staff are not being tested, the firm will have to be sure that the staff have taken in and understood what they have been told and that, if tested, they would score ten out of ten. How can anyone be sure if they have not been tested?

11.5 Systems

Apart from matters covered by the training programme, how will staff know what the ongoing requirements are? With any new regime it is inevitable that change will be brought about in the light of new case law or legislation, new guidance from the courts, NCIS or the Law Society, and the firm's own experience. Changes in the firm itself may also bring about the need to update procedures – opening of new offices may weaken control, new areas of work may heighten the need for checks. Mergers and acquisitions of other practices are also key areas of risk, in addition to the usual changes in personnel through recruitment or hiring of temporary staff.

The ideal solution will be to have the procedures incorporated in the office manual and to have that available centrally and electronically, whether on an intranet or, for smaller firms, a central 'read only' document. That way staff can be sure that they are consulting the latest version.

12. Should you be suspicious?

12.1 Guidance

Criminals may use solicitors in the mistaken belief that legal professional privilege will provide cover; if it appears to, that may be down to misunderstanding by lawyers, but it is an area of considerable complexity as explained in the Law Society's 'Money Laundering Guidance (Pilot – January 2004)' (LS Guidance).[1]

Guidance on what may be suspicious can be found in the Law Society's Money Laundering Warning Card (see **Appendix 13**) and the LS Guidance. Issues to consider include:

1. *The secretive client* – solicitors need to obtain full instructions from the client in order to satisfy themselves that they are giving full and proper advice. If clients seem reluctant to answer questions, is this because they are naturally reticent, or because there is something to hide? This is the type of behaviour that might lead the solicitor onto a trail of enquiry prompting further questions.

2. *Unusual settlement requests* – anything which is unusual or unpredictable or otherwise gives cause for concern should lead to questions about the source of funds.

3. *Settlements by cash* – obviously, criminal activities such as the sale of small quantities of drugs to a large quantity of people can generate large amounts of cash. Similarly, cash-rich businesses can be used as a front to mask cash obtained via criminal activity. Most firms now have a policy of not accepting cash, or at least not accepting it over anything but a very small amount.

4. *Cash being paid into client accounts* – client account details need to be handed to solicitors on the other side, sometimes clients, to enable them to transfer moneys into the firm's account. Nevertheless, those in the accounts department should be vigilant. Firms cannot rely on their banks' procedures and systems. Remember they may well have

---

[1] See www.lawsociety.org.uk/professional/conduct/guideonline/view=page.law?POLICYID=161546.

12. Should you be suspicious?

already reported the incident to NCIS; if they have done so, the failure by the solicitor to report as well will be even more apparent and may prompt investigation.

5. *Surprise payments by way of third party cheques/funds* – as mentioned previously, firms should be alert to the possibility of the client telling the solicitor that the money will be coming in from a United Kingdom clearing bank but the money then comes in from another bank based in a territory which gives rise to suspicion. Again, clients and others need to be telling firms in advance the precise source from which funds are to be expected. Lawyers then need to pass that information onto their accounts staff and they in turn need to be checking that it comes from the source from which it was expected.

6. *Check that the money does in fact come from the client and not a third party* – solicitors have by this time gone through the trouble of obtaining suitable identification evidence. If large sums of money then come in from a third party of whom they have never heard, this may pose problems if it goes unnoticed and they fail to ask the appropriate questions and satisfy themselves that there is nothing suspicious.

7. *Atypical instructions: why has the client chosen this firm?* – is the practice being asked to do something that does not fit in with their normal pattern of business? It could be that the client has been recommended to the firm by an existing client or referral source, or it could be that the client sees an opportunity to undertake a transaction which another firm would not do.

8. *Lack of economic purpose* – solicitors should be alert to instructions which could lead to some financial loss to the client or a third party without a logical explanation, particularly where the client seems unconcerned.

12.2 Examples of areas of suspicion

1. *Conveyancing transaction* – the firm is instructed to sell a property at £45,000. The department dealt with the sale of the adjacent property three weeks ago for £60,000. It might be that the properties are entirely different or that one is in a very poor state of repair. Nevertheless, it could be that the client is attempting to obtain a fast return on the property as it has been purchased with criminal proceeds and does not mind about the selling price as long as it is sold quickly.

2. *Litigation* – the firm is instructed in a commercial litigation action. The client is the defendant. The solicitor believes that the client has an arguable defence, yet the client wants to settle the matter by accepting a payment less than the solicitor would recommend. There could be perfectly legitimate reasons for this or it could be that the action is a fictitious one, that the claimant and defendant are in some way connected and it is merely a means by which money can be passed from one jurisdiction to another. Care should be taken particularly if funds are being routed into and out of the United Kingdom in such a matter. This merits further enquiry.

3. *Instructions from nominees and agents* – again, this is all about knowing the client. Firms are going to some lengths to identify clients and to obtain satisfactory evidence. If it turns out that in fact the clients are merely agents or nominees and that somebody behind the client is not known to the firm at all, the solicitor should be trying to establish identity for the third party. The Money Laundering Regulations 2003 seem to impose a less slightly onerous requirement[2] but it is a risk management issue and the facts may justify a more stringent check than usual. Who is the firm acting for, who is the client, and to whom does the firm owe a duty?

4. *Money transfers* – those where there is a variation between account holder and signatory need fuller enquiry.

5. *Holding money* – being asked to hold money is a cause of particular concern and where there is no underlying transaction the solicitor may be in danger of breaching conduct rules. The firm is a practice of solicitors, not bankers. Solicitors should be very wary if what, in effect, the client is asking them is to provide a banking facility. The solicitor ought to be put in funds to complete a transaction where appropriate and should not be holding funds for any length of time, nor holding funds and making payments out at the direction of the client, nor holding moneys where there is no underlying transaction. Solicitors should also be alert to cases where they are put in funds for transactions which then abort – for example, the clients say they have had an adverse survey and are not proceeding with a purchase – this may be a ruse to use the solicitors' account to clean the funds. The increasingly common practice of simultaneous exchange of contracts and completion increases this risk because the client may provide the full amount required for completion to the solicitors before being contractually bound to purchase.

---

2 See **8.4**.

12. *Should you be suspicious?*

6. *Suspect territory* – if instructed in relation to transactions with an international element, law firms can refer to the Financial Action Task Force website[3] which provides up-to-date information about different countries. Particular care should be taken if a client is introduced through an overseas bank or third party based in countries where the production of drugs, drug trafficking or terrorism may be prevalent. Care should also be taken where funds are being routed into and out of the United Kingdom without a logical explanation. If it is a bank in another country, it might be that the firm's own bank can provide help in relation to identifying it as a mainstream bank.

7. *Settlements reached too easily* – settlements in litigation matters which are reached too early or too easily may be a cause for concern.

8. *Unusual changes in instructions* – solicitors should always be cautious of instructions changed without reasonable explanation.

9. *Changes in transaction circumstances* – be cautious if the transaction takes an unusual turn.

10. *Transfers made 'in error'* – be aware of the risk of moneys being transferred into the firm's account 'by mistake' (overpayments from clients or payments from third parties) and the firm then being asked to return them for the same reasons. Consent from NCIS may be required as well as considering the possibility of constructive trust claims.

12.3 Case studies

The following case studies are genuine with minor changes to preserve confidentiality. Furthermore, although they may not have contravened money laundering legislation at the time, it is thought they would now.

12.3.1 Mortgage fraud

Experience of multiple claims by lenders against professionals in the 1990s shows that many of the frauds committed by borrowers on lenders involve mis-statement of income (possibly unbeknown to the solicitor) or of the purchase price. Allowances against price were common, meaning the full amount appearing on loan documentation is not paid, perhaps indicating the borrower is making no personal contribution to buying the property. Another scam is the sub-sale or back-to-back transaction where there are related transactions and the price increases each time to 'justify' a larger mortgage.

---

3 See www.oecd.org/fatf.

12. Should you be suspicious?

The mortgage advance represents the proceeds of crime. The solicitor may have grounds for suspicion of a mis-statement of income and may be bound to disclose.

The Law Society issued a Green Card to the profession in 1991 identifying several of the warning signs associated with property fraud. The revised version appears in **Appendix 11**.

Case study 1

Stephen, an employed solicitor, acted for Bill. Bill was buying a house with a loan from Evergreen Bank. Stephen had recently acted on the purchase of two other houses for Bill, each mortgaged to a different lender. Stephen carried out no identity checks.

The price on the mortgage documents was £225,000. The bank was lending £200,000 less a £10,000 retention for repairs, conditional on:

1. personal occupation by Bill;
2. the balance of purchase money being provided by Bill without further borrowing; and
3. no other borrowing by Bill on any property.

Bill instructed Stephen that £20,000 would be unpaid but would be secured by a second charge to the seller. Bill never moved in.

Stephen's report on title confirmed compliance with all conditions.

Bill was convicted of mortgage fraud in relation to other properties. Evergreen claimed against Stephen alleging a fraud by Bill on this matter too. It alleged that had Stephen complied with its instructions this would have been discovered. Clearly Stephen was on enquiry that Bill might not have intended moving in, because he had recently acted on the purchase of two other houses. Stephen also knew that there would be a breach of the requirement that there be no further borrowing either on this house or any other.

Lessons

1. The failure of Bill to pay any of the price from his own resources was typical of mortgage fraud and covered by the Law Society's Green Card on mortgage fraud.

2. If the event occurred now there would be a clear risk of Stephen committing the principal money laundering offences (POCA 2002, ss327–329) as well as failure to make a disclosure to NCIS.
3. Failure to implement adequate procedures for identification or for training of staff would expose partners – not just the firm's MLRO – to conviction.

12.3.2 Prime bank instrument fraud

This was the subject of a warning by the Law Society in 1997, with a reissued version of the warning card in 2001 which also appears in the LS Guidance.[4]

In practice, fraudsters tend to approach individuals in small firms using what purports to be the language of international finance, but which is often meaningless jargon. Documents include phrases such as 'prime bank guarantees' and 'good cleared funds of non-criminal origin'.

Practitioners who aspire to a more exciting lifestyle often enter a world where large sums of money pass through their accounts, often with no underlying transaction of the type normally carried out by solicitors. They may be invited to meet investors, sometimes overseas. They may be asked to open US dollar accounts.

Case study 2

Simon was an assistant solicitor with a large and respected West End practice. Alan was a partner in an accountancy firm. Alan asked Simon whether Simon's firm would act for individuals who wanted to invest money in a client company. Simon knew nothing of this company. Alan explained that solicitors were needed because a bank would not deal with 14 individuals but wanted one point of contact.

Investors were given a brochure offering the opportunity to double their money in two months by buying and selling bank debentures. The document set out how the scheme worked: funds would be paid into a solicitor's client account causing the investor to become a client of the solicitor with funds guaranteed by indemnity insurance.

The document explained that this was both secure and profitable and offered clients a guaranteed minimum of an 8% return compared with 'normal deposit interest rates of about 4%' which was the rate prevailing at the time.

---

4 LS Guidance, Annex 14. See **Appendix 12**.

Alan told Simon that the investments would be placed on a blocked deposit account and used to buy and sell letters of credit. He explained that the funds would not be leaving the account. Simon would not be required to provide any advice, all he had to provide was the use of the firm's client account.

Simon hoped this would result in introductions to wealthy individuals who might enhance the firm's practice. Simon spoke to the senior partner, whose only concern was about money laundering, though neither pursued that aspect further.

Simon did not keep a file for this but put everything on his miscellaneous file. The money was paid through a client ledger entitled 'William Green – Miscellaneous', William Green being the partner who supposedly supervised the private client department, including Simon. This was a breach of the Solicitors Accounts Rules because it was in the name of a partner and also failed to separate the funds of the 14 investors.

Investments totalling £2.5m were lost and the investors claimed against both the solicitors and the accountants.

Lessons

1. There was no control over the introduction of new clients.
2. The firm's client account was being used with no underlying transaction. Reference to the security of the firm's indemnity insurance should have set alarm bells ringing.
3. No investigations were made as to the identity and creditworthiness of the investment company.
4. Despite concerns about possible money laundering, no further enquiries were made – only too often, problems of this nature emerge where the warning signs have already been spotted long in advance. The concerns which the senior partner expressed were not misplaced because the investments were taken from clients under false pretences and became the proceeds of crime before they reached Simon's firm. From that point on, Simon's firm was involved in an arrangement which, had it occurred after the POCA 2002 came into force, would have been an offence.
5. The return on investment was far in excess of what was available elsewhere at the time – deals which seem too good to be true usually turn out to be just that.

6. There was no supervision of Simon.
7. Miscellaneous files and client ledger are invariably a recipe for disaster.
8. Firms should never allow client accounts to be opened in the names of partners.
9. Simon knew nothing of the investors' identity and made no enquiry of them. He knew nothing of their needs or objectives in making investments at all.
10. Above all, Simon did not profess to understand the nature of the documents put before him – if he did not understand the nature of the transactions he should never have allowed himself to become involved.

12.3.3 Corporate offences

Recent corporate scandals raise the spectre of money laundering risk for law firms because in many, if not all, cases offences will have been committed which one way or another give rise to proceeds and exposure to involvement in the principal offences.

The problem goes further than those cases however. A wide variety of issues may arise – for example, companies assisting in the purchase of their own shares or, in the course of due diligence on an acquisition, discovering that a target company has committed environmental offences through inadequate systems, which have been tolerated in order to increase profit.

Case study 3

A firm of solicitors acted for a public company for which it had acted for many years since it started as a small business. The company had over 100 outlets of its own and over 200 franchisees. Over a period of six months, £3m was credited in five instalments without warning to the firm's client account by transfer from an Austrian company.

As the company was the firm's only substantial client, the senior partner assumed the payment must be connected with it. He made enquiry and the directors confirmed that the money was in connection with a facility for new franchisees and the Austrian lender was connected with the client's principal supplier. The directors gave instructions as to the application of funds and no enquiry was made of the Austrian lender. The firm did not act for the Austrian lender and no security was put in place.

The money was mainly used to fund new franchisees, few of whom put up any of their own money – any shortfall being dealt with as an 'allowance'. £500,000 was used to fund loans to directors.

Not long afterwards, the client company collapsed and the directors were convicted of fraud.

The Austrian lender claimed against the solicitors on the basis of a constructive trust.

On examination of the solicitors' files, most of the franchisees had used a trade reference from the same double glazing company with considerable doubt as to the authenticity of the documents.

Lessons

1. Firms should always know the source of funds expected into their client account. This enables them to be alert to moneys arriving from unusual or unexpected sources.

2. Firms should not provide a banking facility to clients. Funds should be received from the client or a previously identified source only when necessary to effect a legitimate transaction for the client with an underlying legal purpose. The LS Guidance[5] recommends that care should be taken if funds are routed in or out of the UK with no logical reason.

3. No attempt was made to clarify the scope of the retainer and who was the client *vis à vis* the funds received. Simple questions such as 'who are we acting for?' and 'to whom is a duty of care owed?' would have clarified the firm's position. If the firm was not acting for the lender, then it should have ascertained who was. In that event, it should not have distributed the funds.

4. The firm also ran a high risk of a claim based on a constructive trust.

---

5 LS Guidance, para 6.33.

13. *P v P* AND OTHER CASES

13.1 *P v P*[1]

This was a matrimonial matter – a solicitor acting for a wife in ancillary proceedings, but all solicitors should be aware of it. As this was a matrimonial case the Law Society urges caution before extending it to other areas of practice. The main distinction is the greater duty of disclosure in connection with ancillary relief matters. Nonetheless, it is submitted that the guidance is likely to be of wider application.

13.1.1 *P v P – the decision*

The solicitor and her client were concerned that some of the money which belonged to her husband and which was to be the subject of the proposed ancillary relief settlement may have been derived from tax evasion. The assets involved were thought to be substantial, somewhere in excess of £19m. After unsuccessfully seeking guidance from NCIS, whose response was said to have been misleading, the guidance of the court was sought as both the solicitor and her client were concerned that they might become concerned in an arrangement if they went ahead with a settlement. Following the guidance they had received from NCIS, they were in an untenable position as they had been informed that they could tell neither the opposing solicitors, nor either of the parties and a financial dispute resolution was imminent.

The President of the Family Division, Dame Butler-Sloss held that:

1. The act of informing the client or any other person that a disclosure was to be or had been made to NCIS would itself appear to be a 'disclosure' within the meaning of s333(1) and s342(2) of the Proceeds of Crime Act 2002 (POCA 2002).

2. There was nothing in the POCA 2002, s328 to prevent a solicitor or barrister from taking instructions from a client. However, if, having taken instructions, the solicitor or barrister knew or suspected that

---

[1] [2003] EWHC 2260 (Fam).

13. P v P and other cases

they or their client would become involved in an arrangement that might involve the acquisition, retention, use or control of criminal property, then an authorised disclosure should be made and the appropriate consent sought under s335.

3. The POCA 2002, s333 and s342, which prevent a person from tipping off or prejudicing an investigation, specifically recognise a legal adviser's duty to make the relevant disclosures. A central element of advising and representing a client was the duty to keep the client informed and not to withhold information from the client. The legal professional exemption was lost if a disclosure to a client was made 'with the intention of furthering a criminal purpose'. Unless the requisite improper intention was there, the solicitor should be free to communicate such information to the client as was necessary and appropriate in connection with the giving of legal advice or acting in actual or contemplated legal proceedings.

4. Having complied with the obligations under the POCA 2002, s328, there was nothing in the statute to require a solicitor to delay in informing the client.

5. Where guidance from the court was sought, it would be appropriate for legal advisers to make the application without notice to the other side, making NCIS the respondent to the application. The application would be heard in private and the court should direct that no mechanical recording of the proceedings should be disclosed or transcribed without the leave of the judge.

6. In the circumstances of the instant case, W's legal advisers had been right to make an authorised disclosure to NCIS. It had also been entirely proper for them to approach the court for guidance. As there had been no reply from NCIS by the end of the requisite seven-day period, W's legal advisers had been free to continue dealing with the other side and to inform the other side that a disclosure had been made to NCIS. They would not have been exposed to the risk of prosecution for tipping off or prejudicing an investigation.

13.1.2 P v P – *Law Society and NCIS guidance*

The Law Society has provided a detailed guidance note which appears at **Appendix 10**. Additionally, NCIS amended its 'Guidance to Legal Advisers'[2] as a number of significant issues were clarified.

---

2 See **Appendix 9**.

1. Where somebody in the firm knows or suspects that the proceeds of crime may be involved in a transactional matter that they are handling, and they continue with that matter without making an appropriate disclosure to NCIS, they run the risk of being involved in an arrangement within s328 of the POCA 2002. That is because it is an offence under s328 to enter into an arrangement that a person knows or suspects facilitates (by whatever means) the acquisition, retention, use or control of criminal property by or on behalf of another person.

2. For an arrangement offence to be committed, no money need pass through the solicitor's client account or even be contemplated as having to pass through that account.

3. It does not matter how small the financial benefit from criminal conduct may be, or when or where that conduct took place, as long as it would be a criminal offence if committed in this country. As the definition of criminal conduct is conduct which constitutes an offence in any part of the UK or would constitute an offence if committed there, tax evasion or social security fraud amount to criminal conduct.

It is, of course open to a solicitor to withdraw from a matter in these circumstances. The practical difficulty, however, is the potential for tipping off the client in the way in which the withdrawal from the matter is communicated.

The Law Society guidance note on *P v P*[3] makes it clear in para 7 that:

> It is necessary and appropriate for solicitors, in giving advice to the client or in acting in connection with the legal proceedings, to advise their client that, in the light of their knowledge of suspicion, if they continue to act for the client, both they and their client will commit a money laundering offence unless an authorised disclosure is made to NCIS and the appropriate consent is received from NCIS to continue.

In doing so, however, solicitors must be careful to avoid committing the offences of tipping off (POCA 2002, s333) or prejudicing an investigation (POCA 2002, s342) and should carefully consider the advice given in the LS Guidance, Annex 3, para 19. In the event the client does not consent to the solicitor making an authorised disclosure, the solicitor should withdraw.

Plainly, where a solicitor considers it appropriate to discuss the potential report with the client and the client refuses to consent to the solicitor making an authorised disclosure, the solicitor must withdraw. Whether or not they should discuss it with their client depends on the circumstances. In *P v P*, it is not suggested anywhere in the judgment that the solicitor and the wife whom they represented who made the report to NCIS were in any way

---

[3] 'Money Laundering Guidance (Pilot – January 2004)' (LS Guidance), annex 3. Extract Copyright © The Law Society.

involved in any of the suspected criminal money laundering activities. Where there are concerns about another party, the sensible course will be to consider making a joint report with the client as envisaged in the LS Guidance, Annex 3, para 25.

The position may be different if the solicitors are concerned about their own client. They may consider the greater potential for becoming involved in an offence of tipping off or prejudicing an investigation.

The *P v P* guidance note in the LS Guidance distinguishes between information arising in the regulated sector and the non-regulated sector, namely between relevant and non-relevant business. It was of course prepared prior to 1 March 2004 when the Money Laundering Regulations 2003 came into force in relation to the supply of legal services. On the basis that ancillary relief advice is likely to constitute relevant business, such distinctions are probably now of little practical significance.

13.1.3 P v P – *privilege and matrimonial matters*

Solicitors may in certain circumstances rely on a defence to the POCA 2002, s330 reporting offence if the information came to them in privileged circumstances (see **Chapter 15** where the issue is discussed in more detail).

Much has been written about the special position matrimonial practitioners hold in relation to their clients' financial position when advising on ancillary relief matters. Annex 3, para 11 of the LS Guidance deals with legal professional privilege. It states that, for the purposes of the POCA 2002, legal professional privilege is narrowly drawn. For example, legal professional privilege does not attach to communications between opposing parties in litigation. Therefore, if the knowledge of suspicion arises from a communication between solicitors it will not have come to them in privileged circumstances. To attract privilege, the knowledge must arise from a confidential communication received by the solicitors for the sole or dominant purpose of the proceedings, from their client. Even then, this will not be the case if the purpose of the communication is a criminal one, whether on the part of their client or another. Therefore, even where they subsequently withdraw from the matter because of their suspicions, solicitors must carefully consider whether their knowledge or suspicion arises from privileged circumstances when deciding whether or not they need to make a report.

It seems clear that where a solicitor has gained knowledge or a suspicion of criminal proceeds, the only way they can continue to act to avoid prosecution for a potential money laundering offence is by making a report to NCIS and obtaining the appropriate consent, an 'authorised disclosure'. Whilst waiting for consent, in the interim period, they should of course not take any substantive steps in relation to the matter.[4]

13.1.4 P v P – what should the solicitor tell the client?

P v P also addresses the issue of informing the client following a report being made. Even in circumstances where a privilege defence is properly available to solicitors, there is no absolute duty to tell the client that they have made or intend to make a report to NCIS. From a practical point of view, the most obvious reason to consider discussing this with the client would be where a joint report is likely to be of value. In particular, this might be where the solicitor forms a view that the client is not involved in money laundering activities or it might be where the client themselves actually brings the concern to the attention of the solicitor.

A note of caution – the writers are aware of one case, and doubtless there will be very many more, where the solicitors were acting for the wife and the issue was one of tax evasion through the family company run by the husband. The difficulty which arose was that the wife was company secretary and therefore potentially implicated in the crime.

Even where there is some suspicion that the client might be involved, as the LS Guidance, Annex 3, para 25 makes clear, once the POCA 2002 provisions are explained to them, clients may wish to make their own report or a joint report. They may also, by obtaining consent, give the client protection from commission of the s328 arrangement offence, even if the report is made by, or on behalf of, the suspected party themselves.

13.2 C v S (Money Laundering: Discovery of Documents)[5]

This was a decision under the pre-POCA 2002 legislation that is still relevant. It explains the procedure to be adopted where compliance with an order for disclosure would involve commission of a tipping-off offence.

C obtained a freezing order against the defendants apart from B. C required information as to what had happened to some money and so it obtained from Lightman J a *Norwich Pharmacal* order[6] requiring B to disclose certain

---

4 See **9.6** and **Chapter 6** for further information on making a report and dealing with NCIS.
5 [1999] 1 WLR 1551, CA.
6 See *Norwich Pharmacal Company v Commissioners of Customs & Excise* [1974] AC 152.

papers which were in C's name or in the name of named defendants. All the orders were obtained without notice.

B had made a series of money laundering reports to NCIS. These reports were subject to the tipping-off provisions then in force.[7] B's solicitors sought an assurance from NCIS that there would be no prosecution if it complied with the order. NCIS refused to give any such assurance and indicated that any assurance given would not be watertight because the ultimate decision whether to prosecute rested with the prosecuting authorities.

NCIS made an application under the Police and Criminal Evidence Act 1984, Sch 1 for an order requiring B to produce similar documents to those which Lightman J had ordered to be disclosed.

The Court of Appeal gave the following guidance:[8]

1. As soon as a financial institution is aware that a party to legal proceedings intends to apply for or has obtained an order for discovery which might involve the institution having to give disclosure of information which could prejudice an investigation it should inform NCIS of the position and the material which it is required to disclose.

2. The NCIS will then have the opportunity to identify the material which it does not wish to be disclosed and indicate any preference which it has as to how an application or order should be handled. In doing this it should be born in mind that usually it will not be necessary to disclose any document or part of a document which refers to the fact of the investigation since this will not be relevant to the issues with which the applicant for the order is concerned. A case such as the present is likely to cause particular difficulty because the NCIS did not wish the applicant, C, to know that there was an investigation in progress. However there should be cases where the NCIS is not concerned about the applicant knowing about the investigation. Where this is the position it may be sufficient to make the compliance with the order subject to an appropriate undertaking to keep the relevant information confidential.

3. If NCIS has no objection to partial disclosure the applicant may be satisfied by partial disclosure if it is explained that the alternative is for the matter to be considered by the court. Whether an explanation for the partial disclosure can be given will depend on the attitude of NCIS.

4. If the restricted disclosure is unacceptable to the applicant then the directions of the court will have to be sought. The extent to which the applicant can be informed of the reason for the issue being referred to the court will depend on the circumstances. The circumstances will also influence the way in which the matter is brought before the court. The application can be to set aside the order if it was made ex parte. Alternatively there can be an application for directions. If the order has not been made the problem can be brought to the attention of the court without the need for a separate application. The court will have to be warned in advance of the difficulties. Where a high degree of confidentiality is required a sealed letter can be written to the judge in charge of the relevant court setting out the circumstances and that judge can then put in place the necessary arrangements. In this case we found the provision of a skeleton argument to the court alone setting out the

---

7 Criminal Justice Act 1988, s93D as amended, and replicated in the equivalent provisions of the Drug Trafficking Act 1994.
8 [1999] WLR 1551 at 1555.

background facts and issues and identifying the problem a very convenient way of ensuring that the court is sufficiently informed of the situation.

5. On the issue being brought before the court the degree to which the applicant can be involved and the extent that it is possible for the issues to be resolved in open court again will depend on the circumstances, but the general approach must be to comply with the ordinary principles to the extent that this is possible. If necessary the stratagems which were deployed in this case will have to be used. Where these sort of arrangements are necessary there should always be a transcript prepared and the institution should be required to provide a copy to the applicant when it is informed by the NCIS that there is no longer any requirement for secrecy.

6. In deciding what order should be made the court will have to decide what evidence it requires. In an obvious case a letter from NCIS will suffice. In other cases their attendance will be required. If the court considers this is justified to achieve justice, the NCIS can be made a party.

7. It will be for the NCIS (or other investigating authority) to persuade the court that, were disclosure to be made, there would be a real likelihood of the investigation being prejudiced. If the NCIS did not cooperate with in advancing such a case, the court could properly draw the inference that no such prejudice would be likely to occur and could accordingly make the disclosure order sought without offending the principle in *Rowell v Pratt* and without putting the institution at risk of prosecution.

8. Especially when the applicant can not be heard it is important that the court recognises its responsibility to protect the applicant's interests. The court must have material on which to act if it is to deprive an applicant of his normal rights. The one criticism which can be made in this case of what occurred in the courts below is that they did not have that material. The court should bear in mind that a partial order may be better than no order. It should also consider the desirability of adjourning the issue in whole or in part since the expiry of a relatively short period of time may remove any risk of the investigation being prejudiced. The NCIS will no doubt wish to co-operate with the courts in achieving speedy progress as this will be the most productive way of avoiding prejudicing an investigation and protecting the interests of litigants.

13.3 *Governor and Company of the Bank of Scotland v A Ltd & ors*[9]

This was a decision of the Court of Appeal under the pre-POCA 2002 legislation. The case provides some guidance which may be of assistance to solicitors who are concerned about constructive trust liability and who wish to seek directions or a declaration from the court.

The Bank of Scotland became aware, following communications with the police, that money laundering investigations were being conducted into activities connected with A Ltd. The bank feared that if it paid out money in A Ltd's account it could be liable to third parties as a constructive trustee and, if it did not, an action could be brought and it would not be able to defend itself because the police objected to it revealing what it had been told. This would have constituted a tipping-off offence under the Criminal Justice Act 1988, s93D.

---

9 [2001] EWCA Civ 52.

13. P v P and other cases

The Bank of Scotland applied without notice, in private to Lightman J, seeking directions. Lightman J granted an injunction against the bank, restraining it from making any payment from the accounts. The judge ordered that A Ltd was not to see anything put before the court in support of the application, nor the order itself, nor be informed of its existence. B and C Ltd were joined to the proceedings because they had been responsible for remitting the moneys into A Ltd's accounts.

Lord Woolf CJ, giving the judgment of the court, held that Lightman J was wrong to grant the injunction. It served no useful purpose. He could not envisage circumstances where it would be appropriate to grant an injunction against the only party seeking relief. The bank could have sought directions on the footing that it was at least a putative fiduciary. However, it was unnecessary for the bank to establish its status as a trustee because the court could instead grant a declaration. Whilst recognising the difficult situation in which the bank found itself, there was no point in seeking relief against A Ltd. Instead, the appropriate defendant to any application for directions was the Serious Fraud Office (SFO). If there was a dispute as to whether a payment could be made or disclosure made by the bank, the SFO, on behalf of the police, and the bank should try to resolve it between themselves. If they could not do so, the bank could apply for interim declaratory relief. If proceedings were brought by the customer, the bank would have to take a commercial decision as to whether to contest the proceedings or not. If the proceedings were to be contested, they should be conducted as openly as possible. Consideration should be given as to whether it was desirable for the judge who heard any proceedings against the bank to be different from the judge from whom guidance was sought.

It was of the greatest importance that the use of 'tipping-off' powers was confined to situations where it was appropriate. Banks could call on the assistance of the courts to avoid being unduly prejudiced by these provisions but that must not be regarded as a substitute for financial institutions taking decisions which it should be their commercial responsibility to take. An interim declaration would protect banks from criminal proceedings but it would not automatically protect them against actions by customers or third parties. However, it seemed almost inconceivable that a bank which took the initiative in seeking the court's guidance should subsequently be held to have acted dishonestly so as to incur accessory liability.

13.4 *Tayeb v HSBC Bank Plc & anr*[10]

This case was also decided under the pre-POCA 2002 legislation. The decision largely related to the effect of the banking rules on CHAPS payments and whether a bank could return payment which it regarded as suspicious once the money had been credited to the customer's account. Nonetheless there are some points of wider application which may assist in cases where the firm's account is credited with money as to which they have suspicion.

Mr Tayeb was a Tunisian national with no permanent address in England. In 2000 he opened a savings account at HSBC. On 21 September 2000, almost £1m was transferred from the Libyan corporation General Posts and Telecommunications Company's (GPTC) account with Barclays Bank by CHAPS to Mr Tayeb's HSBC account.

This was payment for a database which GPTC was buying from Mr Tayeb. The transfer was received and credited to Mr Tayeb's account. The database was handed over to GPTC later that day and the transaction completed on the assumption that the transfer had been successfully effected.

In the meantime, an assistant manager at HSBC, who was suspicious of the nature and origin of such a large sum of money, froze Mr Tayeb's account.

Unsatisfied with Mr Tayeb's explanation for the transfer, on 22 September the assistant manager re-transferred the sum by CHAPS to the GPTC account at Barclays. This transfer was made without Mr Tayeb's consent and resulted in GPTC having the database without paying for it.

It was common ground that the circumstances surrounding the transfer of funds justified HSBC in being suspicious, but it was later accepted that the origin of the payment was completely innocent and honest.

It was held that once the CHAPS receipt was authenticated, and therefore unconditionally credited to the account under CHAPS rules, the money should not have been returned. HSBC's assertion that a bank retains an overriding discretion to re-transfer funds already credited to an account without the consent of the customer failed and HSBC was liable to Mr Tayeb.

The judge noted[11] that:

> The JMLSG Money Laundering Guidance Notes 1997, while generally explaining the effect of the 1988 Act, contain specific recommendations as to compliance.

---

10 [2004] EWHC 1529 (Comm).
11 At para [56] of the judgment.

13. P v P and other cases

> 'NCIS "consent" to undertake the transaction following a disclosure is provided to the reporting institution as a defence against a charge of assisting a money launderer. It is not intended to over-ride normal commercial judgment, and a financial sector business is not committed to continuing the relationship with the customer if such action would place the reporting institution at commercial risk. However, it is recommended that before terminating a relationship in these circumstances, the reporting institution should liaise with NCIS or the investigating officer to ensure that the termination does not 'tip-off' the customer or prejudice the investigation in any other way.'

It was held that if a bank has advance warning of a transfer about to be made by CHAPS as to which it already entertains suspicions, it can report the matter to NCIS in advance, or it can withhold authentication while it informs NCIS or, having credited the customer's account following authentification, it can report the matter to NCIS and wait for directions. If it fears that a transfer out of the customer's account is imminent it can temporarily freeze the account and inform NCIS, but with due regard to the dangers of tipping off.

The following passage[12] is helpful in showing that the fact of making an application to the court will tend to displace any suggestion of dishonesty making constructive trust liability unlikely:

> The proposition that a bank which in view of its suspicions about a CHAPS transfer which took the course discussed in paragraphs 62–65 above would be running the risk of liability as a constructive trustee presents itself to me as wholly unrealistic. It finds itself subjected to an electronic transfer. It suspects the origin. If withdrawal appears to be imminent, it withholds authentication for the CHAPS transfer. Alternatively, it informs NCIS and discusses what course should be taken if withdrawal is attempted. If necessary and appropriate, it issues an application for an interim declaration against the Serious Fraud Office. In consequence, it declines its customer's instructions to make payment from the funds received. To characterise the bank's conduct in such circumstances as amounting to dishonest assistance, such as would found a claim against it as constructive trustee by the true beneficiary of the fund would, in my judgment, be inconsistent with the basis of that relief identified in *Royal Brunei Airlines v Tan*,[13] and *Heinl v Jyske Bank*.[14] Far from giving dishonest assistance to the perpetrator of a fraud, the bank would be assisting the beneficiary of the fund by obstructing the course of possibly dishonest conduct.

---

12 At para [75] of the judgment.
13 [1995] 2 AC 378.
14 [1999] Lloyd's Rep Bank 511.

14. CONCERNS FOR PARTICULAR DEPARTMENTS

14.1 Property

For property lawyers, the opportunities for money launderers to use their services is obvious. They are at risk in relation to the 'relevant business' they conduct, but even putting aside the considerations of the regulated sector, they could also fall foul of the principal money laundering offences under ss327 to 329 of the Proceeds of Crime Act 2002 (POCA 2002).

This is against a backdrop of UK property transactions being the current favoured means of money laundering. In its report 'UK Threat Assessment of Serious and Organised Crime 2003' NCIS recorded that:[1]

> In 2002, purchasing property in the UK was the most popular method identified, involving roughly one in three serious and organised crime groups where the method was known. Investment in front companies or high cash businesses came next, followed by simply spending the criminal proceeds to fund a lifestyle, and by transferring cash overseas using bureaux de change and money transmission agencies. Roughly one in 10 groups was known to use bank accounts in the UK, and similar proportions used accounts overseas or transmitted cash through couriers. Fewer groups invested in property overseas, or in financial products, and a small percentage used gambling or alternative remittance systems (for example, 'hawala' banking), although the highly secretive nature of the latter means that this is likely to be understated.

Particular difficulties arise for solicitors who do volume conveyancing work on a nationwide basis which does not afford them the opportunity to see the client. Considerable caution will be needed, as this is particularly high-risk (see **7.10** and **Chapter 8**).

The position may be slightly easier if the instructions are for a remortgage and not a purchase. In some cases these may be one-off transactions below the €15,000 limit which may not require identification evidence for the purposes of the Money Laundering Regulations 2003 (MLR 2003), though whether the solicitor should be proceeding without any evidence at all might be questionable.

The simplest route would be if the lenders are in the regulated sector themselves (which they generally will be), and they either provide written

---

1 See chapter 6 of the NCIS report, entitled 'Money Laundering' at para 6.8 (www.ncis.co.uk).

14. Concerns for particular departments

assurance that the clients have gone through the lenders' money laundering identification procedures, ideally providing copies too, or certify the documentation on the solicitors' behalf.

If that is not possible, certification of original documents by a bank manager, accountant or responsible person, preferably in the regulated sector, may assist.

Where that is not possible, solicitors can consider asking for original documents to be sent to them in accordance with the Law Society's list. Firms may prefer not to ask clients to commit these to the post and may, after conducting their risk assessment, conclude that they will avoid asking clients to send passports or driving licences. It may be useful in these cases to back up any identity evidence with, for example, a letter from the client's bank, council tax statement, and an electronic check on something completely separate such as the electoral register. Documents should be copied carefully, certified and the originals returned.

14.2 Matrimonial

Matrimonial lawyers have been thrust into the limelight in relation to the POCA 2002. This follows the case of *P v P*[2] on which judgment was delivered in October 2003. This is discussed in **13.1**.

As discussed previously, the case addressed various issues regarding the principal money laundering offences (POCA 2002, ss327–329) as well as the offences under s333 and s342, tipping off and prejudicing an investigation. What the case did not address was how far conducting matrimonial work falls with the regulated sector and comprises relevant business for the purposes of the MLR 2003.

As in relation to other work conducted by solicitors, the issue is whether it comprises:

> ... the provision by way of business of legal services by a body corporate or unincorporate, or in the case of the sole practitioner, by an individual and which involves participation of a financial or real property transaction (whether by assisting the planning or execution of any such transaction or otherwise by acting for, or on behalf of, a client in any such transaction).[3]

In practice, albeit that ancillary relief matters are a form of litigation and that on numerous occasions they may be publicly funded, in spite of the Treasury view mentioned in the Law Society's 'Money Laundering

---

2 [2003] EWHC 2260 (Fam).
3 MLR 2003, reg 2(2)(l).

Guidance (Pilot – January 2004)' (LS Guidance), para 3.12, it would appear that until this issue is further clarified, firms ought to err on the side of caution and work on the basis that matrimonial work generally, and ancillary relief matters in particular, form part of relevant business, unless it is clear from the outset that no financial element is going to arise. That being the case, identification should be obtained and record-keeping procedures used for that work.

Plainly, ancillary relief work in matrimonial proceedings is likely to constitute financial or real property transactions and this appears to be the view of the Law Society Professional Ethics helpline, albeit not confirmed in print. Other types of matrimonial work, such as work relating to child law may fall outside relevant business, unless they concern financial aspects.

The guidance of the Law Society and NCIS following the case are discussed at **13.1.2**.

14.3 Criminal work

At present this may appear to be low-risk work because most information will come to a solicitor under the cloak of legal privilege. However, problems are emerging. For example, where a client seeks advice about a mundane motoring offence but, when discussing resources to advise on likely fines, the solicitor discovers the client has illegal income.

Problems arise when instructed on asset recovery proceedings if the solicitor discovers that the prosecution has an incomplete list of assets because the solicitor is then exposed to assisting in concealment, unless the solicitor make a disclosure.

Further problems will emerge if legal aid is restricted because clients who may be well known to be criminal will be paying their ill-gotten gains to the solicitor for fees. The LS Guidance[4] then goes on to indicate the Treasury view, which confirms that certain types of work will not generally be viewed as 'participation in financial transactions', including a payment on account of costs to a solicitor or payment of a solicitor's bill (because the solicitor is not participating in a financial transaction on behalf of the client).

In addition, the money may be received for adequate consideration, however, the refund of any balance at the end of the case may be an issue requiring disclosure and NCIS consent.

---

4 LS Guidance, para 3.12.

14.4 Personal injury and other litigation

This is discussed at **5.2**. As explained, many personal injury practitioners have been taking the view that in principle, their work generally falls outside the definition of relevant business, taking account of the current Treasury view which confirms that participation in litigation would not be within it. There is the risk that view may change.

However personal injury (and other) litigators will be concerned that $P \ v \ P^5$ clearly showed that litigation, in that instance, ancillary relief, could lead solicitors into involvement in a principal money laundering offence, in that case, under the POCA 2002, s328 (an arrangement). Retention of the profits of evading tax may amount to concealment in which the solicitor could also be implicated. Claims which are in some way tainted by fraud and clients who are found to have evaded tax are the main concern.

An MLRO who is notified of matters giving him knowledge or suspicion of money laundering is obliged to report it, whether or not in the regulated sector.

As previously mentioned, the Law Society is apparently considering whether it is able to provide guidance to the effect that personal injury work is not ordinarily considered relevant business and that the strict identification requirements of the MLR 2003 do not ordinarily apply. However, training and awareness of money laundering principles and legislation is still strongly recommended.

---

5 [2003] EWHC 2260 (Fam).

15. Privilege and confidentiality

15.1 Introduction

This is one of the most difficult areas for the money laundering reporting officer (MLRO) and highlights the tension between the duty to the client and obligations to the public at large. If the MLRO is a non-contentious lawyer it is perhaps worth stating that litigation practitioners are usually more informed on the subject and in the first instance it may be worth consulting with a litigation colleague if possible.

This chapter deals with two principal issues:

1. protection from action where disclosure by the solicitor may breach duties to the client; and
2. protection for solicitors who refrain from making disclosures because of their duties to clients.

The problem stems from the general understanding of the profession that clients consult them in confidence and expect that confidence to be maintained. While most clients may be expected to understand that if they have done something wrong, they are in no position to complain about disclosure, the position is harder to explain where it is merely suspicion which has prompted disclosure, and that suspicion proves to be unfounded.

While MLROs may understandably err on the side of caution and make disclosures where privilege issues are complicated, it is clear that a simple policy of 'if in doubt, disclose' is wrong in principle. The risk is that a policy of over-reporting may cause clients' transactions to be delayed with consequent claims for loss.

Solicitors and their staff are under a duty to keep the affairs of clients confidential and that will only be overridden in exceptional circumstances.

The right to withhold documents from production when they are subject to legal professional privilege is that of the client, not the solicitor. Nonetheless, where a third party is seeking disclosure of privileged documents held by a solicitor, the solicitor is duty bound to consider in relation

15. Privilege and confidentiality

to each document whether the client may be entitled to withhold it. In normal circumstances the solicitor might seek the client's consent, but in the context of money laundering that is less straightforward given the risk of tipping off or prejudicing an investigation.

First, it is necessary to distinguish between privilege and confidentiality. Privilege is the *right of the client* to withhold a document from production. Confidentiality on the other hand is the wider, ethical *obligation of the lawyer* not to disclose information. The confusion arises because the confidentiality is generally a pre-condition to the right to claim privilege.

It is worth stating that non-lawyers have real difficulty understanding why lawyers should be concerned about withholding information relating to money laundering from the authorities. It is for this reason that lawyers can expect little sympathy from the public, and perhaps from juries, if they withhold information when they should not have done. The decision-making process in whether to withhold information or make a disclosure is made the more difficult by the increasingly technical issues which arise in determining whether privilege exists. Nonetheless, the reason for the rule is to encourage frank disclosure to legal advisers in confidence without fear. In the absence of legal professional privilege, clients might withhold information from their legal advisers, and it is not in the interests of justice if this were to happen.

15.2 The rules of privilege

In order to assist MLROs reaching a decision on the issue as it affects the facts of a particular case, there are two flowcharts at the end of the chapter, which should be read with the notes which follow them.

15.2.1 Definition of privilege

A good working definition of the test for privilege is to be found in the Police and Criminal Evidence Act 1984 (PACE 1984), s10:[1]

Meaning of 'items subject to legal privilege'
(1) Subject to subsection (2) below, in this Act 'items subject to legal privilege' means ...
   (a) communications between a professional legal adviser and his client or any person representing his client made in connection with the giving of legal advice to the client;
   (b) communications between a professional legal adviser and his client or any person representing his client or between such an adviser or his client or any such representative and any other person made in connection with or in

---

[1] It was held by the House of Lords in *Francis & Francis (a firm) v Central Criminal Court* [1988] 3 WLR 989 to represent a statutory enactment of the common law of privilege.

contemplation of legal proceedings and for the purposes of such proceedings; and

(c) items enclosed with or referred to in such communications and made –

(i) in connection with the giving of legal advice; or

(ii) in connection with or in contemplation of legal proceedings and for the purposes of such proceedings, when they are in the possession of a person who is entitled to possession of them.

(2) Items held with the intention of furthering a criminal purpose are not items subject to legal privilege.

It is important to note the exclusion relating to items held with the intention of furthering a criminal purpose: it is not confined to the intention of the solicitor, nor even the client. It is sufficient that *anyone* has the intention of furthering a criminal purpose. The exception will therefore apply where a third party is seeking to pursue a criminal end, even where neither the solicitor nor the client has that intention – cases where the client is being 'used'.

The next point the solicitor needs to consider is precisely who the client is. Too often, solicitors fail to distinguish between the respective interests of clients when they are acting for more than one client – eg lender/borrower, insurer/insured, co-purchasers – or whatever. Subject to the possibility that one is using the other to pursue a criminal purpose, they each have their rights and the need for separate consideration of their position.

15.2.2 Legal advice privilege

The PACE definition above refers to 'communications between a professional legal adviser and his client or any person representing his client made in connection with the giving of legal advice to the client'. This is a developing area of law and MLROs need to be aware that a particular view on what is privileged may turn out to be subject to vigorous challenge.

In *Three Rivers District Council v Bank of England*[2] the Court of Appeal considered whether advice given by solicitors to the Bank of England on how to present its evidence to the inquiry into the collapse of BCCI was protected by legal advice privilege. The court held that it was not privileged because the dominant purpose of instructing the solicitors was not the obtaining of advice in relation to legal rights and obligations. Set against the background of the litigation which in fact ensued, it is not surprising that the Bank of England would have wanted to seek advice and the decision was therefore surprising to many.

---

2 [2004] EWCA Civ 218.

15. Privilege and confidentiality

Although an appeal to the House of Lords resulted in that decision being overturned,[3] the judgments were still awaited at the time of going to press and the full impact of the appeal cannot yet be assessed. It is particularly significant because the role of a solicitor is ever-changing and increasingly trying to regain the ground the profession once had when it regarded itself as consisting of 'men of affairs'.[4]

15.2.3 Litigation privilege

The definition in PACE 1984 refers to:

> ... communications between a professional legal adviser and his client or any person representing his client or between such an adviser or his client or any such representative and any other person made in connection with or in contemplation of legal proceedings and for the purposes of such proceedings.

It is clear from the authorities that this is narrower than often appreciated and is confined to documents which come into existence either:

1. when litigation has started; or
2. when litigation is reasonably in contemplation.

The litigation, actual or proposed, must have been the sole or dominant purpose of the communications – see *Waugh v British Railways Board*.[5]

15.2.4 Where privilege does not exist

If privilege does exist in relation to a particular client matter, it is important to recognise that it does not extend to all documents which may be on a solicitor's file. Documents and communications which are not privileged include:

1. client ledger;[6]
2. communications which are not obtaining of advice in relation to legal rights and obligations;[7]
3. communications for the purpose of furthering a crime;[8]
4. conveyancing documents;[9]

---

3 Unreported, 29 July 2004.
4 At a time when the profession comprised almost exclusively men!
5 [1979] 3 WLR 150.
6 *Nationwide Building Society v various solicitors* [1999] PNLR 53.
7 *Three Rivers District Council v Bank of England* [2004] EWCA Civ 218.
8 Police and Criminal Evidence Act 1984, s10(2).
9 *R v Inner London Crown Court, ex parte Baines & Baines* [1988] QB 579.

5. diaries;[10]
6. notes of hearings in open court and correspondence or discussions with opposing lawyers, or notes of those discussions;[11]
7. pre-existing documents; and
8. time sheets and records.[12]

15.3 Protection for the solicitor who makes a disclosure

15.3.1 Protected disclosures

Protected disclosures, under the Proceeds of Crime Act 2002, (POCA 2002) s337, as their name implies, give protection against breach of confidentiality. They arise where a person acquires information in the course of their profession which causes them to suspect, or gives reasonable grounds to suspect, that a person is engaged in money laundering. The section provides that a disclosure in the proper manner to a person's MLRO or to NCIS will not give rise to any breach of any restriction on the disclosure of information. The protection applies equally whether the solicitor is in the regulated sector or not. It also applies in circumstances where the disclosure is voluntary.

Two further points arise:

1. *provided* the solicitor *does* suspect money laundering by the person concerned, there is protection from breach of confidentiality, even, it seems, if the suspicion is not justified objectively – ie the facts do not have to be such as would make a reasonable person suspicious; and
2. there is a slightly curious limitation on this protection because under the POCA 2002, s337(4) the disclosure has to be made as soon as is practicable after the information or other matter comes to the discloser – so prompt disclosure is protected, delayed disclosure is not.

15.3.2 Authorised disclosures

An authorised disclosure in accordance with the POCA 2002, s338 is one which may in certain circumstances protect the person disclosing from commission of the principal money laundering offences under s327 (concealment), s328 (arrangement) and s329 (acquisition, use and possession).

---

10 *R v Manchester Crown Court, ex parte Rogers* [1999] 1 WLR 832.
11 *Parry v News Group Newspapers Ltd* (1990) 140 NLJ 1719.
12 *R v Manchester Crown Court, ex parte Rogers* [1999] 1 WLR 832.

15. Privilege and confidentiality

This will be of particular relevance to solicitors who are concerned that their own clients are embarking on a course of conduct which may lead to the commission of an offence. Situations where this may arise are easy to envisage, for example:

1. the matrimonial client who agrees a financial settlement with a tax-evading spouse;
2. the property-buying client whose income is inconsistent with the number of mortgaged properties he has bought; or
3. the former employee whose dismissal for dishonesty was procedurally unfair and on whose behalf the solicitor has negotiated a settlement.

Note that it does not relieve the solicitors from any other liability, such as a constructive trust.[13]

15.4 Protection for the solicitor who does not make a disclosure

In some circumstances, particularly where privilege in fact applies, there may be protection for a solicitor who does not make a disclosure. It is essential to note however, that the protection described in the following paragraphs is protection *only* in relation to the reporting obligations applying to the regulated sector.

Separate consideration is given later to whether the solicitor – inside or outside the regulated sector – who fails to disclose might still be guilty of the principal offence of concealment.

The requirement to disclose arises under the POCA 2002, s330 when, in the course of business in the regulated sector, a person acquires knowledge, suspicion, or reasonable grounds for knowledge or suspicion, that another person is engaged in money laundering. Section 330(6) provides that a person does not commit an offence under the section if:

1. they have a reasonable excuse for not disclosing the information or other matter;
2. they are a 'professional legal adviser' and the information or other matter came to them in 'privileged circumstances'.

Under the POCA 2002, s330(10), information or other matter comes to a professional legal adviser in privileged circumstances if it is communicated or given to them:

---
13 See **4.7.2** and **13.4**.

(a) by (or by a representative of) a client of his in connection with the giving by the adviser of legal advice to the client,

(b) by (or by a representative of) a person seeking legal advice from the adviser, or

(c) by a person in connection with legal proceedings or contemplated legal proceedings.

However, s330(11) provides that it does not come to the lawyer in privileged circumstances if it is communicated or given with the intention of furthering a criminal purpose.

The term 'professional legal adviser' gives rise to some difficulty. Many staff in a solicitor's office may acquire confidential information but not be legally qualified and may be involved in a support role. They are subject to the same duties of confidentiality as their employers but are not professional legal advisers. These include secretaries, accounts staff and others in a support role. However, the Money Laundering Regulations 2003 (MLR 2003), reg 7(6) widens the definition of professional legal adviser to include 'any person in whose hands information or other matter may come in privileged circumstances'. The definition therefore includes non-qualified employees of solicitors including secretaries and experts such as accountants and doctors instructed in connection with litigation. At the time of going to press the Home Office was carrying out an informal consultation on whether the privilege exception should be extended to accountants, auditors and tax advisers carrying out comparable work to lawyers.[14]

However, there may still be doubt as to whether the MLRO, or even the expert's MLRO, who receives information from another member of staff does so in privileged circumstances, as the client is not then seeking legal advice in confidence from the MLRO. The Law Society's 'Money Laundering Guidance (Pilot – January 2004)' (LS Guidance),[15] as yet untested and without Treasury approval, is that in those circumstances the MLRO may fall back on the alternative defence of 'reasonable excuse'.

It is easy to envisage that the solicitor may genuinely believe that information is privileged but is unaware of, say, a third party's criminal purpose in using the solicitor's client. In those circumstances, taking the provision at face value, there might appear to be no defence against non-disclosure because there would be no privilege. The solicitor may have

---

14 'The Proceeds of Crime Act 2002 & The Money Laundering Regulations 2003: Obligations of Accountants to Report Money Laundering – An Informal Consultation', 4 August 2004, see www.homeoffice.gov.uk/docs3/accountant_obligations.pdf.
15 LS Guidance, para 4.36.

15. Privilege and confidentiality

two defences in this situation – first, lack of criminal intent,[16] and second, reliance on 'other reasonable excuse'.

15.5 Dangers to avoid in practice

Once the solicitor has received information relating to proceeds of crime, even though it is received in privileged circumstances, he or she is then in a difficult position. The issue is discussed in some detail in the LS guidance on *P v P*.[17] A number of the issues arising from that guidance, such as informing clients and opponents about disclosure and the risks of tipping off, are dealt with in **13.1**. The case to which that relates was a matrimonial case, and the advice states that solicitors should be extremely cautious about extending it to other types of work. Nonetheless, the guidance is helpful, in the writers' view, in identifying the issues which need to be addressed.

If there is a distinction to be drawn between ancillary relief proceedings and other types of legal work, it arises from what the judge in the case described as follows:

> … there is an enhanced duty of full and frank disclosure upon legal professionals acting in family proceedings, and particularly in ancillary relief proceedings … In accordance with this duty of full and frank disclosure in financial disputes between spouses, details of the size and description of family assets and actual or potential debts are crucial to the attempts of the legal advisers to settle these cases and to the FDR process … If financial irregularities are discovered and investigated, it may diminish the value of the assets, the subject of the ancillary relief proceedings. The purpose of the FDR would be frustrated if the judge or district judge did not have the true facts and the parties were unable to negotiate a genuine settlement in the absence of the requisite knowledge as to the true value of the assets.[18]

The solicitor can clearly advise clients on their obligations under the POCA 2002. However, almost anything else runs the risk of committing one of the principal money laundering offences under the POCA 2002, s327 (concealment), s328 (arrangement) and s329 (acquisition, use and possession). The options at this stage therefore, if there are further steps needed on behalf of the client, are:

---

16 LS Guidance, para 4.38 cites Lord Rooker, the government spokesman in the House of Lords, as saying during the passage of the Proceeds of Crime Bill: 'The criminal law is quite clear: where a criminal offence is silent as to its mental element, the courts must read in the appropriate mental element. Therefore, in circumstances where a legal adviser did not know that information was not legally privileged, the courts would read in a requirement that he could not be convicted unless he did know.' (Hansard, 27 May 2002, col 1078).
17 LS Guidance, Annex 3.
18 *P v P* [2003] EWHC 2260 (Fam), para 60.

1. authorised disclosure, seeking consent to proceed, taking no further steps unless and until consent is forthcoming; or
2. withdraw.

In either case the solicitor will need to consider carefully the risk of committing offences of tipping off under s333 of the POCA 2002 or prejudicing an investigation under s342 of the POCA 2002. These provisions are considered in more detail in **4.5.4**. If the solicitor withdraws, they still need to consider whether to make a disclosure. Solicitors in the regulated sector must disclose unless privilege applies.

However, that still leaves open the question of whether the solicitor who does not make a disclosure might be guilty of concealment under s327 of the POCA 2002. The scenario is easy to envisage. The matrimonial solicitor discovers on examination of his client's accounts that his own client has not been disclosing all his income to the Inland Revenue. The solicitor realises that concluding a financial settlement may amount to an arrangement and decides to cease acting. The solicitor decides not to make a disclosure. He puts the papers back in the file and sends them off for storage. What defence does the solicitor have if he is charged with an offence of aiding and abetting concealment of criminal property under s327?

The answer is not entirely easy. The section 330(6) privilege defence is quite clear in its wording in that it applies only to offences under that section, ie breaches of the disclosure requirements in the regulated sector.

Section 327(2) also provides little assistance as a possible defence. The most relevant provision, at first sight, is in s327(2)(b) which provides that a person does not commit an offence if 'he intended to make such a disclosure but had a reasonable excuse for not doing so'. Here the solicitor may have thought that privilege was a reasonable excuse for not disclosing, but they fail in their defence at the first hurdle because they cannot establish that they intended to make a disclosure.

The LS Guidance[19] states that it is unlikely that the solicitor commits an offence by failing to make a disclosure upon withdrawal in circumstances such as this because otherwise the section 330(6) privilege defence would be made redundant. The basis for that proposition is not explained further however and it must be the case that the position is unclear, and the only certainty is that where privilege exists on the facts, it provides a defence to the disclosure obligations of those in the regulated sector under that section.

---

19 LS Guidance, para 4.52.

15. Privilege and confidentiality

All solicitors, whether in the regulated sector or not, must be concerned that they commit an offence of concealment, or at least aiding and abetting it, by simply withdrawing and not making a disclosure in these circumstances. These are the same provisions which apply to all members of the public. The reader will therefore understand if solicitors take what appears to be the easy option and make a disclosure in every such case regardless of privilege and regardless of whether they are in the regulated sector or not. The following case study illustrates some of the problems which may arise in the commercial arena and which may also touch on areas such as matrimonial practice. Note also that a mediator who happens to be a solicitor or barrister cannot claim the professional legal adviser exemption from making a disclosure because mediators do not give legal advice.

15.6 Case study

15.6.1 *The facts*

There is a highly acrimonious dispute between shareholders of a long-established family company which runs a small supermarket. There are three main shareholders. Two of them, Bill and Penny, are directors. The third shareholder, Charlie, is not a director. Charlie lives abroad, and has become increasingly disenfranchised by Bill and Penny. He is anxious to sell his shares, not only to put the affairs of the company behind him, but also to fund a rather expensive divorce. Bill and Penny are proposing to buy him out.

There is a dispute over the share valuation, with Charlie alleging serious irregularities in the accounts. Litigation has commenced but the matter has been referred to mediation. Bill and Penny are represented by their solicitor, Shaun. The parties appoint Mary as their mediator. She is not a lawyer, but is an accredited mediator.

During the course of the mediation, Mary presses Bill and Penny to explain a payment from the company to a supplier in which Bill and Penny have a substantial interest. Their explanation is decidedly vague and satisfies neither the mediator nor Shaun. On instructions from Bill and Penny, the mediator communicates the explanation to Charlie and his solicitor, Al, who are equally unimpressed and suspect a fraud on the company.

The parties reach the point where Bill and Penny say they cannot fund a higher settlement than is currently on offer. Pressed further by the mediator in a private session, it emerges that the money which Bill and Penny are proposing to put towards a settlement is to be borrowed by them from the company's bank. As evidence of this, they produce a letter from the bank which Shaun has not seen before. The letter shows the extent of the agreed facility. The letter concludes that the facility is subject to a guarantee by the company.

The mediator asks if she can show the letter to Charlie and Al, which they agree to as it seems likely to put some pressure on Charlie to settle at the sum on offer.

15.6.2 *The issues*

Shaun is dissatisfied with the explanation of the payment by the company to its supplier. Depending on the facts, he may have grounds to suspect theft of company property. If so, he should advise Bill and Penny to disclose this to NCIS jointly with him. If they do not agree, he may consider that the information is privileged, and that he is therefore under no obligation to disclose it to his MLRO. He will be considering carefully, however, whether there may be any reason for privilege not applying, because if it does not, he may be at risk of a disclosure offence under s330 of the POCA 2002. He may well decide to disclose in any event out of concern over the risk of committing a separate offence of aiding and abetting concealment. If he does suspect a crime and discloses it promptly, he is protected from any breach of confidence action.

Al suspects a crime. Information from an opponent is not subject to legal professional privilege. He advises Charlie that they should report this to NCIS jointly.

Mary, the mediator, is not in the regulated sector and is under no statutory duty under s330 of the POCA 2002 to report her concerns about the payment to NCIS. She may however be concerned that by not notifying NCIS, she may be party to an offence of concealment. She may disclose voluntarily in any event and, as the information came to her in the course of her profession, she will be protected from any liability for breach of confidence.

Shaun's second concern is the bank loan for purchase of Charlie's shares, guaranteed by the company. This is potentially an offence of assisting in the purchase of the company's own shares;[20] it is not going to be possible to comply with the 'whitewash' provisions of ss156 to 158 Companies Act 1985 on the day of the mediation, though this may be a possibility given more time. Proceeding to settle as matters stand on the day of mediation will put all present at risk of committing money laundering

---

20 Companies Act 1985, s151.

offences, either as principal or aiding and abetting – for an arrangement, acquisition, use and possession, and possibly concealment.

Shaun could in theory try and seek consent from NCIS to proceed in this way but in the context of a mediation and the timescales involved that is unlikely to be a practical course. It would be perfectly proper for him to advise Penny and Bill that to proceed in this way would involve the commission of an offence and, if they are by chance still intent on proceeding, he should cease acting. Upon ceasing to act he will wish to consider whether the safe course is to make a disclosure in any event because of the risk of being party to an offence of concealment.

Al should advise Charlie not to accept payment for his shares in the knowledge of the illegal assistance. Again, NCIS consent is unlikely to be a viable option in the available timescale.

If Mary facilitated a settlement involving illegal assistance, she too could be guilty of principal money laundering offences. Even though she is not in the regulated sector, she is under the same obligations as everyone else in relation to the principal offences. It will not be viable for her to seek NCIS consent, unless theoretically the mediation were to be adjourned, exercising all due caution over the risk of tipping off. The more realistic course for her is to say that any settlement must be funded in some other way and that she cannot continue the mediation if the parties insist on using the illegal bank loan.

All in all, the mediation seems unlikely to result in a settlement on the day. It might be possible to reach an agreement in principle with a view to the company subsequently complying with ss156 to s158 of the Companies Act 1985. Concerns over the unexplained payment to the supplier remain to be disclosed to NCIS as outlined above.

15. Privilege and confidentiality

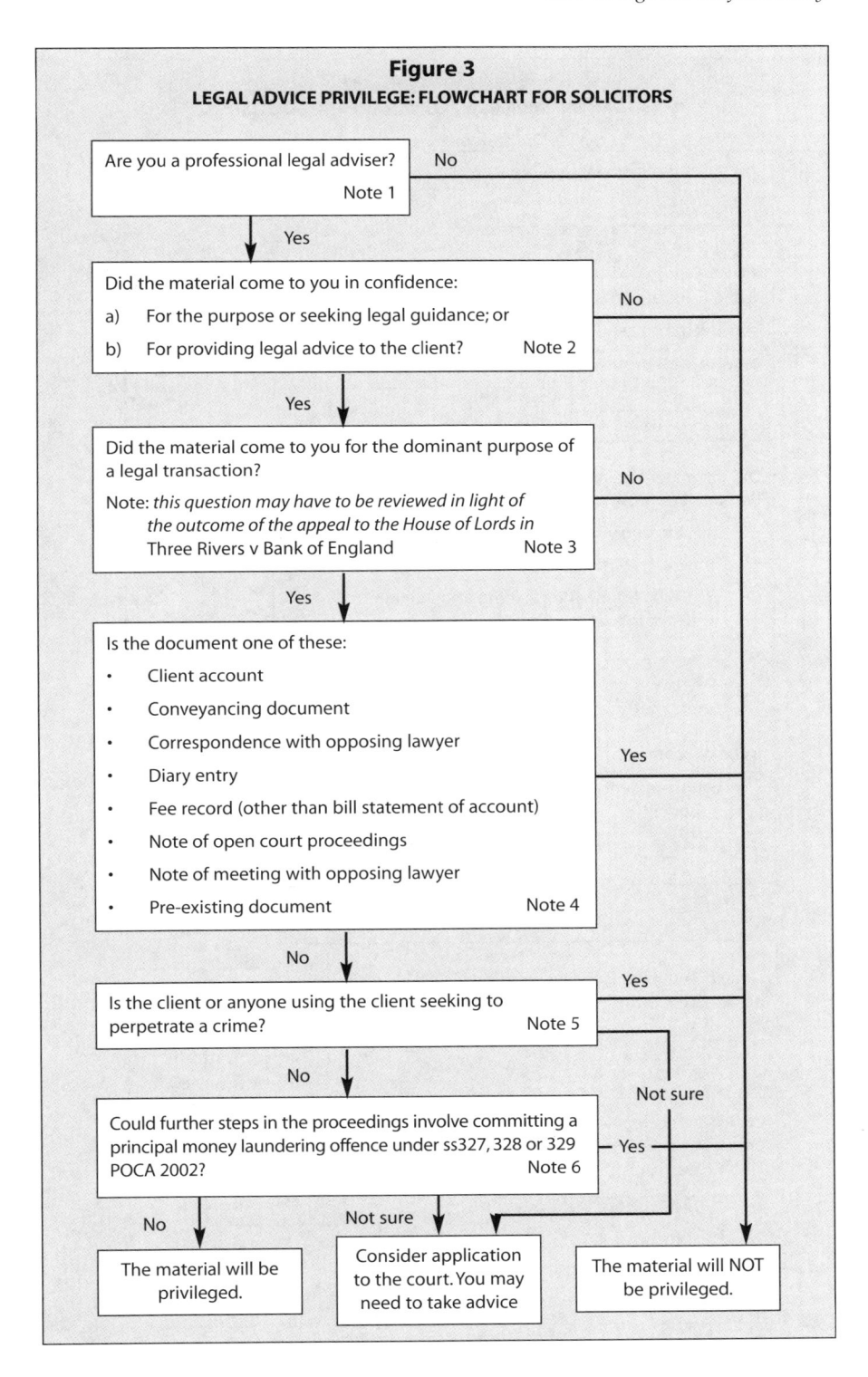

Figure 3
LEGAL ADVICE PRIVILEGE: FLOWCHART FOR SOLICITORS

```
┌─────────────────────────────────────────┐
│ Are you a professional legal adviser?   │──No──────────┐
│                               Note 1    │              │
└─────────────────────────────────────────┘              │
                 │ Yes                                    │
                 ▼                                        │
┌─────────────────────────────────────────┐              │
│ Did the material come to you in         │              │
│ confidence:                             │──No──────────┤
│ a) For the purpose or seeking legal     │              │
│    guidance; or                         │              │
│ b) For providing legal advice to the    │              │
│    client?                     Note 2   │              │
└─────────────────────────────────────────┘              │
                 │ Yes                                    │
                 ▼                                        │
┌─────────────────────────────────────────┐              │
│ Did the material come to you for the    │              │
│ dominant purpose of a legal             │──No──────────┤
│ transaction?                            │              │
│ Note: this question may have to be      │              │
│   reviewed in light of the outcome of   │              │
│   the appeal to the House of Lords in   │              │
│   Three Rivers v Bank of England        │              │
│                               Note 3    │              │
└─────────────────────────────────────────┘              │
                 │ Yes                                    │
                 ▼                                        │
┌─────────────────────────────────────────┐              │
│ Is the document one of these:           │              │
│  • Client account                       │              │
│  • Conveyancing document                │              │
│  • Correspondence with opposing lawyer  │──Yes─────────┤
│  • Diary entry                          │              │
│  • Fee record (other than bill          │              │
│    statement of account)                │              │
│  • Note of open court proceedings       │              │
│  • Note of meeting with opposing lawyer │              │
│  • Pre-existing document      Note 4    │              │
└─────────────────────────────────────────┘              │
                 │ No                                     │
                 ▼                          Yes           │
┌─────────────────────────────────────────┐──────────────┤
│ Is the client or anyone using the       │              │
│ client seeking to perpetrate a crime?   │              │
│                               Note 5    │              │
└─────────────────────────────────────────┘              │
                 │ No          Not sure                   │
                 ▼            ─────────────┐              │
┌─────────────────────────────────────────┐              │
│ Could further steps in the proceedings  │              │
│ involve committing a principal money    │──Yes─────────┤
│ laundering offence under ss327, 328 or  │              │
│ 329 POCA 2002?                Note 6    │              │
└─────────────────────────────────────────┘              │
         │ No         │ Not sure                          │
         ▼            ▼                                   ▼
┌──────────────┐ ┌──────────────────┐ ┌──────────────────┐
│ The material │ │ Consider         │ │ The material will│
│ will be      │ │ application to   │ │ NOT be           │
│ privileged.  │ │ the court. You   │ │ privileged.      │
│              │ │ may need to take │ │                  │
│              │ │ advice           │ │                  │
└──────────────┘ └──────────────────┘ └──────────────────┘
```

133

15. Privilege and confidentiality

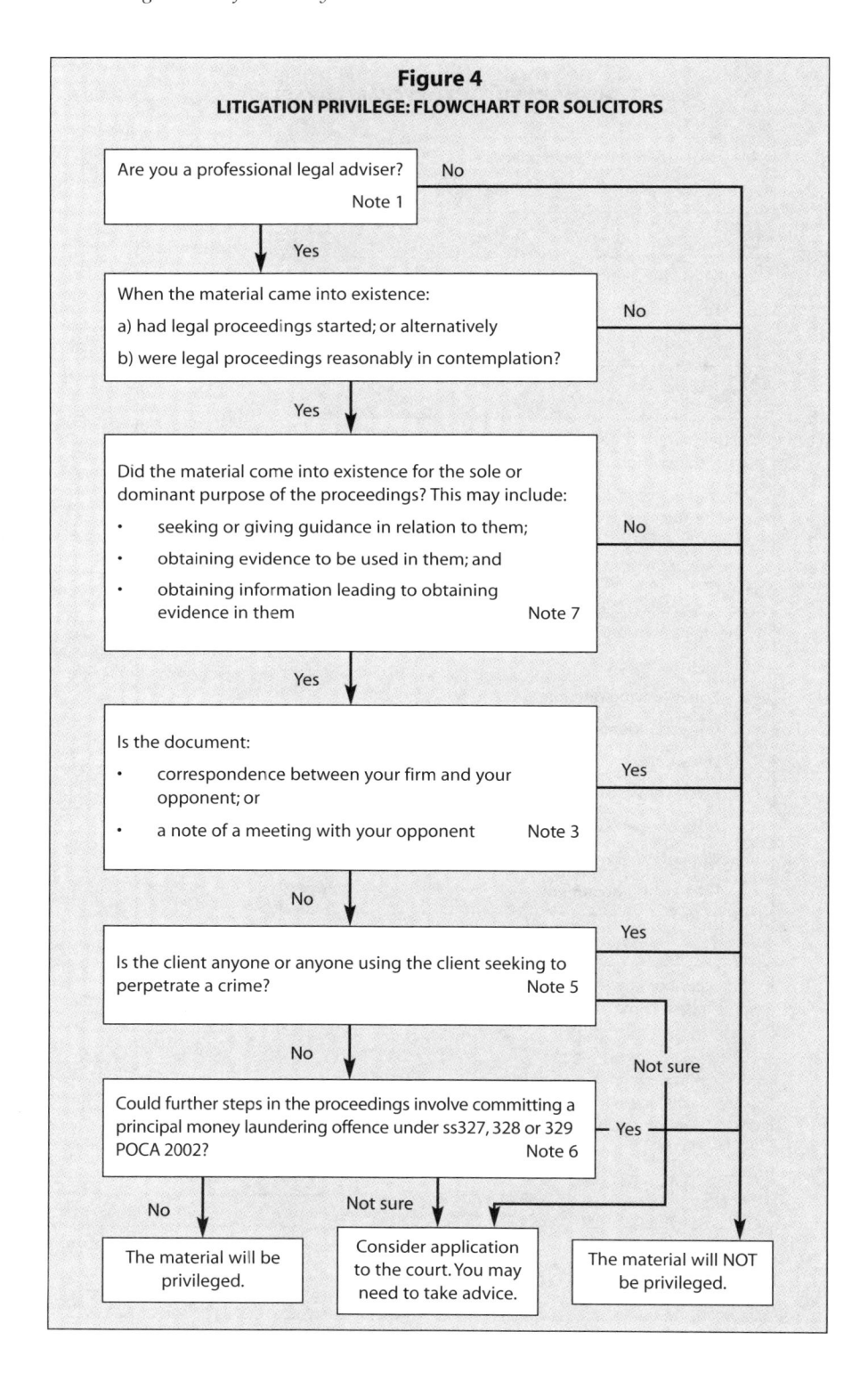

Figure 4
LITIGATION PRIVILEGE: FLOWCHART FOR SOLICITORS

- Are you a professional legal adviser? **Note 1**
  - No → The material will NOT be privileged.
  - Yes ↓
- When the material came into existence:
  a) had legal proceedings started; or alternatively
  b) were legal proceedings reasonably in contemplation?
  - No → The material will NOT be privileged.
  - Yes ↓
- Did the material come into existence for the sole or dominant purpose of the proceedings? This may include:
  - seeking or giving guidance in relation to them;
  - obtaining evidence to be used in them; and
  - obtaining information leading to obtaining evidence in them **Note 7**
  - No → The material will NOT be privileged.
  - Yes ↓
- Is the document:
  - correspondence between your firm and your opponent; or
  - a note of a meeting with your opponent **Note 3**
  - Yes → The material will NOT be privileged.
  - No ↓
- Is the client anyone or anyone using the client seeking to perpetrate a crime? **Note 5**
  - Yes → The material will NOT be privileged.
  - No ↓
- Could further steps in the proceedings involve committing a principal money laundering offence under ss327, 328 or 329 POCA 2002? **Note 6**
  - Yes → Consider application to the court. You may need to take advice.
  - Not sure → Consider application to the court. You may need to take advice.
  - No → The material will be privileged.

Notes to flowcharts

Note 1

Regulation 7(6) of the MLR 2003 amends POCA 2002 s330(6) to widen the definition of professional legal adviser to include 'any person in whose hands information or other matter may come in privileged circumstances'. The definition therefore includes non-qualified employees of solicitors including secretaries and experts such as accountants and doctors instructed in connection with litigation.

See **15.4** on the position of experts reporting matters to their MLROs.

Note also that a mediator who happens to be a solicitor or barrister cannot claim the professional legal adviser exemption from making a disclosure because mediators do not give legal advice.

Note 2

Communications between a lawyer (acting in their capacity as a lawyer) and the client are privileged if they are confidential and for the purpose of seeking legal advice from the lawyer or providing legal advice to the client subject to exceptions described in the following notes.

Note 3

The Court of Appeal in *Three Rivers District Council & anr v Governor of Company of the Bank of England*[21] held that the material must have come to the lawyer for the dominant purpose of a legal transaction. The House of Lords has allowed an appeal but at the time of going to press the reasons for the decision were still awaited and this point will therefore need careful review in the light of the decision.

Note 4

A number of categories of documents have been held by the courts not being covered by advice and privilege. See the list at **15.2.4**.

Note 5

Has the client sought advice in order to perpetrate a crime? Although it is acceptable for a lawyer to advise a client on how to stay within the law and avoid committing a crime, a client is not entitled to privilege where they

---

21 [2004] EWCA Civ 218.

instruct the lawyer in order to obtain advice which the client admits is in relation to carrying out an offence. If the lawyer suspects that their client is attempting to involve them in a fraud, provided there is strong evidence,[22] the lawyer may release themselves.

Otherwise the solicitor may apply to the court for an order.[23] Note that the exception applies where a third party intends the communications between the lawyer and client to be for the purpose of committing a crime and where, for example, an innocent client is being used by a third party.

Note 6

Solicitors need to be particularly astute to avoid committing offences because clearly no privilege can apply here.

Note 7

See *Waugh v British Railways Board*.[24]

Note 8

Correspondence with your firm and your opponent is not privileged.[25]

Notes of a meeting with an opposing lawyer are not privileged.[26]

---

22 *O'Rourke v Darbishire* [1920] AC 581.
23 *Finers v Miro* [1991] 1 WLR 35.
24 [1979] 3 WLR 150.
25 *Parry v News Group Newspapers Ltd* (1990) 140 NLJ 1719.
26 *Ibid*.

16. INTERNATIONAL ASPECTS

16.1 Relevance to domestic firms

This chapter applies to most firms, even if at first glance it appears otherwise.

For many firms the international aspects of compliance may appear few and there will be no need to understand foreign law. For others, it will be their bread and butter work and some of the issues affecting those firms are dealt with in this chapter and elsewhere in the book.

However, even those with no overseas work should be aware of the wider ramifications that the legislation may have for them. A large professional indemnity claim, handled on behalf of insurers, is described in the case study which follows and provides an illustration of how even small provincial firms can be affected by this.

16.2 Case study

A three-partner firm in a provincial town became caught up in an international bank instrument fraud with judgment against one partner in the American courts for nearly $200 million. The partner, perhaps finding that his branch office high street work lacked some of the spice of life, was approached by an individual purporting to be an international financier. The solicitor was invited to travel to the United States to meet those behind the scheme and was unwilling to admit that he did not understand the documents put before him which were full of meaningless jargon.

The deal involved a purported American bank which was not licensed under American securities laws and several British Virgin Islands companies. Lines of credit were available with profit of between 2% and 4% per 'trade'. The extraordinary nature of this proposal is revealed when it becomes apparent that the trades were supposed to take place almost weekly resulting in an annual profit of approximately 400% on each investment.

The partner opened a US dollar client account, which would be unusual for a small firm of this type. When the partner concerned was out of the office, cheques were signed by another partner without enquiry. It barely needs stating that if it sounds too good to be true, it probably is. A number of foreign individuals made substantial claims resulting in the judgment mentioned above and the demise of the practice. Whether the partner was merely incredibly naïve, or worse, remains unresolved. However, the case merits mentioning for a number of reasons:

1. a point which all lawyers should understand, it demonstrates how essential it is that whatever work one is doing for a client, the lawyer must understand the nature of the transaction and its purpose;
2. it highlights the dangers of becoming involved in areas of practice with which the practitioner is unfamiliar;
3. it highlights the need for a risk assessment when taking on new work, an issue which some firms will be addressing as part of their compliance with the Lexcel Standard 2004 or as part of general good practice;
4. it emphasises the need for partners signing cheques to understand the need to be on enquiry when a cheque out of the ordinary requires signing;
5. it demonstrates the need for partners to understand what their other partners are doing and to implement systems of audit and supervision across all levels of the practice; and
6. it shows how a small high street practice can become immersed in international money laundering issues.

Although the facts in this case occurred before the implementation of Proceeds of Crime Act 2002 (POCA 2002), and did not therefore constitute money laundering at the time, they are by no means unique and it is easy to see how a solicitor could become embroiled in committing offences under the POCA 2002.

16.3 Overseas clients

Increasingly, firms may find they have overseas clients through the simple fact of increased mobility and established clients finding work overseas. Clients may be paid abroad and issues may arise on whether tax should or should not be paid in the United Kingdom, with the inevitable potential for error or fraud. Solicitors may act on comparatively routine conveyancing or trusts and probate work and find that they are unwittingly becoming involved in the principal money laundering offences as they become involved in arrangements or transactions.

Generally, the lawyer doing United Kingdom work can avoid the need to understand foreign criminal law because the POCA 2002, s340(2) defines criminal conduct as conduct which constitutes an offence in the United Kingdom or would do so if it occurred there. There is no reference to anything constituting an offence abroad being material to the commission of an offence under the POCA 2002. Where the client is already established, the firm may already be able to establish identity from existing records. Those firms taking on new overseas clients will need to think carefully about their acceptance procedures.

16.4 Instructions from foreign lawyers

When accepting instructions from foreign lawyers, the solicitor will first need to consider whether the client is the foreign lawyer or that lawyer's lay client. The Law Society's 'Money Laundering Guidance (Pilot – January 2004)' (LS Guidance)[1] advises that:

> You must also consider whether your client is instructing you as principal or agent. Where the client is or appears to act for another person then, in addition to obtaining evidence of identity in relation to the client, under Regulation 4(3)(d), you must also take reasonable measures to establish the identity of a principal for whom that client is acting, and under Regulation 6 you must maintain records in relation to that evidence. This obligation to take reasonable measures is rather less than the obligation to obtain satisfactory evidence in relation to the client, but it must still be complied with.

16.5 Identification checks

In practice, at least when undertaking business in the regulated sector (and they will doubtless wish to do a risk assessment in other cases) solicitors will want to be satisfied as to the identity of both the instructing lawyer and the lay client. The difficulty with taking an absolute approach to identification, by requiring normal identification in all cases and not just those involving work in the regulated sector, is that it may prevent the firm taking perfectly lawful instructions from entirely reputable clients. So, for example, emergency instructions to obtain an injunction on behalf of a client complaining of infringement of intellectual property rights may not be fulfilled in time if, for example, the solicitor requires the personal attendance of two directors with passports and utility bills, resulting in loss of instructions or even loss to the client with the possibility of a damages claim. If, on the other hand, the client is accepted without further enquiry, there is the risk that the client will instruct the firm on other, regulated sector work in future. Care is therefore needed.

---

1 LS Guidance, para 3.70. Extract © Copyright The Law Society.

16. International aspects

Attention will also have to focus on residents of countries which have not adequately implemented the 40 recommendations of the Financial Action Task Force (FATF). FATF Recommendation 21 states:

> Financial institutions should give special attention to business relationships and transactions with persons, including companies and financial institutions, from countries which do not or insufficiently apply the FATF Recommendations. Whenever these transactions have no apparent economic or visible lawful purpose, their background and purpose should, as far as possible, be examined, the findings established in writing, and be available to help competent authorities.[2]

FATF has, since 2000, published a list of 'Non-Co-operative Countries and Territories' (NCCTs) but in 2002 it announced that no more names would be added, at least for 12 months, because the assessments were part of a wider review by the International Monetary Fund. Solicitors will need to have regard to:

1. the current list of NCCTs;[3]
2. any notices issued by the Bank of England Sanctions Unit from time to time as part of the international effort to cut off the flow of money to individual terrorists and terrorist organisations;[4] and
3. public information generally available in the media concerning named terrorists and terrorist organisations.

Corruption by some government leaders and public officials is an increasing issue. These are referred to as politically exposed persons or 'PEPs'. They include senior political figures, or their immediate family and close associates. Often their wealth is at odds with the poverty of much of the rest of their countries. The proceeds of their crimes are frequently transferred abroad and concealed through private companies and trusts, sometimes in the names of relatives or other associates. Lawyers should particularly be on their guard where they know that the client, or proposed client, is a senior political figure or connected with one.

Where it is possible to meet new potential clients who are not normally resident in the UK, passports or national identity cards will be appropriate for the evidence of the name of the customer. As in any other case it is important to keep copies of the pages containing the relevant information including reference numbers, date, and country of issue or the relevant information should be recorded in the firm's records. Where copies are kept, the solicitor should certify the copy examined against the original

---

[2] See www1.oecd.org/fatf/FATDocs_en.htm. Extract © FATF.
[3] To be found at www.fatf-gafi.org or www.jmlsg.org.uk.
[4] See www.bankofengland.co.uk.

and the date of the examination. Information on other pages such as visas should also be noted. As in all other cases, the solicitor should keep a clear copy of the photograph (in black and white, not colour).

The LS Guidance advises[5] that where a prospective client is a national of, or resident in, a country on the FATF list of NCCTs, solicitors should consider whether they need to carry out further checks to find out exactly who the client is and what their business is before accepting instructions. Separate evidence of the prospective client's permanent residential address should also be obtained, ideally from an official document such as a national identity card or driving licence where these have not been used as evidence of name. Note that in Hong Kong and the Gulf States, PO Box numbers are normally used but solicitors should be satisfied (personally or through an agent) that the prospective clients' residential address can be physically located by way of a recorded description or other means.[6] As an alternative the LS Guidance advises that confirmation may be obtained from a qualified lawyer who confirms that the client is known to him or her and lives or works at the address given.[7]

Difficulties may arise in identifying whether a foreign passport, identity card or driving licence is genuine. The Law Society advises[8] solicitors must be reasonably satisfied that the document is a genuine passport or national identity card, and if in doubt as to whether it is genuine, they could ask advice from an embassy or consulate official for the country concerned.

Where a local lawyer is used as part of the identification process, solicitors should check they are registered to practise; often this may be possible through the website of the appropriate law society or bar association or through a reputable directory. They should also keep a copy of the relevant entry from the website as part of their records.

The Law Society also advises[9] that evidence of identity may be obtained through a reputable credit or financial institution in the applicant's home country or country of residence. However, particular care should be taken when relying on evidence provided by a third party to ensure that the client's true identity and current permanent address have been confirmed and it would be wise to ask for certified copies of the evidence on which the institution relied.

---

5 LS Guidance, para 3.87.
6 *Ibid*, para 3.88.
7 *Ibid*.
8 *Ibid*, para 3.86.
9 *Ibid*, para 3.89.

16. International aspects

Where it is not possible to meet the client, because the client is overseas, the solicitor should ask for documents to be certified by an embassy, consulate or high commission of the country of issue or an overseas lawyer whose identity has been verified as above. Other possible solutions include certification by a lawyer from the country of issue or by staff in the registry of a UK higher education institution in the case of international students.[10] The guidance issued by the Council of Licensed Conveyancers to its members[11] also suggests its members can rely on certification by a principal or a member of the senior management within the practice having sufficient experience in the recognition of such documents issued in the country concerned.

16.6 Firms with overseas offices

Those firms which practise overseas will however need to comply with local laws. Particular attention should be paid to the United States because of the extra-territorial effect of its legislation, which is covered below. Firms with overseas offices will wish to consider whether to introduce the same client identification procedures in those offices as well. In any event they may also be bound by overseas legislation.

16.7 United States of America: the PATRIOT Act

All firms with any United States connections will need to be aware of the USA PATRIOT Act[12] (The Uniting and Strengthening America by Providing Appropriate Tools to Intercept and Obstruct Terrorism Act). This came into force on 26 October 2001. Many of its provisions are extra-territorial. It is wide-ranging. Apart from money laundering it covers crime, transporting hazardous materials, counterfeiting and immigration.

Procedural requirements on banks are increased. These include enhanced procedures for certain types of account to detect money laundering. US banks are prohibited from maintaining certain accounts for foreign 'shell' banks – those with no physical presence in the country. The Treasury Secretary is required to set minimum standards for identification of clients opening accounts. Significantly, this includes consulting lists of known or suspected terrorists or organisations provided by the government.

---

10 LS Guidance, para 3.92.
11 See www.conveyancer.org.uk/yogiP/UploadFiles/
CLCGuidanceHandbookFinalVersion.PDF at para 3.C.53.
12 See www.epic.org/privacy/terrorism/hr3162.html.

Bulk cash smuggling is prohibited with penalties of confiscation and imprisonment of up to five years. In broad terms, this applies when a person knowingly conceals $10,000 or more and attempts to transport it out of the United States.

There are provisions relating to foreign corruption offences, and provision for forfeiture of proceeds of foreign crimes found in the United States. There is also a prohibition on providing material support or resources knowing and intending that it will be used for terrorism. In addition it provides for certain offences involving chemical weapons, terrorist attacks and violence against mass transportation systems, sabotage of nuclear facilities or fuel, and damaging or destroying interstate pipeline facilities.

The Act contains provisions to assist enforcement. There are also various prohibitions on biological weapons and on transporting hazardous materials.

16.8 Corporate offences

One international aspect corporate lawyers need to be aware of is ss765–766 of the Income and Corporation Taxes Act 1988 (ICTA 1988), which provides for certain transactions to require prior consent from the Treasury.

Under s766 of ICTA 1988, companies, their officers and advisers may be guilty of criminal offences if a transaction requiring special consent takes place without such consent. The person needs to know that the actions were unlawful under s765(1) in order to be guilty of a criminal offence (s766(1)). However, this is unlikely to help greatly in practice: s766(2) puts the burden of proof as to the person's state of knowledge on to the individual in the case of directors.

It is likely that the commission of an offence under this section would result in there being proceeds of the crime.

16.9 419s

The NCIS website reports that the West African organised crime has a big impact on the economy of the UK and other major industrialised countries. The main activities are fraud, personal identity theft and corporate impersonation, with strong intelligence to suggest that funds obtained through fraud fund drug trafficking and other major crime.

Commonplace among West African criminals is advance fee fraud, or '419' fraud, so called after the relevant section of the Nigerian penal code. Many solicitors will have seen letters, faxes and e-mails of this type. The author

16. International aspects

generally purports to be a senior government or central bank official (not necessarily in West Africa), or related to such a person, who has over-inflated a contract. In return for helping to smuggle money out of the country, the recipient of the letter is offered up to 30%. Once the target has been drawn into the scam, requests are made for assistance with legal and administrative costs. Victims have lost hundreds of thousands of pounds in some cases. The general rule applies – if it sounds too good to be true, it probably is.

NCIS also advises that West African criminals are experts in exploiting the criminal possibilities of the web. For example, they may 'spoof' legitimate banking websites – the fake site is sometimes more impressive than the real site – or spoof e-mail addresses belonging to genuine senior banking staff.

Criminals also use the anonymity offered by the Internet to reply to advertisements for articles such as motor vehicles, vessels and even residential property. People are duped into parting with their goods and funds in return for counterfeit cheques.

NCIS has previously advised on its website that it does not wish to be notified of preliminary 419 notifications direct unless they are truly extraordinary (eg linked to terrorism), but that they should instead should be sent to local law enforcement, details of which are obtainable on telephone number 020 7238 8012. The advice was however removed from the NCIS website shortly before going to press. Similar advice remains on other official websites such as that of the Financial Services Authority.[13]

The NCIS website guidance previously advised that e-mails received can also be forwarded to the abuse facility of the appropriate Internet service provider (ISP). These e-mails should be addressed to abuse@'the ISP name' (eg abuse@yahoo.com). By this method, the ISPs can terminate any accounts that abuse their systems.

Remember however that the LS Guidance warns[14] that the position may change if there is knowledge or suspicion that money has actually changed hands, in which case a report may be necessary in order to comply with the reporting obligations under the POCA 2002.

---

[13] See www.fsa.gov.uk/consumer/01_WARNINGS/scams/mn_advance_caught.html.
[14] LS Guidance, para 7.33.

17. Changes in the firm's practice

Money laundering reporting officers (MLROs) will need to be involved in any change in the firm's practice.

This will be relevant where:

1. a practice incorporates, whether as a limited liability partnership (LLP) or limited company;
2. a practice dissolves;
3. a practice is taken over;
4. a sole practitioner or all the partners retire;
5. practices merge;
6. there are lateral hires of partners or teams, particularly when they are bringing clients with them; or
7. the Law Society intervenes.

A variety of issues will arise. In essence, those who acquire will want to know what they are acquiring, those whose practices are acquired will want to be sure that someone else will look after the compliance with their (largely non-delegable) obligations to the highest standards.

Those who are ceasing to practise will be concerned to ensure that records continue to be kept and that there remains a central point of contact for any queries. There may be issues involving the professional indemnity insurers – if they arise from a notification to the insurers on risk before dissolution, those insurers need to be kept informed. If on the other hand they were not notified then, the insurers of the 'successor practice' as defined under the Law Society's Minimum Terms and Conditions[1] will be involved; practitioners need to be sure they know which firm's insurers are relevant and who the contact point is.

Incorporation, whether as an LLP or limited company, raises issues of client identification and record retention. See **8.10** for a discussion on this

---

1 'Minimum Terms and Conditions of Professional Indemnity Insurance for Solicitors and Registered European Lawyers in England and Wales'. See www.lawsociety.org.uk//documents/downloads/Minimum terms and conditions_2003.pdf.

17. Changes in the firm's practice

and the possible issues over changes in a partnership. The obligation to retain records will remain with the individual partners in the former firm. Due diligence when acquiring practices will have to include checks on the adequacy of procedures and record keeping in the firm being acquired, and the scope and extent of training and compliance. Staff who join the new firm will have to be trained to the new firm's standards.

The Joint Money Laundering Steering Group advises that firms that undergo mergers, take-overs or internal reorganisations need to ensure that records of identity verification and transactions will be readily retrievable for the required periods when rationalising computer systems and physical storage arrangements.[2]

Interventions by the Law Society raise several issues – some take place simply because a sole practitioner has died or abandoned the clients– but in other cases there is clear reason to be on guard for possible money laundering and other dishonesty. Any retained staff will have to be advised fully as to their obligations and the correct channel for communication of reports.

---

[2] See 'Prevention of Money Laundering Guidance Notes for the UK Financial Sector', 2003 edition, para 7.4.

18. Solicitors employed outside private practice

18.1 Application

This section applies to solicitors employed in commerce and industry, local government and otherwise not in private practice.

The critical distinction to make at the outset is between those whose employers are in the regulated sector and those who are not. All solicitors are subject to the general law – which also applies to any member of the public – not to commit the principal offences relating, eg, to concealing, arrangements, acquisition, use and possession of property and tipping off and prejudicing an investigation (described in more detail in **Chapter 4**). They are also subject to the notification requirements under the Terrorism Act 2000 (TA 2000).

Only those in the regulated sector are required to appoint a nominated officer and comply with the notification requirements under the Proceeds of Crime Act 2002 (POCA 2002).

18.2 The regulated sector

Solicitors' employers are in the regulated sector if they undertake 'relevant business'. Apart from the banking and investment sector, reg 2 of the Money Laundering Regulations 2003 (MLR 2003) defines this as including, in summary:

1. various deposit taking and investment activities;
2. National Savings Bank activities;
3. activities carried on under the National Loans Act 1968;
4. operating a bureau de change;
5. banking services (see below);
6. estate agency work;
7. operating casinos;

18. Solicitors employed outside private practice

8. activities of insolvency practitioners;
9. advice from tax advisers;
10. services of accountants;
11. services of auditors;
12. legal services involving participation in a financial or real property transaction;
13. formation, operation or management of companies or trusts; and
14. dealing in goods which involve accepting cash payments of €15,000 or more.

Readers should refer to the precise wording in the MLR 2003 which are set out in **Appendix 2**.

The provision defines relevant 'business' – those listed in points 9–13 all include reference to the provision of services 'by way of business', the rest do so by necessary implication given their nature. Although solicitors employed by local authorities may be involved in the sale of property, for example, they are therefore unlikely to find themselves in the regulated sector. Contrast this with the position of an in-house lawyer working for a property developer who will be providing legal services by way of business and which involve participation in real property transactions.

Banking services are those listed in Annex 1 to the Banking Consolidation Directive[1] but are for convenience set out in the MLR 2003, Sch 1. These include a wide variety of activities and merit listing in full:

1. Acceptance of deposits and other repayable funds.
2. Lending.
3. Financial leasing.
4. Money transmission services.
5. Issuing and administering means of payment (eg credit cards, travellers' cheques and bankers' drafts).
6. Guarantees and commitments.
7. Trading for own account or for account of customers in—
   (a) money market instruments (cheques, bills, certificates of deposit, etc.);
   (b) foreign exchange;
   (c) financial futures and options;
   (d) exchange and interest-rate instruments;
   (e) transferable securities.

---

[1] Directive 2000/12/EC.

8. Participation in securities issues and the provision of services related to such issues.
9. Advice to undertakings on capital structure, industrial strategy and related questions and advice as well as services relating to mergers and the purchase of undertakings.
10. Money broking.
11. Portfolio management and advice.
12. Safekeeping and administration of securities.
13. Credit reference services.
14. Safe custody services.

A wide cross-section of in-house lawyers will therefore be affected by the provisions.

18.3 Guidance for solicitors whose employers are in the regulated sector

Solicitors who are in the regulated sector should apply the guidance provided by their employers, guidance issued by any relevant regulator or trade association, in many cases the Joint Money Laundering Steering Group, or, in the absence of any such guidance, the aspects of the Law Society's 'Money Laundering Guidance (Pilot – January 2004)' (LS Guidance) that relate to the obligations on individuals and relevant businesses.

Individuals or businesses involved in the provision of management consultancy services should note that they could be within the scope of the duty to report under the POCA 2002, ss330 and 331 and the requirements of the MLR 2003 because they may supply the service of forming, operating or managing companies.

Money service operators and high-value dealers are regulated by HM Customs and Excise, as set out in the MLR 2003, Part III.

18.4 Solicitors whose organisations have an MLRO

Where a solicitor's employer has nominated an MLRO, or similar officer, suspicions should normally be reported to that person. If for any reason that is not possible or appropriate, individuals may report directly to NCIS.

18.5 Confidentiality

Businesses and individuals are covered by the confidentiality override provisions contained in both the POCA 2002 and the TA 2000. The

18. Solicitors employed outside private practice

protection covers voluntary reports of money laundering, where the information giving rise to knowledge or suspicion did not arise in the context of relevant business.

19. LIABILITY AND PROFESSIONAL INDEMNITY

19.1 Key areas of potential liability

Areas of potential liability include:

1. delay causing loss of interest and consequential losses;
2. delay resulting in loss of transactions;
3. claims for the return of money by clients;
4. claims for the return of money by third parties who claim to be entitled;
5. ceasing to act at a critical point in a transaction;
6. breach of confidence through unnecessary notification to NCIS; and
7. redress for inadequate professional services.

There is some overlap between these areas.

The main area on which the Law Society's 'Money Laundering Guidance (Pilot – January 2004)' (LS Guidance) focuses[1] is constructive trusteeship. Some thought is given to the possibility of negligence claims, mainly from delay, though the LS Guidance[2] suggests that the fact there is only one known civil claim against an intermediary arising from delay[3] means it may be less likely in practice than might be expected.

However, this may be down to a number of factors, not least the fact that solicitors have only been in the regulated sector since 1 March 2004, and that although they had certain obligations prior to that date, there was far less awareness of solicitors' duties and risks than there is now.

19.2 Constructive trusts

The Proceeds of Crime Act 2002 (POCA 2002) does not provide civil remedies for victims of crime, merely a mechanism for the state to confiscate the

---

[1] See LS Guidance, Chapter 5.
[2] *Ibid*, para 5.21.
[3] *A v Bank of Scotland* [2002] 1 WLR 751.

proceeds in the hands of the wrongdoer. Liability arises where the courts in equity impress the money held by an intermediary with a trust in favour of another, generally the true owner. Where the rightful owner of the funds is a client there will generally be a fiduciary obligation and it is this which underpinned many of the claims by mortgage lenders against solicitors in the 1990s. However, mere negligence or breach of contract by itself does not amount to breach of fiduciary duty: there has to be either dishonesty or a conscious preference of one client (or the solicitor's own interests) over another.[4]

Liability under a constructive trust generally arises in one or other of the following circumstances:

1. knowing receipt; or
2. dishonest assistance.

19.2.1 Knowing receipt

This arises where the recipient of the funds uses the money for their own benefit. A claimant must show that its assets have been taken in breach of fiduciary duty or in breach of trust, that the solicitor (or other defendant) has received the money beneficially, or that the funds are traceable to the solicitor, and knowledge on the part of the defendant that the assets are traceable to a breach of fiduciary duty or trust which makes it unconscionable that the solicitor should retain them.

Knowledge for these purposes is not limited to actual knowledge but includes constructive knowledge and may include 'Nelsonian blindness' – wilfully shutting one's eyes to the obvious, recklessly failing to make enquiries which an honest and reasonable person would make, or knowledge of circumstances which would put an honest and reasonable person on enquiry.[5]

In one case a solicitor became involved in advising a fraudster on a purported commercial transaction of some complexity. The solicitor's fees were paid out of the proceeds and the rest taken by the fraudster. The solicitor was found not to have been dishonest. Accordingly, although he was held liable to repay his fees with interest, he was not liable for the remainder of the money taken by the fraudster.

---

[4] *Bristol and West Building Society v Mothew* [1996] 4 All ER 698.
[5] See *Bank of Credit & Commerce International (Overseas) Ltd & ors v Akindele* [2000] 3 WLR 1423 and the cases referred to in it.

19.2.2 Dishonest assistance

Liability under this head requires a breach of trust or fiduciary duty by someone other than the defendant in which the defendant assisted, dishonesty by the defendant in doing so, and loss to the claimant.

The initial breach of trust need not be dishonest but, for there to be liability, the assistance by the defendant must be. Dishonesty is judged objectively and includes cases where the defendant deliberately closes his or her eyes or chooses not to ask questions for fear of learning something he or she would sooner not know.[6] It does however require more than suspicion, even though the suspicion may have been enough to trigger a report to NCIS.[7] It also emphasises the point that consent from NCIS operates only to avoid criminal liability under the POCA 2002 and does not affect any other issues of civil liability nor, perhaps, criminal liability under other provisions (though doubtless a defendant to criminal proceedings in those circumstances would seek to establish an abuse of process defence).

From a practical point of view, the general view is that the fact of a disclosure report to NCIS makes it less likely that the solicitor will be found liable under a constructive trust. The LS Guidance suggests[8] that this is because the disclosure report is likely to be seen as a badge of honesty. It is unlikely that solicitors will be found liable as constructive trustees when they act in accordance with directions of the court. Since then, there has been support for this point in *Tayeb v HSBC Bank Plc & anr*.[9] However, when issues of solicitor dishonesty do arise in practice they are analysed in excruciating detail and generally involve not only a detailed examination of the documents but also intensive questioning of the solicitor.

A dishonest solicitor will not be entitled to indemnity from the firm's insurers (though other, honest, members of the firm generally will be entitled). This practice developed in the days of the Solicitors Indemnity Fund when solicitors were interviewed in conference with counsel as part of the process of reaching a determination of the issue. The practice is now followed by a number of open market insurers. It is territory most solicitors will not wish to explore.

Solicitors who become concerned about the source of funds they are holding and the correct identity of the rightful owner may, rarely, wish to consider

---

6 *Twinsectra Ltd v Yardley* [2002] 2 AC 164.
7 *Bank of Scotland v A Ltd* [2000] All ER (D) 864.
8 LS Guidance, para 5.17.
9 [2004] EWHC 1529 (Comm). See **13.4** for more details on this case.

19. Liability and professional indemnity

an application to the court for directions. They should however consult with their professional indemnity insurers first and may be entitled to legal representation, as explained later in this chapter.

19.3 Negligence claims

The problems outlined at the beginning of this chapter can be illustrated through a case study.

19.3.1 Case study 1

The solicitor is acting on a house sale and purchase. The client, a builder, is moving up-market from a small terraced house to a grand, historic house in a fine location. On first taking instructions, the solicitor was concerned about how the client, who is not ostensibly wealthy, could fund this transaction. The client explained this by saying that he had recently received a substantial inheritance. The solicitor made further enquiry to provide confirmation of this and obtained a photocopy of the grant of probate and will from the solicitors acting on the estate.

Contracts were exchanged on both houses.

Completion is now approaching and the solicitor has just heard that the sole principal of the practice which acted on the estate, and who provided the photocopy grant of probate, has been arrested on money laundering charges and the Law Society has intervened in the practice. The solicitor is concerned and asks the Law Society's intervening agents to confirm that the photocopy of the probate and will were genuine. In fact they are, but the solicitor agent mentions that the client seems to have been involved with the suspect solicitor in a number of other transactions which have yet to be investigated. The solicitor is greatly concerned and the firm's money laundering reporting officer (MLRO) notifies NCIS. NCIS responds in the seven-day period and refuses consent to proceed, imposing the 31-day moratorium.

The date for completion is three days away. The client telephones the solicitor to confirm everything is in hand for completion as he is finalising arrangements with the removal company. The solicitor, troubled about what he can say, tells the client – wrongly – that there are some concerns about the title to the new property. The client probes more deeply and the solicitor is unable to expand on this explanation. The client complains to the firm's senior partner.

Eventually, a week after the contractual completion date, NCIS give their consent to the transaction proceeding. Claims come in for interest on the delayed transactions, additional removal costs and other consequential losses which are said to have been incurred by other parties as well as the client. The client complains about his solicitor misleading him as to defects in title when in fact there were none.

19.3.2 Case study 2

Delay resulting in loss of transactions

There is a contract race. The client comes to the solicitor's office with a substantial amount of cash for the deposit. The solicitor is concerned about the client's inadequate explanation as to the source of the money and refuses to accept it. Another party ends up buying the house and sells it soon afterwards for development at a price substantially higher. The client claims against the solicitor for the difference between the price he was going to pay and the price for which the other buyer has sold it.

19.4 Claims for the return of money by clients

This can also be illustrated by a case study.

There is a contract race, but with the additional complication that the solicitor is holding the client's deposit money which he had in readiness for exchange of contracts, the parties having originally expected to exchange before completion. The solicitor had a number of suspicions about his client. He notified NCIS and they consented to the transaction proceeding.

The solicitor is on the point of exchange when the client reports that he has heard rumours of a proposed new road scheme and does not wish to proceed.

The client asks for the return of his deposit. The return of money to the client is not the same transaction as the one to which NCIS consent was sought previously (completion of the purchase), so the MLRO notifies NCIS again and seeks consent. NCIS refuses.

Other problem cases might include a solicitor ceasing to act part way through a transaction when there is no provision in the letter of engagement allowing him to withdraw. NCIS might consent to a transaction proceeding, but only after a completion date has passed causing a claim for interest and perhaps other damages if a conveyancing chain was disrupted. Notification where suspicions proved to be unwarranted might also cause such delay.

19.5 Managing these risks

It would be unwise to assume that all these risks and others can be eliminated. This is a new and rapidly developing aspect of practice and there are many lessons yet to be learned, some no doubt the hard way. It has yet to be seen how the courts will decide aspects of liability when there may be conflicting tensions of public policy – on the one hand, encouraging professionals to report suspicions to NCIS to aid the war on crime while on the other hand, protecting clients who may be innocent of any wrongdoing. As a matter of policy, where a loss has to be allocated between two parties and one of those parties is insured, the courts will often tend to allocate the loss to the insured party, which is small comfort to the professional who already shoulders the burden of substantial premiums, not to mention excesses on policies.

There are however steps which can be taken to try and limit the risk. These include controlling the client relationship more effectively through appropriate terms of engagement, and ensuring that insurers are notified promptly when events happen which might result in a claim.

19.6 Limiting liability through terms of engagement

There are many potential obstacles to limiting liability through terms of engagement, but that is not a reason for not trying. Even though an exclusion may not ultimately be effective, it may at least give the solicitor a negotiating position. In addition, it is not only terms directly limiting liability which will be of assistance, but also (as will be seen) those which set out clearly the responsibilities of the client. The potential obstacles to limiting liability include commercial ability to impose terms, legislation and Law Society rules.

In practice, solicitors who act for institutional clients, which insist on their own terms of engagement, may have difficulty imposing terms which limit liability. The more routine the service provided, the less able a firm may be to impose terms – there is always another firm down the road.

An exclusion clause is unlikely to help protect against third-party claims, for example by lenders, and in this context it is worth noting that some lenders are now asking solicitors to provide a certificate of title without the solicitor having any retainer to act for them.

Even so, the areas of risk with most frequent exposure will probably arise with private clients, and though it may not be possible in practice to

19. Liability and professional indemnity

restrict liability to a mortgage lender, it may be possible to do so with the buyer or indeed clients in other areas of private client work.

19.6.1 Unfair Contract Terms Act 1977

The Unfair Contract Terms Act 1977 requires any exclusion to be fair and reasonable having regard to the circumstances which were or ought reasonably to have been known to or in the contemplation of the parties when the contract was made. The courts will strive to find a way round exclusions – see, for example, *St Albans DC v ICL*[10] and *South West Water v ICL*.[11] Where they allow an exclusion, equality of bargaining power is often a significant reason, suggesting that there is more chance of an exclusion being upheld against a business client than a private client. In the context of money laundering compliance, the prospects of a clause being upheld are probably at their highest where the client is also in the regulated sector.

19.6.2 Restrictions imposed by rules of professional conduct

The Law Society's Guide to Professional Conduct provides:

> 12.11 Limitation of liability by contract
>
> Although it is not acceptable for solicitors to attempt to exclude by contract all liability to their clients, there is no objection as a matter of conduct to solicitors seeking to limit their liability provided that such limitation is not below the minimum level of cover required by the Solicitors' Indemnity Rules. (© The Law Society)

The cover currently required by the Solicitors' Indemnity Insurance Rules is, in broad terms, £1,000,000.

19.6.3 Solicitors Act 1974, s60(5)

This provides, in relation to a contentious business agreement, that

> A provision in such an agreement that the solicitor shall not be liable for negligence, or that he shall be relieved from any responsibility to which he would otherwise be subject as a solicitor, shall be void.

It is a moot point whether this operates as a total bar on limiting liability or only prohibits complete exclusion of liability. The provision has two limbs to it and this may need careful analysis. The first limb of the provision prevents solicitors using terms which provide that they shall not be liable for negligence. There may be circumstances where the matters complained of, for example delay while waiting for NCIS approval, constitute a potential

---

10 [1996] 4 All ER 481.
11 [1999] BLR 420.

breach of contract but do not amount to negligence. Although at first sight this seems more likely to occur in non-contentious work, to which the section has no application, a client might, for example, complain of delay in making a payment into court in civil proceedings, thus losing protection on costs. More importantly, the provision will also be applicable to matrimonial proceedings where many of the more difficult areas of liability are expected to arise. The second limb of the provision prevents solicitors from seeking to be relieved of responsibility. It may be that that provision does not refer to monetary limits on liability but to other responsibilities and duties which a solicitor on the court record has as an officer of the court. More detailed consideration of the Solicitors Act 1974, s60(5) is beyond the scope of this work.

Terms should include provision to ensure that if any parts are found not to comply with legislation or Law Society rules, only the offending parts are affected and not all the terms. It is also important that the firm does not seek to exclude liability arising from fraud or dishonesty on the part of a partner or member of staff.

In addition of course it is essential to ensure that the terms are in fact agreed by the client, ideally by signing a copy of them. Bear in mind too the risk that terms may be varied orally or in correspondence.

19.6.4 Terms of engagement in practice

There are many areas where terms might seek to mitigate the firm's risk, including those outlined in the case studies at the beginning of this chapter.

Liability for wrongfully reporting either a client or another party to a transaction for suspected money laundering and causing:

1. completion of a contract to be delayed or aborted with claims for interest and consequential losses from the client and other parties claiming against the client; or
2. loss of a contract race; or
3. delay in paying client money into court,

is worth considering. It is not without difficulty, because the ability to rely on the term might in practice be limited by the provisions relating to tipping off in s333 of the POCA 2002 and those relating to prejudicing an investigation under s342. However, there may be cases where that is not a problem and it would be unwise to dismiss out of hand the possibility of such a term providing some protection.

19. Liability and professional indemnity

There are two reasons why the tipping off and prejudice provisions might not always be a problem in practice. First, the client may already know of the notification to NCIS where, for example, there has been a joint notification by solicitor and client. The knowledge may even mean there is no claim in the first place. Second, there may be other circumstances in which the disclosure does not in fact constitute an offence, for example, because the solicitor (with due cause, perhaps because of advice from NCIS) does not know or suspect that the disclosure is likely to prejudice an investigation[12] or the disclosure is made in connection with legal proceedings or contemplated legal proceedings.[13]

Suffice to say, each case must be looked at carefully on its own facts with due regard to the full provisions of ss333 and 342 before deciding to rely or not to rely on a contract term seeking to restrict liability in these circumstances. Note, in particular, that the exceptions to these offences do not apply if they are made with the intention of furthering a criminal purpose. When considering the position under the tipping off and prejudice provisions it is advisable to revisit the LS Guidance on *P v P*[14] even though that carries a note of caution that the case to which it refers specifically relates to ancillary relief proceedings in matrimonial matters. It is also advisable to seek guidance from NCIS.

19.6.5 Terms relating to form of payment of funds

One particular area where it should be possible to control the solicitor-client relationship and help limit exposure is in connection with payment of funds. Solicitors will wish, for example, to guard not only against the client turning up on the day of completion with a case full of used bank notes, but also the client who has told the solicitor in advance that money will come from a source which the solicitor regards as acceptable, perhaps the client's usual bank, but then at the last moment payment comes from some other, more suspicious, source. It would therefore seem sensible to provide first that the firm will not accept cash and second for prior notification as to the source of funds.

So far as excluding payment in cash is concerned, solicitors will need to bear in mind the risks which attach to sale at auction and they will want to be consulted before the auction to ensure the client, and in turn the solicitor, is not bound to accept payment in cash.

---

12 POCA 2002, ss333(1) and 342(3).
13 *Ibid*, ss333(3) and 342(4).
14 LS Guidance, Annex 3 and see **Appendix 10**.

For non-cash payments, ideally the terms should require the client to identify the source of funds at the outset or with a minimum of, say, 14 days' notice, giving the solicitor the right to refuse to accept payment from any other source, and excluding liability where the client fails to comply with this. This way the firm should not be put under undue pressure to complete in haste and should have time to investigate and, if appropriate, seek consent from NCIS. Terms should also guard against clients, or third parties purportedly on their behalf, remitting excessive money to the firm's account and seeking reimbursement without the solicitor having adequate opportunity to check the source of the funds – a common trap for the unwary.

19.6.6 Reserving the right to cease acting

Reserving the right to cease acting is important. In particular, solicitors need to bear in mind that although NCIS may consent to a transaction proceeding, it does not in itself absolve the solicitor of any liability, either civil or criminal, arising otherwise than under the POCA 2002. It is always possible that NCIS consent to a transaction proceeding because the client is suspected to be committing criminal activity but the police are not yet ready to proceed. Bear in mind that it may not always be possible to explain fully to the client why the firm is unwilling to continue to act.

A potential problem arises on ceasing to act, that the client will immediately ask for the file to be sent to a new solicitor. The danger lies in the possibility that the solicitor may inadvertently release records which the firm is required by law to retain. Precisely what records the solicitor is required[15] to retain remains to be established – this is discussed in **Chapter 10**.

19.6.7 Mediations

Mediators and solicitors acting for parties in mediations will need to have regard to the risk of having to withdraw from a mediation for fear of committing the predicate offences, such as facilitating concealment or an arrangement, resulting in a substantial waste of costs and a lost opportunity for settlement.

19.6.8 Confiscation proceedings

Those who advise clients in proceedings by the Asset Recovery Agency may wish to inform clients in terms of engagement, that if they become

---

15 By the MLR 2003, reg 6(2).

aware that the client has assets of which the Agency are unaware, they will be bound to notify NCIS. The issue is discussed in the LS Guidance.[16] The solicitor who fails to notify NCIS risks committing a concealment offence under the POCA 2002, s327, a facilitation offence under s328 and, if in the regulated sector, failure to disclose under s330. Further discussion of confiscation proceedings is beyond the scope of this work.

19.6.9 Other terms

Compliance with the guidance of the Law Society or the courts, such as that in *P v P*,[17] for example as to withholding information from the client pending approval of NCIS, may constitute a technical breach of the solicitor's obligations as the client's agent to provide information to the client, and terms may usefully address this too.

Overall, terms of engagement offer an opportunity to raise client awareness of the issues and lay down markers at the outset. How thoroughly clients read terms may be open to question, but a covering letter would usefully encourage them to do so, particularly in relation to these aspects.

19.7 Insurance implications

19.7.1 Policy requirements

Professional indemnity policies under the Law Society's 'Minimum Terms and Conditions of Professional Indemnity Insurance for Solicitors Registered in England and Wales 2004' (LS Minimum Terms)[18] invariably require firms to notify circumstances which may give rise to a claim, and firms fail to do so at their peril because they may find, as explained in more detail below, that they are effectively uninsured for the claim or have to pay an additional premium, despite the apparent protection in the policy against non-disclosure.

The requirement means that insurers have a greater opportunity to become involved early on and, if appropriate, help with remedial action. It is worth bearing in mind that insurers may be able to help with practical advice because their involvement as insurers of many firms may mean they will have greater exposure to the problems and their solutions than most firms. It will also mean that the firm may be entitled to the costs of an application to the court for directions where that is appropriate.

---

16 LS Guidance, paras 4.55-4.58.
17 [2003] EWHC 2260 (Fam).
18 See www.lawsociety.org.uk/professional/professionalinsurance.law.

19. Liability and professional indemnity

In the past, firms might have become aware of a problem but, in the days of the Solicitors Indemnity Fund, were under no obligation to report anything short of a claim. It is important to understand what constitutes a 'claim' or a circumstance. Both are defined in the LS Minimum Terms. The definitions are as follows:

> 8.2 '**Circumstances**'
>
> Circumstances means an incident, occurrence, fact, matter, act or omission which may give rise to a Claim in respect of civil liability.
>
> 8.3 '**Claim**'
>
> Claim means a demand for, or an assertion of a right to, civil compensation or civil damages or an intimation of an intention to seek such compensation or damages. For these purposes, an obligation on a Firm and/or any Insured to remedy a breach of the Solicitors' Accounts Rules 1998 (as amended from time to time), or any rules which replace the Solicitors' Accounts Rules 1998 in whole or in part, shall be treated as a Claim, and the obligation to remedy such breach shall be treated as a civil liability for the purposes of clause 1, whether or not any person makes a demand for, or an assertion of a right to, civil compensation or civil damages or an intimation of an intention to seek such compensation or damages as a result of such breach. (© The Law Society)

Clearly this requires that insurers should be notified as soon as the firm realises something has given rise to a loss or claim – or may be about to.

Policy wordings vary but the following from a Zurich Professional policy is typical:

> The Insured shall give notice in writing to the Insurer immediately of any Circumstance of which the Insured shall become aware that may give rise to a loss or Claim against the Insured...

Clearly therefore, where a firm identifies – or should identify – that it is approaching a difficult point because of the money laundering legislation, it should be putting insurers on notice because they may wish to become involved and even though it is early days for everyone concerned, their wider experience on behalf of other firms may make their assistance invaluable. It will enable the insurer to help in any application to the court for directions if this is appropriate, and the firm may have the benefit of the cover for costs, which are dealt with below.

Where a firm fails to comply with these requirements, insurers may rely on the reimbursement provisions in the LS Minimum Terms relating to prejudice. These provide as follows:

> 7.2 The insurance may provide that each Insured who –
> (a) committed; or
> (b) condoned (whether knowingly or recklessly) –
>   (i) non-disclosure or misrepresentation; or

> (ii) any breach of the terms or conditions of the insurance; or
>
> (iii) dishonesty or any fraudulent act or omission –
>
> will reimburse the Insurer to the extent that is just and equitable having regard to the prejudice caused to the Insurer's interests by such non-disclosure, misrepresentation, breach, dishonesty, act or omission, provided that no Insured shall be required to make any such reimbursement to the extent that any such breach of the terms or conditions of the insurance was in order to comply with any applicable rules or codes laid down from time to time by the Council of the Law Society of England and Wales, or in the Law Society publication "Keeping Clients – a Client Care Guide for Solicitors" as amended from time to time. The insurance must provide that no non-disclosure, misrepresentation, breach, dishonesty, act or omission will be imputed to a body corporate unless it was committed or condoned by, in the case of a company, all directors of that company, or, in the case of a limited liability partnership, all members of that limited liability partnership.
>
> The insurance must provide further that any right of reimbursement contemplated by this clause 7.2 against any person referred to in clauses 1.3(d), 1.5(d) or 1.7(d) (or against the estate or legal personal representative of any such person if they die or become legally incapacitated) is limited to the extent that is just and equitable having regard to the prejudice caused to the Insurer's interests by that person having committed or condoned (whether knowingly or recklessly) dishonesty or any fraudulent act or omission. (© The Law Society)

Although these provisions therefore appear to provide some protection for non-disclosure, most practitioners will not wish to test how far they protect them in practice. There have been examples of firms facing substantial personal liability when insurers took issue with the extent of the disclosure they had given.

19.7.2 Which insurers should you notify?

This section addresses two issues. First, the policy year in which a claim falls, particularly bearing in mind that the firm may have changed insurers, and second, for firms with top-up insurance and/or cover for their excess (deductible), whether other insurers need to be notified.

It is important to understand how professional indemnity cover operates. Policies are written on a 'claims made' basis which is quite different from motor or employers' liability insurance. If you have a car accident, the insurers who deal with the claim will be those on risk at the time you had the accident. Likewise with employers liability insurance, hence the losses which have crippled many in the insurance markets due to exposure to disease claims caused by asbestos decades ago, which were not taken into account when cover was agreed at the time.

In contrast, a professional indemnity claim will, broadly speaking, fall to be dealt with by the insurers who issued the policy in the policy year in which the claim is made, or, if earlier, when circumstances were notified to insurers.

19. Liability and professional indemnity

So, for example, if:

1. the solicitor became concerned about a client's activities in August 2004 and notified the insurers then;
2. it becomes necessary to involve them further in January 2005 after the renewal,

then the matter will be dealt with by the insurers to whom the firm notified circumstances in August 2004, ie the insurers for the policy year from September 2003 to October 2004 (as all solicitors' insurance covers the same period – a one-off 13 month period).

There is increased awareness of police investigations into solicitors in connection with conveyancing matters completed some years ago. Careful consideration needs to be given to such cases to see whether there are any potential civil claims, perhaps by mortgage lenders, which need to be notified to insurers. Considerable caution is needed before disclosing confidential client files to the police voluntarily. Those who are asked to be interviewed under caution would do well to seek legal advice from solicitors with specialist serious fraud experience before doing so.

The reader will appreciate from what is set out above that even though the mistake may have been in January 1999, when firms were all covered by Solicitors Indemnity Fund, it will not be covered by Solicitors Indemnity Fund, because no claim was made while the Fund was on risk and, because the firm was presumably unaware of any concern at the time, did not notify circumstances to the Fund. Remember that the fact that a previously notified circumstance has turned into a claim is a material fact to be notified when seeking insurance on renewal.

As mentioned above, the firm also needs to consider whether there are any other insurers covering different layers for the same period of indemnity who need to be notified, whether excess infill or top-up. This has a particular significance, and problems arise in practice, when a claim comes in for substantially more than expected. For example, the firm may recognise that there is a problem involving a few thousand pounds. It notifies the firm's primary insurers, who cover the first £1m. When the claim comes in the client has suddenly come to the conclusion that he has far more substantial consequential losses than they anticipated. The claim is now very substantial indeed. Generally, top-up insurers will want to be notified of a claim where the reserve for damages and claimant's costs has reached half the limit of indemnity provided by insurers of the layer below. So, for a firm with a £1m primary policy and a separate top-up policy, insurers should be notified when the reserve is £500,000 or more.

Solicitors should also bear in mind that sometimes there can be an issue about whether claims should be 'aggregated', ie a number of claims treated as one claim with one excess and one limit of indemnity. This is a technical area beyond the scope of this work, but firms should be considering that in those circumstances, although individual claims are comparatively small, whether they will be treated as one large claim and hence need to be notified to top up insurers.

19.7.3 Notifying brokers

Readers may have expected this question to appear before the question about notifying insurers. There are three reasons for discussing it here:

1. primary responsibility for notifying insurers will usually rest with the insured, though often in practice it is done via the brokers;
2. it is notification to the insurers which is critical, particularly where a firm is notifying circumstances which must be received by insurers before the end of the policy year to ensure any subsequent claim is covered; and
3. readers need to understand who needs to know about a claim or circumstance and why.

Some of the larger insurers who have their own claims team will in practice deal directly with the insured and bypass the broker. But this does not obviate the need to keep the broker informed. Reasons for this may include the need to inform other insurers – excess infill or top up, and to ensure the broker has all available claims information in readiness for the next renewal, although again the primary responsibility for the proposal form must at all times remain with the insured. Nonetheless, the broker is a vital additional safeguard in the process.

19.7.4 Communicating with insurers and brokers

The LS Guidance advises notifying the MLRO of the insurers in these circumstances.[19] While that may be appropriate for the smaller insurers with only a few risks, it is unlikely to be the most workable solution so far as insurers are concerned. At the time of writing some of the larger insurers are considering nominating, or already have nominated, an individual in their claims teams to deal with money laundering-related notifications so

---

19 LS Guidance, para 5.22.

19. Liability and professional indemnity

that the relevant expertise in solicitor-related notifications can be built up as soon as possible.

19.7.5 What happens when insurers are notified?

On reading this section readers will start to appreciate where the hidden cost of claims lies, even before any additional premium or excess payment is incurred. Much depends on who the insurers are. Some insurers have their own claims team who may deal with the matter from start to finish. Others appoint solicitors or insurance brokers to deal with at least some of the early stages. Some send the more difficult cases and generally most or all litigated cases out to panel solicitors. They may allow insureds to handle claims themselves, perhaps agreeing to pay a non-profit charging rate. However, in the context of money laundering, it is quite likely that the firm will be looking for a helping hand.

Policies will require that notification is in writing. Insurers will also want a claims report form completed. Many provide this electronically, enabling their insureds to keep it on hand for prompt completion when needed. If the solicitors have it already, they should start completing it the moment they realise that they need to notify a matter to insurers – it helps save time which may be important if there is remedial action to be taken.

They should start preparing to deal with the inevitable requests they are going to receive from insurers or solicitors instructed by them as soon as possible.

Information that the insurers are likely to want includes:

1. the file;
2. other material documents;
3. a statement from the case handler; and
4. if there are proceedings, or are likely to be imminently, a list of partners to acknowledge service.

They will also require co-operation in dealing with the claim.

Caution will be needed in taking a statement from the case handler if they are suspected of being involved.

It is helpful if the file is tidy – without destroying or materially altering its contents – and useful if it is in some semblance of order and complete, so any unfiled letters and attendance notes should be put on the file.

Inevitably there will be correspondence about it going forward, so if the file is likely to be requested by insurers or panel solicitors it is often a good idea to prepare a copy at this stage. If the matter is current this will be necessary anyway. There is something to be said for paginating it before copying as this can make it much easier to refer to documents in correspondence. Draft documents may be important to show how a final version developed and it can be useful to put them in the right order.

It should be remembered that there may be documents which are not on the file but are relevant to the issues, particularly accounting records and diaries. If staff are still using paper diaries, make sure they are not thrown out. If there are diary entries relevant to the claim it may be helpful to include copies with the file, perhaps redacting entries relating to other clients.

The work should be checked to ensure it was done on standard terms and whether there is a copy on the file. Terms change from time to time, so it is a good idea to see if a copy is still available, particularly if it may contain some information on the firm's terms for money laundering compliance.

It should be borne in mind that there may be other files which are relevant too. These may include other files relating to the same client. Can these be disclosed to insurers? They can, provided there is a claim – by making a claim, the client waives the right to confidentiality.[20] There may be more difficulty however where the notification to insurers is precautionary and there is no claim, which in the context of money laundering concerns may not be uncommon. The client has not waived their right to confidentiality. If the client has sought the solicitor's advice where there is an intention on the part of the client or a third party to further criminal activity, clearly there will be no duty of confidentiality, but this will probably leave a large tranche of cases where the facts are less clear cut. What can the solicitor do then? There is no simple answer. However, it is submitted that the duty of confidentiality is not absolute, there is a wide duty to cooperate with insurers under a statutory scheme of insurance which was set up in the public interest, compliance with the money laundering provisions is also required in the public interest, and there may therefore be an argument that a solicitor may make disclosure to the insurers and their solicitors for the purpose of seeking legal advice.

A pragmatic approach to the problem would suggest that it is better to err on the side of disclosure to insurers. It is useful to obtain a statement at an early stage even if only in a rudimentary form to cover the firm against the risk of

---

20 *Lillicrap v Nalder & Son* [1993] 1 WLR 94, [1993] 1 All ER 724.

19. Liability and professional indemnity

the staff member becoming unavailable in future. If there is a paginated copy of the file available as suggested above, and cross-referenced to the document page numbers in the statement, this can be very helpful.

A list of partners will be required to acknowledge service of any proceedings. Generally, as a matter of good practice, the partners on whose behalf service is acknowledged will be those who were equity partners (including fixed share equity partners) at both the date of the alleged act giving rise to the claim and at the date of service of proceedings.

Briefly, the reason for this is that a judgment can only be enforced without permission of the court against a person who was a partner at the time of the alleged act (otherwise they would not be liable to the claimant) and who has acknowledged service. Salaried partners may also be liable but it is good practice to leave their position protected by not acknowledging on their behalf, as in order to succeed against them a claimant would have to establish that they were held out as partners to the claimant and that the claimant relied on that holding out in their dealings with the firm.[21]

19.7.6 Co-operation with insurers

Co-operation with insurers and their solicitors is an important area and it is one where even some of the best firms fall down. This is no doubt due to a variety of factors – claims are unwelcome and the file may inevitably be a mental block file, and it is often dead time which will not be chargeable. As a matter of practice, it is a good idea if the primary contact with the insurer is not the person responsible for the file giving rise to the claim, indeed in the context of money laundering it may well be appropriate for it to be the MLRO. This makes co-operation easier and means that the person who is the point of contact in the firm may have a more detached view of things.

It is important to put things in order as soon as possible because it is quite possible that matters will move on fast with the need for civil proceedings, or perhaps a request by the police for possession of the file.

Insurance policies will provide for firms to cooperate, some containing wider provisions than others, and if the insured's failure to cooperate prejudices insurers, they may seek to recover the additional outlay from those in the firm who are responsible.

---

21 See *Nationwide Building Society v Lewis & anr* [1998] 2 WLR 915.

19.7.7 Costs

Costs can be a serious issue. There are many points in the LS Guidance where it is noted that firms may wish to seek legal advice on their position. In addition, a firm may wish to seek guidance from the court as to how to deal with a particular situation such as distribution of funds which it is holding. Provided there is a potential loss which might give rise to a claim, there will generally be cover under the firm's professional indemnity policy – subject of course to strict compliance with the terms, particularly as to seeking prior approval.

Costs of this nature fall within the definition of 'Defence costs' in clause 8.5 of the LS Minimum Terms which provides as follows:

> Defence Costs mean legal costs and disbursements and investigative and related expenses reasonably and necessarily incurred with the consent of the Insurer in –
> (a) defending any proceedings relating to a Claim; or
> (b) conducting any proceedings for indemnity, contribution or recovery relating to a Claim; or
> (c) investigating, reducing, avoiding or compromising any actual or potential Claim; or
> (d) acting for any Insured in connection with any investigation, inquiry or disciplinary proceeding.
>
> Defence Costs do not include any internal or overhead expenses of the Firm or the Insurer or the cost of any Insured's time. (© The Law Society)

Sub-paragraph (c) will be the most significant for these purposes. Note however that there is only cover where the costs have been incurred with the consent of the insurer, hence the need to notify as soon as possible.

20. Conclusion: a risk-based approach

20.1 Introduction

The potential loss of livelihood for individuals and reputational damage for firms inevitably causes a huge fear factor. Given the complexity of professional practice, the inevitable question is: 'Where do we start?'

A few questions serve to identify the problem:

1. Do you apply the procedures to all areas of practice?
2. Do you train all staff or only some of them?
3. How do you guard against acting for money launderers?
4. How do you guard against being involved in transactions or other substantive offences?

The list could almost be endless.

As in all areas of risk, there is a choice:

1. do nothing, and hope the problem will go away; or
2. plan a strategy, assess the risks and implement a strategy to deal with them.

Either way, of course, things may still go wrong. But the benefit of the second approach is that, in addition to reducing the risk of things going wrong in the first place, you may have better prospects of avoiding prosecution and civil liability or, if unfortunate enough to be prosecuted, may have more prospect of persuading a jury of your innocence.

Particularly given the risk of committing a crime without realising it (eg because one's senses were not aroused at the time by reasonable grounds for suspicion, perhaps through overwork, shortage of time, late night working to conclude a corporate deal, or simply failure to appreciate the significance of facts of which one was aware) the only viable approach can be to take the second course and deal with this like any other area of risk

20. Conclusion: A risk-based approach

– identify the vulnerabilities, both generally and specifically as they affect the firm, and identify the likelihood of them occurring. It goes without saying that the likely impact of anything going wrong will in all cases be high – the only difference will be the length of the sentence.

What appears therefore to be good practice is in fact underlined by the Money Laundering Regulations 2003 (MLR 2003). As explained previously, under reg 3, all firms in the regulated sector must 'establish such procedures of internal control and communication as may be appropriate for the purposes of forestalling and preventing money laundering'. The Law Society's 'Money Laundering Guidance (Pilot – January 2004)' (LS Guidance)[1] advises that this means that each firm must consider how it conducts its practice, and whether, in addition to the arrangements for reporting and training,[2] there are any procedures which should be introduced to satisfy this regulation 3 requirement.

20.2 Assessing the risk

In all but the smallest firms it is unlikely that the money laundering reporting officer (MLRO) will know all the clients and may have little understanding of the practical aspects of the work of all the firm's departments, which may include those giving the firm the greatest exposure. Clearly there is a case for the initial assessment of risk being done by a working party drawn from the firm's fee-earning and accounts departments. The people involved in the process should be of sufficient seniority and experience to identify the risk and help the MLRO in their job of communicating the message to the rest of the firm.

They will want to take account of their own particular areas of exposure having regard to the work they do. In doing this it will be helpful to have regard to any available data. More will doubtless emerge in due course but at present there is some information on the NCIS website in a document entitled 'United Kingdom Threat Assessment of Serious and Organised Crime 2003'.[3] The following extract is relevant to this:

> 6.8... In 2002, purchasing property in the UK was the most popular method identified, involving roughly one in three serious and organised crime groups where the method was known. Investment in front companies or high cash businesses came next, followed by simply spending the criminal proceeds to fund a lifestyle, and by transferring cash overseas using bureaux de change and money transmission agencies. Roughly one in 10 groups was known to use bank accounts in the UK, and similar proportions used accounts overseas or

---

1 LS Guidance, para 6.1.
2 Discussed in the LS Guidance, paras 3.16–3.27.
3 See www.ncis.co.uk/ukta/2003/threat06.asp.

transmitted cash through couriers. Fewer groups invested in property overseas, or in financial products, and a small percentage used gambling or alternative remittance systems (for example, 'hawala' banking), although the highly secretive nature of the latter means that this is likely to be understated...

6.10 Serious and organised criminals frequently launder cash through legitimate and quasi-legitimate businesses. These businesses are often owned or part-owned by the criminals or by close associates, although legitimate businessmen may also be duped into providing the means for laundering criminal proceeds. The businesses typically have a high cash turnover, since this makes it easier for criminally acquired cash to be mixed in with legitimate funds, for example, restaurants, nightclubs, fast food outlets, tanning salons, taxi firms and car sales or repair companies. The same businesses may support money-making criminality, for example providing the means to transport drugs or the venue where they are sold.

The firm may act for cash-based businesses but, in doing its risk assessment, should appreciate that that *by itself* is not suspicious, though it may put practitioners on enquiry.

Other problem areas identified include cancelled transactions. Conveyancing solicitors and their staff need to be alert to the risk of receiving money as part payment for a property purchase which does not then proceed at the last minute, perhaps because the client says he has been advised there is a structural problem or an issue such as a road development of which he says he was previously unaware; the client then asks for the deposit to be refunded. Aborted transactions are an area which the firm may therefore, as a matter of policy, wish to flag up as requiring further investigation.

Discretionary trusts are another problem area the firm with a private client department will wish to consider in undertaking their risk assessment. However firms will need to have regard to the fact that their obligations under the Proceeds of Crime Act 2002 (POCA 2002) are not by any means limited to the 'professional' criminal but cover the full ambit of criminal activity including tax evasion; it is this which gives rise to the biggest problem for the average practitioner, with, for example, the particular problems of matrimonial practice.

20.3 Systems and policies

Whatever systems and policies are put in place, they should not be viewed as a standalone money laundering risk management policy – they must be integral to the firm's systems.

By way of illustration, as explained in some detail earlier, the money laundering legislation requires firms to have client identification procedures and the Law Society has given guidance on what constitutes adequate identification evidence. Likewise, institutional lenders require solicitors to

20. Conclusion: A risk-based approach

check identity, but the documents recommended by the Law Society as being adequate for general purposes do not all satisfy the requirements of lenders set out in the Council of Mortgage Lenders' *Handbook*. So although a firm may have satisfied the money laundering legislation and breathed a sigh of relief in the process, it may still be exposed to a claim by an institutional lender for failing to satisfy their contractual requirements.

Firms also need to consider how they will react to changing circumstances, for example a client changing address during a transaction. If the client is moving to the new house they are buying and on which the solicitor is acting, that is only to be expected. But it is not enough for firms to adopt a simple tick box approach to compliance and assume that because they have satisfied the requirements on identification checks, that is the end of the matter. Although the regulations do not require a further check during the currency of the transaction, practitioners need also to be aware, as a completely separate issue, of the wider picture on compliance.

Consider this scenario, which is not as uncommon as might be supposed. A husband instructs the solicitor to act on the sale of the jointly owned matrimonial home. The solicitor has acted for both husband and wife on the purchase in recent times and does not repeat his identification checks. So far, so good in relation to money laundering compliance, though all may not be well on other fronts. In fact, the marriage is breaking down and the husband is purporting to sell the house without his wife's knowledge, intending to make off with the proceeds. Realising belatedly that the solicitor will write to them with documents for signature, he rents another house and tells the solicitor they have moved out. The rented address is very near the house they are selling, and when asked about the temporary move, the client is evasive.

The solicitor is not required by the regulations to carry out another identification check but the additional facts – the rented address nearby and the unsatisfactory response - may put him or her on enquiry that both client and solicitor are both about to become involved in an arrangement. The solicitor needs to consider the position most carefully because this will give rise to issues of notifying NCIS, deciding whether to continue to act or not, whether or not to seek NCIS consent, and tipping off.

Turning back to the identification issues generally, firms may wish in any event to consider what they regard as acceptable evidence. For example, the LS Guidance[4] suggests a cheque drawn on an account in the name of the client with a bank in the UK or EEA as acceptable evidence, an issue discussed at **8.8**.

---

4 LS Guidance, para 3.84.

20. Conclusion: A risk-based approach

All the systems and policies in the world will not help unless they are applied rigorously in practice, however, and that leads on to two further considerations – training, and auditing for compliance – discussed further below.

The issues covered below involve a variety of policy decisions. There is no single policy which can work for all firms given the enormous variety in firms' practices. For example, some firms will have greater exposure to clients who have difficulty satisfying identification requirements, perhaps because they are elderly and have no passports or driving licences. Other firms will be exposed to the problems of volume remortgage work with clients scattered around the country.

The risk-based approach to implementing a money laundering strategy has been endorsed in other sectors, notably by the Joint Money Laundering Steering Group and the Financial Services Authority (FSA) and there is every reason for law firms to adopt a similar approach, indeed the MLR 2003, reg 3 might be interpreted as making it mandatory.

Firms which undertake financial services business under direct regulation of the FSA will have other, separate considerations to take into account and are outside the scope of this book. Indeed, whether as a matter of policy to continue carrying out that type of work given all the other attendant risks is, in itself, worth keeping under review.

Solicitors will wish to consider whether to put established clients through identification procedures. Most will probably opt not to do so in the majority of cases, though many banks have had no such reservations about requiring existing customers to prove their identity. Those considering incorporation, whether as a limited liability partnership or limited liability company, should consider the issue on whether they need to recheck identity.

20.4 Documentation

Compliance will mean that firms will have to document their procedures and the application of them in practice. This will help practitioners learn from their experience and, through introducing consistency of approach, should ultimately help mitigate some of the cost of compliance.

MLROs will wish to document the factors they have considered in deciding whether or not to make a disclosure or seek NCIS approval to a transaction for at least five reasons:

1. if a decision not to disclose subsequently proves to have been mistaken, it may assist in justifying to the authorities the stance taken at the time;

20. Conclusion: A risk-based approach

2. if a decision to disclose subsequently proves to have been mistaken, it may assist in resisting a client's claim or complaint, whether for breach of confidentiality, delay or loss of a transaction;
3. if external legal advice is needed, or advice from insurers, it will help in giving proper instructions;
4. it will assist in a structured review of policies and procedures to ensure the firm is learning as much as possible to protect it and its clients' interests;
5. it will help demonstrate compliance with the requirements of the MLR 2003, reg 3 (the requirement to establish procedures of internal control and communication).

Firms will also need to ensure they have a documented audit trail showing all changes which have been made to their policy, office manuals and training material and how and when those changes were communicated to each and every member of staff.

Establishing a written policy will help maintain consistency, not only between decisions made by the MLRO and his or her deputy, but also between individual case handlers and indeed in the MLRO's own decision making. In an article entitled 'Lawyers As Risk Managers', Andrew M Whittaker, general counsel to the FSA explains:

> Any organisation needs to work on the basis of a single, consistent view of the law. Any other approach would be dysfunctional. So we need procedures to ensure that advice we give is consistent. This does not mean that consistency is a virtue above all else. There is no virtue in being consistently wrong or consistently right, but unhelpful. If we are to aim for consistency, we need to recognise that this is as much an issue for the first person who gives advice on a subject as for those who do so afterwards. It means talking to colleagues, thinking round the subject and ensuring that the conclusions we reach work all round, not just in the particular case before us. This is a necessary part of our accountability as a legal team, rather than a collection of sole practitioners.[5]

Clearly it is not going to be possible or desirable to try and identity every problem scenario at the outset. What is required is an attempt at identifying the issues which are most likely to occur with a measure of protection against the rest.

Solicitors relying on advice on the NCIS website would be well advised to save or print a copy as the website is constantly changing and advice relied upon may disappear.

Telephone discussions with NCIS should also be carefully documented in an attendance note and solicitors should consider whether to write to

---

5 *Butterworths Journal of International Banking and Financial Law*, January 2003, pp6-7, published by LexisNexis UK.

20. Conclusion: A risk-based approach

NCIS confirming those discussions, particularly when they relate to guidance, or refusal to give guidance, on what to tell clients and others when concerned about the risk of tipping off.

20.5 Do you apply the systems across all the practice?

One's initial reaction may be to ask why a firm should try and make life harder for itself than it needs to – if part of the practice is doing unregulated work, why apply the same rigorous compliance systems to it?

There are many reasons why a firm might wish to subject itself to more onerous internal procedures than are strictly required by law. First, there is the possibility of a client being able to instruct the firm on regulated business 'through the back door', by instructing the firm first on business which is not regulated. Second, there is the risk of staff becoming involved in the commission of a variety of substantive offences.

Leading on from the first point, an initial instruction may be for a transaction below €15,000. There are two potential problems here – first, aggregation with other transactions taking the matter over the limit, and second the inevitability of fluctuation in the value of the Euro with the associated risk of a transaction going over the limit at a later date. As the LS Guidance[6] points out, the MLR 2003 do not, unlike previous regulations, provide a common date for a valuation of €15,000. The Treasury has indicated that it will be up to the courts to identify what rate will apply. It is therefore far safer to apply consistent policies across the practice.

The LS Guidance points out[7] that solicitors should remain vigilant about clients avoiding identification checks by purposefully entering into a number of transactions below the €15,000 limit, adding that if such tactics are suspected, identification should be obtained, and the suspicions reported to the MLRO or NCIS. The danger from the firm's point of view is that in seeking identification, perhaps on the second or third transaction when it has not done previously, it may be alerting the client and, if notification has been given to NCIS, it may amount to tipping off.

With regard to involvement in the substantive offences, it is not difficult to think up examples. First, there are the money laundering requirements in relation to drugs and terrorism which have applied for years. Second, there is the risk of becoming involved, perhaps in litigation, in concluding a settlement which constitutes an arrangement contrary to the POCA 2002.

---

6 LS Guidance, para 3.30.
7 *Ibid*, para 3.31.

20. Conclusion: A risk-based approach

Third, there is always the possibility of committing another substantive offence outside the POCA 2002, for example tax fraud – bear in mind that NCIS consent technically is only a defence to a charge under the POCA 2002 and not to other offences such as tax fraud. Whether the authorities would prosecute in those circumstances may be open to doubt, and proceedings may be susceptible to challenge for abuse of process, but one can well envisage circumstances where it might be alleged that disclosure was given less fully than it should have been, opening up risks of prosecution for other offences.

Firms should also give thought to whether they are exposed to the risk of acting in cases where there may be terrorist involvement. The offences of providing funds to terrorists only require proof of reasonable cause for suspicion; the LS Guidance warns[8] that terrorists may be funded from legitimately obtained income, which includes charitable donations, and it can be difficult to know at what stage legitimate earnings become terrorist assets. It may be advisable in appropriate circumstances, depending on the nature of the firm's practice and client base, for firms to refer to the consolidated sanctions list of the names of suspected terrorists maintained by the Bank of England on its website.[9] Nonetheless, the LS Guidance also warns that suspicion should never be based solely on stereotypical images of certain groups or categories of people.[10]

Staff need to be aware of all these risks. Overall, it is probably far easier in most cases to be consistent across the whole practice. It also means that the firm is increasing its protection against the risk of a variety of other potential misdemeanours giving rise, for example, to claims for constructive trust.

20.6 Transactions

When firms assess the risks they face they will need to consider the type of problems they may encounter on the business they handle. Some help will be found in the Law Society's 'Money Laundering Warning Card'.[11] This is worth studying in more detail. In particular it highlights the following:

- Settlements by cash
- Surprise payments by way of third party cheque
- Money transfers where there is a variation between the account holder or the signatory

---

8 LS Guidance, para 2.36.
9 See www.bankofengland.co.uk/sanctions/sanctionsconlist.htm.
10 LS Guidance, para 6.12.
11 *Ibid*, Annex 5. Reproduced in full at **Appendix 13**.

20. Conclusion: A risk-based approach

- Requests to make regular payments out of client account
- Settlements which are reached too easily

The Warning Card also advises watching out for unusual instructions, drawing attention to the following:

- Why has the client chosen your firm? Could the client find the same service nearer their home?
- Are you being asked to do something that does not fit in with the normal pattern of your business?
- Be cautious if instructions change without a reasonable explanation
- Be cautious about transactions which take an unusual turn

The Card warns that solicitors should watch out in particular for use of their client accounts:

- Using solicitors' client accounts to transmit money is useful to money launderers
- Do not provide a banking facility if you do not undertake any related legal work
- Be cautious if you are instructed to do legal work, receive funds into your client account, but then the instructions are cancelled and you are asked to return the money either to your client or a third party

Cancelling or withdrawing from transactions is a particular risk area because it is the easiest way of cleaning and disguising the source of money without the inconvenience of having to enter into a substantive transaction such as buying a property the client does not really want. From the client's perspective it is even worth sacrificing a deposit.

If the firm is instructed in transactions with an international element you can refer to the Financial Action Task Force website[12] which provides up to date information about different countries.

The LS Guidance[13] advises that one should be cautious if a client is introduced by an overseas bank or third party based in a country where drug production and trafficking or terrorism may be prevalent.

Firms need to take care if funds are being routed into and out of the UK without a logical explanation. In particular, they need to be alert to loss-making transactions, where instructions could lead to financial loss to the client or a third party without a logical explanation, particularly where the client seems unconcerned. Avoid confusing movements of funds between different accounts, institutions or jurisdictions without apparent reason.

---

12 See www.oecd.org/fatf.
13 LS Guidance, para 3.33.

20. Conclusion: A risk-based approach

In short, do all members of the firm *understand* the transactions they are being asked to implement for their clients? If they do not understand them fully the firm should not be acting. A test to consider – could the fee-earners explain the transactions they are handling to their secretaries? If not, why not? One of the authors has for many years asked his secretary if she understands the matters which are current, and the only negative answer was in relation to a matter which the writer did not fully understand himself! It is a useful test. Although it is not part of a secretary's role or training to understand, for example, the intricacies of the Taxes Acts, it should be possible to explain the nature of the transaction to one. After all, if fee-earners cannot do so, how will they explain it to a jury? They may have chosen their secretaries but will have little choice over jury selection.

In short, lawyers are only there to implement the clients' wishes, and if they do not understand their clients' wishes it is difficult to see how they can realistically hope to implement them adequately.

These pointers are all very well, however, but those responsible for the firm's money laundering policy will need to consider how they prevent them happening in their firm – whether through training, internal controls or a combination of the two.

Another area of concern to bear in mind is the completion money for a transaction coming in from a source other than the expected one. These issues tend to arise at short notice before completion when the pressure is on, minimising the opportunity for the firm to spot the issue, and maximising the pressure on the firm to proceed if it does spot it.

In formulating a risk management policy, firms should maximise their bargaining position in refusing payments from unexpected sources. Consider for example whether the firm's terms of engagement might give the right to agree the source of funds a certain period in advance and to refuse them if they come from some other source. It may not be the way lawyers, as a profession, have been used to doing business but times have changed, the challenges and regulation which they face have moved on, and they have to rise to the occasion to meet them. In formulating their terms they will have to have regard to the client's contractual obligations, so it would make sense to determine the proposed source of funds at the pre-contract stage and for it to be agreed with the client as the only method by which the transaction may be completed without further agreement from the firm and the risk of enquiries required by law delaying the process.

20.7 Disclosures

The LS Guidance advises that:[14]

> NCIS has been known to reject reports in which a reason for suspicion has not been provided. In explaining the reasons for suspicion you may include an explanation of the background to the retainer, making clear the identity of the suspected person or organisation and why there are suspicions surrounding them. Taking time to set out clear reasons should help the NCIS respond more quickly.

Whether or not there is power to reject reports, solicitors who seek consent to a transaction, in assessing their prospects of obtaining consent *and* avoiding prosecution for an offence which is not prescribed by the POCA 2002, would do well to give as much information as they can without going beyond the bounds of an unauthorised breach of confidentiality. In saying that, the writer recognises that it is probably easier said than done! Furthermore, the guidance to accountants, which is not of course binding on lawyers but is nonetheless helpful, is as follows:

> NCIS or the law enforcement authority undertaking an investigation will contact the business (usually the MLRO) if they have any queries about the disclosure. Businesses and individuals should be cautious in responding to requests for additional information, and generally route them through the MLRO, to ensure their response is covered by appropriate protection against claims for breach of confidentiality. Except for requests for clarification or explanation of material already included within a suspicion report made to NCIS, it is recommended that disclosure of further information takes place only:
>
> - in response to a Court order or other legal powers requiring disclosure, such as those available to the Serious Fraud Office; or
> - after careful consideration, and documenting the justification for making a disclosure in the public interest.[15]

20.8 Training

Careful thought needs to be given to training. Who to train, how to train them, what training to give them, whether to test them, and the frequency of retraining are all issues requiring a risk assessment.

20.9 Communication

Apart from matters covered by the training programme, how will staff know what the requirements are from time to time? With any new regime it is inevitable that change will be brought about in the light of new case law or legislation, new guidance form the courts, NCIS or the Law Society, and the firm's own experience. Changes in the firm itself may

---

14 LS Guidance, para 7.7. Extract © The Law Society.
15 Anti-Money Laundering (Proceeds of Crime And Terrorism), Second Interim Guidance for Accountants, February 2004, para 20.4.

also bring about the need to update procedures – opening of new offices may weaken control, new areas of work may heighten the need for checks. Mergers and acquisitions of other practices are also key areas of risk, in addition to the usual changes in staff through recruitment or hiring of temporary staff.

The ideal solution will be to have the procedures incorporated in the office manual and to have that available centrally and electronically, whether on an intranet or, for smaller firms, a central 'read-only' document. That way staff can be sure that they are consulting the latest version.

20.10 The money laundering reporting officer

The identity of the MLRO and any deputies must be readily identifiable to all. While on the subject, it is difficult to see how firms will generally be able to manage compliance if there is no deputy – these are matters which by law simply cannot wait until his or her return from holiday.

The seniority of the MLRO is important. An assessment will have to be made as to whether the person is sufficiently senior to challenge the most senior partners, request information and call for files. Anything less will not suffice.

There is a further point to consider in relation to the MLRO. To quote Caesar, 'Who will guard the guards themselves?' The point has some significance for partners, because although employees will generally discharge their notification duties under the legislation by reporting matters to the MLRO, the same is not true of partners, because they are not employees.[16] Nor do partners have any defence of lack of training. (Salaried partners who are truly classed as such, however, may be employees. In practice most are probably self-employed fixed-share partners.)

The partners will therefore wish to be satisfied that the MLRO is discharging his or her functions to their satisfaction.

20.11 Enforcement

It is essential that there is an internal system of enforcement. Some control can be brought into the client opening procedures by centralising the system through the accounts department, which for many firms will mean that fee-earners cannot record time until they have done all they

---

[16] See POCA 2002, s337(5), preserving an anomaly which existed under the previous legislation.

are required to do. That may operate as an incentive for fee-earners to comply.

Disciplinary sanctions need to be considered too. Breach of money laundering requirements could be disastrous for the firm and for individuals, so it must be made clear that in the absence of reasonable excuse it will be regarded as gross misconduct.

20.12 Auditing for compliance

Self-evidently it is no use having the finest money laundering policies in the profession if they are not being applied. Many firms already undergo audit by external assessors for quality systems such as Lexcel, ISO 9001 or by the Legal Services Commission. Those firms and others may have internal audit. Those who do not, may wish to consider whether they should start now to see that their procedures are being followed.

Is it possible, for example, for staff to act for friends and relatives without going through the normal file opening processes? General experience of law firms suggests that it is rather easy – with either no file being opened on the accounts system at all, which rather defeats the protection on which many firms rely, or by 'laundering' a matter through a 'miscellaneous' or 'general' file, either opened in the name of the client or of the fee earner concerned.

Clearly all this has to stop. A trawl of matters for those with 'general' or 'miscellaneous' in their description is a worthwhile exercise, but once it is known that is open to checking other ways to beat the system will doubtless emerge and random file selection will always be an important part of audit, though it should not be the only basis of file selection.

Is it possible for new matters to be undertaken for existing clients without going through the normal procedures? Again this offers opportunities for non-compliance, particularly if client identification checks are only carried out in relation to 'relevant business' – a client may instruct on, say, a personal injury matter without any checks being carried out, and then instruct the firm to act on a conveyancing matter. The solicitor can easily be lulled into a false sense of security. The only truly safe course is to undertake the checks for all clients.

Firms will doubtless wish to consider, particularly if they have no audit process at present (apart from under the Solicitors Accounts Rules 1998), whether they wish to retain an outside practice to undertake an audit for compliance.

20.13 Record keeping

Records of identification evidence must be kept for five years after the last transaction for the client. This may give rise to an offence if the evidence is kept on the first file opened and the file is destroyed after, say, six years, while other matters are more current. There is also the risk that different departments will act for the same client, and the department which has relied on another department's identification checks may continue acting until some years later. Firms need to consider therefore where the evidence will be kept, and a central store in the accounts department may commend itself in many cases. The issue is discussed in **Chapter 10**.

Records need to be kept for five years. File retrieval from archives is probably the area of practice where solicitors fare worst. The examples of solicitors being sued and unable to trace the file are legion. Never before have they faced the risk of prosecution; perhaps this will focus minds on archiving systems and responsibility for them.

20.14 The 'reasonable excuse' defence

The risk assessment issue here is: 'When are you going to act in a particular way, knowing that the only defence to a criminal charge will be the defence of "reasonable excuse"?' In what circumstances can you proceed knowing that your only defence, if called to account, will be one of 'reasonable excuse'?

The general view, as yet unsupported by any authority, is that the term 'reasonable excuse' will be very narrowly construed. Threats of physical violence are the possible reason cited by commentators.

Some solicitors have queried whether the test would be satisfied where, for example, material facts are discovered shortly before completion of a transaction and notifying NCIS would cause delay in a conveyancing chain. This view is untenable for two reasons. First, it seems barely credible that the public policy, as decided by Parliament, of preventing the funding of criminal activity including terrorism could properly be subverted for pure personal or commercial expedience. Second, and more significantly, it is hard to see how the solicitor, armed with knowledge that the transaction is in some way tainted, could not expose him or herself to the risk of personal involvement in an arrangement resulting in criminal liability for a primary money laundering offence.

20. Conclusion: A risk-based approach

There is one further issue however, which is in relation to legal professional privilege. The LS Guidance[17] advises as follows:

> A further anomaly appears to have arisen in the relationship between the failure to disclose offence under section 330 and that under section 331 which applies to a nominated officer. Under section 330, if the information is received by a professional legal adviser in privileged circumstances, no offence is committed by failing to make the requisite report. However, if the adviser makes a report to his nominated officer, although that information came to the professional legal adviser in privileged circumstances, it could be that the nominated officer has not received the information in privileged circumstances (even if he is a professional legal adviser) and therefore may not be able to rely upon the section 330 privilege defence even though the information is privileged. It is the Law Society's view that in such circumstances a nominated officer has a reasonable excuse under section 331(6) for not disclosing.

Clearly it is deeply unsatisfactory to have to rely on such an approach. Firms and their MLROs will have to make policy decisions on how to proceed. Although the LS Guidance[18] sets out fully the solicitor's duty to maintain confidentiality, it does not perhaps go as far as the guidance issued to accountants which warns of the risks of civil action for breach of that duty where it is not expressly permitted, or one should perhaps say required, by statute.

This issue raises the desirability of contract terms limiting liability for breach. They may not be a complete solution but are perhaps the best hope one can have of achieving a sensible compromise. Firms are inevitably going to err on the side of caution and report out of an abundance of caution, but they do have to recognise the risks of liability, albeit non-criminal, inherent in that course too. Policy decisions will have to be made on the use of terms limiting liability and whether the firm will act for clients who refuse to accept those terms.

20.15 Privilege

Legal professional privilege may be a legitimate reason for not making a disclosure to NCIS, but it is a closely circumscribed and developing area of law and one that is often easier to state than to apply in practice. It would be highly undesirable to find that a newly recruited, unqualified member of staff with relatively little experience had taken it upon themselves to decide whether or not a matter was privileged and, on the basis of that decision, whether or not to notify a matter to the MLRO.

Furthermore, if the only reason not to notify is a claim of privilege, then the firm cannot continue to act or it will be exposed to a risk of committing substantive offences and to civil liability.

---

17 LS Guidance, para 4.36. Extract © The Law Society.
18 See *ibid*, paras 4.1 to 4.22.

20. *Conclusion: A risk-based approach*

That being so, it must follow that a firm's procedures should make it clear that the decision to withhold notification on grounds of privilege can only be decided by nominated individuals, probably the MLRO or his or her deputy, but if that is the approach to be taken firms will also have to take account of the privilege issue (or lack of privilege) relating to MLROs identified in the previous section.

20.16 Involvement of insurers

Careful thought will need to be given to notifying insurers in cases where it proves impossible to obtain consent from NCIS to a transaction proceeding in time. Firms are generally required to notify insurers of circumstances which may give rise to a claim and this would clearly be such a circumstance. The LS Guidance advises[19] that NCIS should be informed of the urgency. The Guidance continues:

> Insurance companies have their own nominated officer, and if possible solicitors should contact the nominated officer to explain the reasons for the notification. In case of doubt, particularly in relation to the tipping-off offence, contact Professional Ethics.

This will therefore require the firm's MLRO to liaise with the professional indemnity contact partner. The LS Guidance might not be entirely appropriate, given the fact that insurers' MLROs may be far removed from the professional indemnity arena. Insurers need to consider their approach and the process for claims departments. This is an early stage of development in a difficult area of law and it is highly desirable that they focus money laundering-related notifications on a select team within their claims departments, if they have one, so that the maximum opportunity is obtained for learning from experience and consistency of approach. Insurers will be exposed to increasing numbers of urgent notifications involving requests for guidance and payment of costs where, for example, transactions are about to be delayed with consequent exposure to claims for damages and interest, or directions are needed from the court as to the disposal of funds held in a solicitor's client account.

20.17 Other reporting obligations

Solicitors are less exposed to reporting obligations than accountants but there are nonetheless obligations which arise in practice. They may, for example, be asked to confirm to the auditors whether they know of any

---

19 LS Guidance, para 5.22. Extract © The Law Society.

liabilities. Those who act for listed American companies may have obligations under the Sarbanes-Oxley Act. Those who have such obligations will need to consider the risk of tipping off. For most firms, obligations of this nature will probably not be a large problem, but that may mean the risks are more readily overlooked when they do arise.

20.18 Decision-making

It is highly desirable that MLROs adopt a policy of noting the reasons for the decisions they make, recording the factors they have taken into account. The retrospective application, perhaps years later, of an objective test to the question of whether a solicitor should have realised that a money laundering offence had been committed means that MLROs must be able to demonstrate what they knew at the time and what weight they gave to each fact. Otherwise there is a very real danger that facts discovered subsequently will be attributed to them and enhance substantially the risk of conviction. It is highly likely that the matters complained of will not stand out in the MLRO's mind years after the event and reconstruction of the facts as known at the time will be essential.

20.19 And finally...

Most of the points outlined above involve policy decisions by the firm. The authors' view is that in practice this necessitates the firm documenting its risk assessment and how it is going to proceed. If the firm has a reasonable policy and the policy has been applied, then even if sometimes things go wrong, it will greatly enhance the prospects of avoiding prosecution or, if the worst comes to the worst, explaining the position to a jury.

It is also highly desirable that the policy is reviewed at least annually to see that it is still appropriate in the light of any changed regulations, reported decisions, LS Guidance and practical experience, changes in the firm's practice and changes in practice generally.

To illustrate the last point, government proposals to reintroduce means testing to publicly funded criminal work, for example, may increase the risk for criminal solicitors who may in future become aware of clients failing to disclose income in their application for public funding.

Firms will also wish to look at the level of their reporting relative to the numbers of instructions. Home Office Minister Bob Ainsworth is reported as saying:

20. Conclusion: A risk-based approach

> The number of suspicious transactions [notified by] the legal profession is very low indeed. It simply cannot be a reflection of the genuine occasions that exist. We do expect to see that there will be a substantial increase in suspicious transaction reports from the legal profession.[20]

Although there is insufficient data yet to think of benchmarking, it may not be surprising if the authorities give thought to this at some point in the future. They may be surprised, for example, if a firm with a high volume conveyancing practice and a large matrimonial practice makes no notifications at all in the first year.

In a number of areas the authors have recommended action which goes beyond current LS Guidance. In doing so, they have had regard to current practice in the financial services industry and the Joint Money Laundering Steering Group guidance. They have also had regard to the requirement in the MLR 2003 to have 'systems of internal control', which may be construed more onerously with the benefit of hindsight in years to come given the general sea change in corporate governance.

Firms which aim only for the bare minimum in the field of compliance are courting disaster.

Appendix 1: Proceeds of Crime Act 2002, Part 7 and Part 8, chapter 1

PART 7

MONEY LAUNDERING

Offences

327 Concealing etc

(1) A person commits an offence if he –

    (a) conceals criminal property;

    (b) disguises criminal property;

    (c) converts criminal property;

    (d) transfers criminal property;

    (e) removes criminal property from England and Wales or from Scotland or from Northern Ireland.

(2) But a person does not commit such an offence if –

    (a) he makes an authorised disclosure under section 338 and (if the disclosure is made before he does the act mentioned in subsection (1)) he has the appropriate consent;

    (b) he intended to make such a disclosure but had a reasonable excuse for not doing so;

    (c) the act he does is done in carrying out a function he has relating to the enforcement of any provision of this Act or of any other enactment relating to criminal conduct or benefit from criminal conduct.

(3) Concealing or disguising criminal property includes concealing or disguising its nature, source, location, disposition, movement or ownership or any rights with respect to it.

328 Arrangements

(1) A person commits an offence if he enters into or becomes concerned in an arrangement which he knows or suspects facilitates (by whatever means) the acquisition, retention, use or control of criminal property by or on behalf of another person.

(2) But a person does not commit such an offence if –

    (a) he makes an authorised disclosure under section 338 and (if the disclosure is made before he does the act mentioned in subsection (1)) he has the appropriate consent;

    (b) he intended to make such a disclosure but had a reasonable excuse for not doing so;

    (c) the act he does is done in carrying out a function he has relating to the enforcement of any provision of this Act or of any other enactment relating to criminal conduct or benefit from criminal conduct.

329 Acquisition, use and possession

(1) A person commits an offence if he –

    (a) acquires criminal property;

    (b) uses criminal property;

    (c) has possession of criminal property.

(2) But a person does not commit such an offence if –

Appendix 1

(a) he makes an authorised disclosure under section 338 and (if the disclosure is made before he does the act mentioned in subsection (1)) he has the appropriate consent;

(b) he intended to make such a disclosure but had a reasonable excuse for not doing so;

(c) he acquired or used or had possession of the property for adequate consideration;

(d) the act he does is done in carrying out a function he has relating to the enforcement of any provision of this Act or of any other enactment relating to criminal conduct or benefit from criminal conduct.

(3) For the purposes of this section –

(a) a person acquires property for inadequate consideration if the value of the consideration is significantly less than the value of the property;

(b) a person uses or has possession of property for inadequate consideration if the value of the consideration is significantly less than the value of the use or possession;

(c) the provision by a person of goods or services which he knows or suspects may help another to carry out criminal conduct is not consideration.

330 Failure to disclose: regulated sector

(1) A person commits an offence if each of the following three conditions is satisfied.

(2) The first condition is that he –

(a) knows or suspects, or

(b) has reasonable grounds for knowing or suspecting, that another person is engaged in money laundering.

(3) The second condition is that the information or other matter –

(a) on which his knowledge or suspicion is based, or

(b) which gives reasonable grounds for such knowledge or suspicion, came to him in the course of a business in the regulated sector.

(4) The third condition is that he does not make the required disclosure as soon as is practicable after the information or other matter comes to him.

(5) The required disclosure is a disclosure of the information or other matter –

(a) to a nominated officer or a person authorised for the purposes of this Part by the Director General of the National Criminal Intelligence Service;

(b) in the form and manner (if any) prescribed for the purposes of this subsection by order under section 339.

(6) But a person does not commit an offence under this section if –

(a) he has a reasonable excuse for not disclosing the information or other matter;

(b) he is a professional legal adviser and the information or other matter came to him in privileged circumstances;

(c) subsection (7) applies to him.

(7) This subsection applies to a person if –

(a) he does not know or suspect that another person is engaged in money laundering, and

(b) he has not been provided by his employer with such training as is specified by the Secretary of State by order for the purposes of this section.

(8) In deciding whether a person committed an offence under this section the court must consider whether he followed any relevant guidance which was at the time concerned –

(a) issued by a supervisory authority or any other appropriate body,

(b) approved by the Treasury, and

(c) published in a manner it approved as appropriate in its opinion to bring the guidance to the attention of persons likely to be affected by it.

(9) A disclosure to a nominated officer is a disclosure which –

(a) is made to a person nominated by the alleged offender's employer to receive disclosures under this section, and

(b) is made in the course of the alleged offender's employment and in accordance with the procedure established by the employer for the purpose.

(10) Information or other matter comes to a professional legal adviser in privileged circumstances if it is communicated or given to him –

(a) by (or by a representative of) a client of his in connection with the giving by the adviser of legal advice to the client,

(b) by (or by a representative of) a person seeking legal advice from the adviser, or

(c) by a person in connection with legal proceedings or contemplated legal proceedings.

(11) But subsection (10) does not apply to information or other matter which is communicated or given with the intention of furthering a criminal purpose.

(12) Schedule 9 has effect for the purpose of determining what is –

(a) a business in the regulated sector;

(b) a supervisory authority.

(13) An appropriate body is any body which regulates or is representative of any trade, profession, business or employment carried on by the alleged offender.

331 Failure to disclose: nominated officers in the regulated sector

(1) A person nominated to receive disclosures under section 330 commits an offence if the conditions in subsections (2) to (4) are satisfied.

(2) The first condition is that he –

(a) knows or suspects, or

(b) has reasonable grounds for knowing or suspecting, that another person is engaged in money laundering.

(3) The second condition is that the information or other matter –

(a) on which his knowledge or suspicion is based, or

(b) which gives reasonable grounds for such knowledge or suspicion, came to him in consequence of a disclosure made under section 330.

(4) The third condition is that he does not make the required disclosure as soon as is practicable after the information or other matter comes to him.

(5) The required disclosure is a disclosure of the information or other matter –

(a) to a person authorised for the purposes of this Part by the Director General of the National Criminal Intelligence Service;

(b) in the form and manner (if any) prescribed for the purposes of this subsection by order under section 339.

(6) But a person does not commit an offence under this section if he has a reasonable excuse for not disclosing the information or other matter.

(7) In deciding whether a person committed an offence under this section the court must consider whether he followed any relevant guidance which was at the time concerned –

(a) issued by a supervisory authority or any other appropriate body,

(b) approved by the Treasury, and

(c) published in a manner it approved as appropriate in its opinion to bring the guidance to the attention of persons likely to be affected by it.

(8) Schedule 9 has effect for the purpose of determining what is a supervisory authority.

(9) An appropriate body is a body which regulates or is representative of a trade, profession, business or employment.

Appendix 1

332 Failure to disclose: other nominated officers

(1) A person nominated to receive disclosures under section 337 or 338 commits an offence if the conditions in subsections (2) to (4) are satisfied.

(2) The first condition is that he knows or suspects that another person is engaged in money laundering.

(3) The second condition is that the information or other matter on which his knowledge or suspicion is based came to him in consequence of a disclosure made under section 337 or 338.

(4) The third condition is that he does not make the required disclosure as soon as is practicable after the information or other matter comes to him.

(5) The required disclosure is a disclosure of the information or other matter –

(a) to a person authorised for the purposes of this Part by the Director General of the National Criminal Intelligence Service;

(b) in the form and manner (if any) prescribed for the purposes of this subsection by order under section 339.

(6) But a person does not commit an offence under this section if he has a reasonable excuse for not disclosing the information or other matter.

333 Tipping off

(1) A person commits an offence if –

(a) he knows or suspects that a disclosure falling within section 337 or 338 has been made, and

(b) he makes a disclosure which is likely to prejudice any investigation which might be conducted following the disclosure referred to in paragraph (a).

(2) But a person does not commit an offence under subsection (1) if –

(a) he did not know or suspect that the disclosure was likely to be prejudicial as mentioned in subsection (1);

(b) the disclosure is made in carrying out a function he has relating to the enforcement of any provision of this Act or of any other enactment relating to criminal conduct or benefit from criminal conduct;

(c) he is a professional legal adviser and the disclosure falls within subsection (3).

(3) A disclosure falls within this subsection if it is a disclosure –

(a) to (or to a representative of) a client of the professional legal adviser in connection with the giving by the adviser of legal advice to the client, or

(b) to any person in connection with legal proceedings or contemplated legal proceedings.

(4) But a disclosure does not fall within subsection (3) if it is made with the intention of furthering a criminal purpose.

334 Penalties

(1) A person guilty of an offence under section 327, 328 or 329 is liable –

(a) on summary conviction, to imprisonment for a term not exceeding six months or to a fine not exceeding the statutory maximum or to both, or

(b) on conviction on indictment, to imprisonment for a term not exceeding 14 years or to a fine or to both.

(2) A person guilty of an offence under section 330, 331, 332 or 333 is liable –

(a) on summary conviction, to imprisonment for a term not exceeding six months or to a fine not exceeding the statutory maximum or to both, or

(b) on conviction on indictment, to imprisonment for a term not exceeding five years or to a fine or to both.

Consent

335 Appropriate consent

(1) The appropriate consent is –

(a) the consent of a nominated officer to do a prohibited act if an authorised disclosure is made to the nominated officer;

(b) the consent of a constable to do a prohibited act if an authorised disclosure is made to a constable;

(c) the consent of a customs officer to do a prohibited act if an authorised disclosure is made to a customs officer.

(2) A person must be treated as having the appropriate consent if –

(a) he makes an authorised disclosure to a constable or a customs officer, and

(b) the condition in subsection (3) or the condition in subsection (4) is satisfied.

(3) The condition is that before the end of the notice period he does not receive notice from a constable or customs officer that consent to the doing of the act is refused.

(4) The condition is that –

(a) before the end of the notice period he receives notice from a constable or customs officer that consent to the doing of the act is refused, and

(b) the moratorium period has expired.

(5) The notice period is the period of seven working days starting with the first working day after the person makes the disclosure.

(6) The moratorium period is the period of 31 days starting with the day on which the person receives notice that consent to the doing of the act is refused.

(7) A working day is a day other than a Saturday, a Sunday, Christmas Day, Good Friday or a day which is a bank holiday under the Banking and Financial Dealings Act 1971 (c. 80) in the part of the United Kingdom in which the person is when he makes the disclosure.

(8) References to a prohibited act are to an act mentioned in section 327(1), 328(1) or 329(1) (as the case may be).

(9) A nominated officer is a person nominated to receive disclosures under section 338.

(10) Subsections (1) to (4) apply for the purposes of this Part.

336 Nominated officer: consent

(1) A nominated officer must not give the appropriate consent to the doing of a prohibited act unless the condition in subsection (2), the condition in subsection (3) or the condition in subsection (4) is satisfied.

(2) The condition is that –

(a) he makes a disclosure that property is criminal property to a person authorised for the purposes of this Part by the Director General of the National Criminal Intelligence Service, and

(b) such a person gives consent to the doing of the act.

(3) The condition is that –

(a) he makes a disclosure that property is criminal property to a person authorised for the purposes of this Part by the Director General of the National Criminal Intelligence Service, and

(b) before the end of the notice period he does not receive notice from such a person that consent to the doing of the act is refused.

(4) The condition is that –

(a) he makes a disclosure that property is criminal property to a person authorised for the purposes of this Part by the Director General of the National Criminal Intelligence Service,

(b) before the end of the notice period he receives notice from such a person that consent to the doing of the act is refused, and

(c) the moratorium period has expired.

(5) A person who is a nominated officer commits an offence if –

(a) he gives consent to a prohibited act in circumstances where none of the conditions in subsections (2), (3) and (4) is satisfied, and

(b) he knows or suspects that the act is a prohibited act.

(6) A person guilty of such an offence is liable –

(a) on summary conviction, to imprisonment for a term not exceeding six months or to a fine not exceeding the statutory maximum or to both, or

(b) on conviction on indictment, to imprisonment for a term not exceeding five years or to a fine or to both.

(7) The notice period is the period of seven working days starting with the first working day after the nominated officer makes the disclosure.

(8) The moratorium period is the period of 31 days starting with the day on which the nominated officer is given notice that consent to the doing of the act is refused.

(9) A working day is a day other than a Saturday, a Sunday, Christmas Day, Good Friday or a day which is a bank holiday under the Banking and Financial Dealings Act 1971 (c. 80) in the part of the United Kingdom in which the nominated officer is when he gives the appropriate consent.

(10) References to a prohibited act are to an act mentioned in section 327(1), 328(1) or 329(1) (as the case may be).

(11) A nominated officer is a person nominated to receive disclosures under section 338.

Disclosures

337 Protected disclosures

(1) A disclosure which satisfies the following three conditions is not to be taken to breach any restriction on the disclosure of information (however imposed).

(2) The first condition is that the information or other matter disclosed came to the person making the disclosure (the discloser) in the course of his trade, profession, business or employment.

(3) The second condition is that the information or other matter –

(a) causes the discloser to know or suspect, or

(b) gives him reasonable grounds for knowing or suspecting, that another person is engaged in money laundering.

(4) The third condition is that the disclosure is made to a constable, a customs officer or a nominated officer as soon as is practicable after the information or other matter comes to the discloser.

(5) A disclosure to a nominated officer is a disclosure which –

(a) is made to a person nominated by the discloser's employer to receive disclosures under this section, and

(b) is made in the course of the discloser's employment and in accordance with the procedure established by the employer for the purpose.

338 Authorised disclosures

(1) For the purposes of this Part a disclosure is authorised if –

(a) it is a disclosure to a constable, a customs officer or a nominated officer by the alleged offender that property is criminal property,

(b) it is made in the form and manner (if any) prescribed for the purposes of this subsection by order under section 339, and

(c) the first or second condition set out below is satisfied.

(2) The first condition is that the disclosure is made before the alleged offender does the prohibited act.

(3) The second condition is that –

(a) the disclosure is made after the alleged offender does the prohibited act,

(b) there is a good reason for his failure to make the disclosure before he did the act, and

(c) the disclosure is made on his own initiative and as soon as it is practicable for him to make it.

(4) An authorised disclosure is not to be taken to breach any restriction on the disclosure of information (however imposed).

(5) A disclosure to a nominated officer is a disclosure which –

(a) is made to a person nominated by the alleged offender's employer to receive authorised disclosures, and

(b) is made in the course of the alleged offender's employment and in accordance with the procedure established by the employer for the purpose.

(6) References to the prohibited act are to an act mentioned in section 327(1), 328(1) or 329(1) (as the case may be).

339 Form and manner of disclosures

(1) The Secretary of State may by order prescribe the form and manner in which a disclosure under section 330, 331, 332 or 338 must be made.

(2) An order under this section may also provide that the form may include a request to the discloser to provide additional information specified in the form.

(3) The additional information must be information which is necessary to enable the person to whom the disclosure is made to decide whether to start a money laundering investigation.

(4) A disclosure made in pursuance of a request under subsection (2) is not to be taken to breach any restriction on the disclosure of information (however imposed).

(5) The discloser is the person making a disclosure mentioned in subsection (1).

(6) Money laundering investigation must be construed in accordance with section 341(4).

(7) Subsection (2) does not apply to a disclosure made to a nominated officer.

Interpretation

340 Interpretation

(1) This section applies for the purposes of this Part.

(2) Criminal conduct is conduct which –

(a) constitutes an offence in any part of the United Kingdom, or

(b) would constitute an offence in any part of the United Kingdom if it occurred there.

(3) Property is criminal property if –

(a) it constitutes a person's benefit from criminal conduct or it represents such a benefit (in whole or part and whether directly or indirectly), and

(b) the alleged offender knows or suspects that it constitutes or represents such a benefit.

(4) It is immaterial –

(a) who carried out the conduct;

(b) who benefited from it;

(c) whether the conduct occurred before or after the passing of this Act.

Appendix 1

(5) A person benefits from conduct if he obtains property as a result of or in connection with the conduct.

(6) If a person obtains a pecuniary advantage as a result of or in connection with conduct, he is to be taken to obtain as a result of or in connection with the conduct a sum of money equal to the value of the pecuniary advantage.

(7) References to property or a pecuniary advantage obtained in connection with conduct include references to property or a pecuniary advantage obtained in both that connection and some other.

(8) If a person benefits from conduct his benefit is the property obtained as a result of or in connection with the conduct.

(9) Property is all property wherever situated and includes –

(a) money;

(b) all forms of property, real or personal, heritable or moveable;

(c) things in action and other intangible or incorporeal property.

(10) The following rules apply in relation to property –

(a) property is obtained by a person if he obtains an interest in it;

(b) references to an interest, in relation to land in England and Wales or Northern Ireland, are to any legal estate or equitable interest or power;

(c) references to an interest, in relation to land in Scotland, are to any estate, interest, servitude or other heritable right in or over land, including a heritable security;

(d) references to an interest, in relation to property other than land, include references to a right (including a right to possession).

(11) Money laundering is an act which –

(a) constitutes an offence under section 327, 328 or 329,

(b) constitutes an attempt, conspiracy or incitement to commit an offence specified in paragraph (a),

(c) constitutes aiding, abetting, counselling or procuring the commission of an offence specified in paragraph (a), or

(d) would constitute an offence specified in paragraph (a), (b) or (c) if done in the United Kingdom.

(12) For the purposes of a disclosure to a nominated officer –

(a) references to a person's employer include any body, association or organisation (including a voluntary organisation) in connection with whose activities the person exercises a function (whether or not for gain or reward), and

(b) references to employment must be construed accordingly.

(13) References to a constable include references to a person authorised for the purposes of this Part by the Director General of the National Criminal Intelligence Service.

PART 8

INVESTIGATIONS

CHAPTER 1

INTRODUCTION

341 Investigations

(1) For the purposes of this Part a confiscation investigation is an investigation into –

(a) whether a person has benefited from his criminal conduct, or

(b) the extent or whereabouts of his benefit from his criminal conduct.

(2) For the purposes of this Part a civil recovery investigation is an investigation into –

(a) whether property is recoverable property or associated property,

(b) who holds the property, or

(c) its extent or whereabouts.

(3) But an investigation is not a civil recovery investigation if –

(a) proceedings for a recovery order have been started in respect of the property in question,

(b) an interim receiving order applies to the property in question,

(c) an interim administration order applies to the property in question, or

(d) the property in question is detained under section 295.

(4) For the purposes of this Part a money laundering investigation is an investigation into whether a person has committed a money laundering offence.

342 Offences of prejudicing investigation

(1) This section applies if a person knows or suspects that an appropriate officer or (in Scotland) a proper person is acting (or proposing to act) in connection with a confiscation investigation, a civil recovery investigation or a money laundering investigation which is being or is about to be conducted.

(2) The person commits an offence if –

(a) he makes a disclosure which is likely to prejudice the investigation, or

(b) he falsifies, conceals, destroys or otherwise disposes of, or causes or permits the falsification, concealment, destruction or disposal of, documents which are relevant to the investigation.

(3) A person does not commit an offence under subsection (2)(a) if –

(a) he does not know or suspect that the disclosure is likely to prejudice the investigation,

(b) the disclosure is made in the exercise of a function under this Act or any other enactment relating to criminal conduct or benefit from criminal conduct or in compliance with a requirement imposed under or by virtue of this Act, or

(c) he is a professional legal adviser and the disclosure falls within subsection (4).

(4) A disclosure falls within this subsection if it is a disclosure –

(a) to (or to a representative of) a client of the professional legal adviser in connection with the giving by the adviser of legal advice to the client, or

(b) to any person in connection with legal proceedings or contemplated legal proceedings.

(5) But a disclosure does not fall within subsection (4) if it is made with the intention of furthering a criminal purpose.

(6) A person does not commit an offence under subsection (2)(b) if –

(a) he does not know or suspect that the documents are relevant to the investigation, or

(b) he does not intend to conceal any facts disclosed by the documents from any appropriate officer or (in Scotland) proper person carrying out the investigation.

(7) A person guilty of an offence under subsection (2) is liable –

(a) on summary conviction, to imprisonment for a term not exceeding six months or to a fine not exceeding the statutory maximum or to both, or

(b) on conviction on indictment, to imprisonment for a term not exceeding five years or to a fine or to both.

(8) For the purposes of this section –

(a) 'appropriate officer' must be construed in accordance with section 378;

(b) 'proper person' must be construed in accordance with section 412.

APPENDIX 2: THE MONEY LAUNDERING REGULATIONS 2003, SI 2003/3075

PART I

GENERAL

Citation, commencement etc

1-(1) These Regulations may be cited as the Money Laundering Regulations 2003.

(2) These Regulations come into force –

(a) for the purposes of regulation 10 in so far as it relates to a person who acts as a high value dealer, on 1st April 2004;

(b) for the purposes of regulation 2(3)(h), on 31st October 2004;

(c) for the purposes of regulation 2(3)(i), on 14th January 2005;

(d) for all other purposes, on 1st March 2004.

(3) These Regulations are prescribed for the purposes of sections 168(4)(b) and 402(1)(b) of the 2000 Act.

(4) The following Regulations are revoked –

(a) the Money Laundering Regulations 1993[1];

(b) the Financial Services and Markets Act 2000 (Regulations Relating to Money Laundering) Regulations 2001[2];

(c) the Money Laundering Regulations 2001[3].

Interpretation

2-(1) In these Regulations –

'the 2000 Act' means the Financial Services and Markets Act 2000;

'applicant for business' means a person seeking to form a business relationship, or carry out a one-off transaction, with another person acting in the course of relevant business carried on by that other person in the United Kingdom;

'applicant for registration' means an applicant for registration as a money service operator, or as a high value dealer;

'the appropriate judicial authority' means –

(a) in England and Wales, a magistrates' court,

(b) in Scotland, the sheriff,

(c) in Northern Ireland, a court of summary jurisdiction;

'authorised person' has the meaning given by section 31(2) of the 2000 Act;

'the Authority' means the Financial Services Authority;

---

[1] SI 1993/1933, amended by SI 1994/1696, SI 1998/1129, SI 2000/2952, SI 2001/3641 and 3649.

[2] SI 2001/1819.

[3] SI 2001/3641.

'the Banking Consolidation Directive' means Directive 2000/12/EC of the European Parliament and of the Council of 20th March 2000 relating to the taking up and pursuit of the business of credit institutions as last amended by Directive 2002/87/EC of the European Parliament and of the Council of 16th December 2002[4];

'business relationship' means any arrangement the purpose of which is to facilitate the carrying out of transactions on a frequent, habitual or regular basis where the total amount of any payments to be made by any person to any other in the course of the arrangement is not known or capable of being ascertained at the outset;

'cash' means notes, coins or travellers' cheques in any currency;

'the Commissioners' means the Commissioners of Customs and Excise;

'constable' includes a person commissioned by the Commissioners and a person authorised for the purposes of these Regulations by the Director General of the National Criminal Intelligence Service;

'EEA State' means a State which is a contracting party to the agreement on the European Economic Area signed at Oporto on 2nd May 1992 as it has effect for the time being;

'estate agency work' has the meaning given by section 1 of the Estate Agents Act 1979[5] save for the omission of the words '(including a business in which he is employed)' in subsection (1) and includes a case where, in relation to a disposal or acquisition, the person acts as principal;

'high value dealer' means a person who carries on the activity mentioned in paragraph (2)(n);

'the Life Assurance Consolidation Directive' means Directive 2002/83/EC of the European Parliament and of the Council of 5th November 2002 concerning life assurance[6];

'justice' means a justice of the peace or, in relation to Scotland, a justice within the meaning of section 307 of the Criminal Procedure (Scotland) Act 1995[7];

'money laundering' means an act which falls within section 340(11) of the Proceeds of Crime Act 2002[8] or an offence under section 18 of the Terrorism Act 2000[9];

'the Money Laundering Directive' means Council Directive 91/308/EEC of 10th June 1991 on prevention of the use of the financial system for the purpose of money laundering as amended by Directive 2001/97/EC of the European Parliament and of the Council of 4th December 2001[10];

'money service business' means any of the activities mentioned in paragraph (2)(d) (so far as not excluded by paragraph (3)) when carried on by way of business;

'money service operator' means a person who carries on money service business other than a person who carries on relevant business falling within any of sub-paragraphs (a) to (c) of paragraph (2);

'nominated officer' has the meaning given by regulation 7;

'officer' (except in regulations 7, 10 and 27) has the meaning given by section 1(1) of the Customs and Excise Management Act 1979[11];

---

4 OJ L 126, 26.5.2000, p1; OJ L 35, 11.2.2003, p1.

5 1979 c 38. Section 1 was amended by the Law Reform (Miscellaneous Provisions) (Scotland) Act 1985 (c 73), Schedule 1, Pt I, para 40, the Planning (Consequential Provisions) Act 1990 (c 11), Schedule 2, para 42, the Planning (Consequential Provisions) (Scotland) Act 1997 (c 11), Schedule 2, para 28 and by SI 2001/1283.

6 OJ L 345, 19.12.2002, p1.

7 1995 c46.

8 2002 c29.

9 2000 c11.

10 OJ L 166, 28.6.1991, p77; OJ L 344, 28.12.2001, p76.

11 1979 c2.

Appendix 2

'officer in overall charge of the investigation' means the person whose name and address are endorsed on the order concerned as being the officer so in charge;

'one-off transaction' means any transaction other than one carried out in the course of an existing business relationship;

'operator' means a money service operator;

'recorded information' includes information recorded in any form and any document of any nature whatsoever;

'registered number' has the meaning given by regulation 9(2);

'relevant business' has the meaning given by paragraph (2);

'the review procedure' means the procedure under regulation 21;

'satisfactory evidence of identity' has the meaning given by paragraphs (5) and (6);

'supervisory authority' has the meaning given by paragraphs (7) and (8);

'tribunal' means a VAT and duties tribunal.

(2) For the purposes of these Regulations, 'relevant business' means –

    (a) the regulated activity of –

        (i) accepting deposits;

        (ii) effecting or carrying out contracts of long-term insurance when carried on by a person who has received official authorisation pursuant to Article 4 or 51 of the Life Assurance Consolidation Directive;

        (iii) dealing in investments as principal or as agent;

        (iv) arranging deals in investments;

        (v) managing investments;

        (vi) safeguarding and administering investments;

        (vii) sending dematerialised instructions;

        (viii) establishing (and taking other steps in relation to) collective investment schemes;

        (ix) advising on investments; or

        (x) issuing electronic money;

(b) the activities of the National Savings Bank;

(c) any activity carried on for the purpose of raising money authorised to be raised under the National Loans Act 1968[12] under the auspices of the Director of Savings;

(d) the business of operating a bureau de change, transmitting money (or any representation of monetary value) by any means or cashing cheques which are made payable to customers;

(e) any of the activities in points 1 to 12 or 14 of Annex 1 to the Banking Consolidation Directive (which activities are, for convenience, set out in Schedule 1 to these Regulations) when carried on by way of business, ignoring an activity falling within any of sub-paragraphs (a) to (d);

(f) estate agency work;

(g) operating a casino by way of business;

(h) the activities of a person appointed to act as an insolvency practitioner within the meaning of section 388 of the Insolvency Act 1986[13] or Article 3 of the Insolvency (Northern Ireland) Order 1989[14];

---

12 1968 c13.

13 1986 c45.

14 SI 1989/2405 (NI 19).

(i) the provision by way of business of advice about the tax affairs of another person by a body corporate or unincorporate or, in the case of a sole practitioner, by an individual;

(j) the provision by way of business of accountancy services by a body corporate or unincorporate or, in the case of a sole practitioner, by an individual;

(k) the provision by way of business of audit services by a person who is eligible for appointment as a company auditor under section 25 of the Companies Act 1989[15] or Article 28 of the Companies (Northern Ireland) Order 1990[16];

(l) the provision by way of business of legal services by a body corporate or unincorporate or, in the case of a sole practitioner, by an individual and which involves participation in a financial or real property transaction (whether by assisting in the planning or execution of any such transaction or otherwise by acting for, or on behalf of, a client in any such transaction);

(m) the provision by way of business of services in relation to the formation, operation or management of a company or a trust; or

(n) the activity of dealing in goods of any description by way of business (including dealing as an auctioneer) whenever a transaction involves accepting a total cash payment of 15,000 euro or more.

(3) Paragraph (2) does not apply to –

(a) the issue of withdrawable share capital within the limit set by section 6 of the Industrial and Provident Societies Act 1965[17] by a society registered under that Act;

(b) the acceptance of deposits from the public within the limit set by section 7(3) of that Act by such a society;

(c) the issue of withdrawable share capital within the limit set by section 6 of the Industrial and Provident Societies Act (Northern Ireland) 1969[18] by a society registered under that Act;

(d) the acceptance of deposits from the public within the limit set by section 7(3) of that Act by such a society;

(e) activities carried on by the Bank of England;

(f) any activity in respect of which an exemption order under section 38 of the 2000 Act has effect if it is carried on by a person who is for the time being specified in the order or falls within a class of persons so specified;

(g) any activity (other than one falling within sub-paragraph (f)) in respect of which a person was an exempted person for the purposes of section 45 of the Financial Services Act 1986[19] immediately before its repeal;

(h) the regulated activities of arranging deals in investments or advising on investments, in so far as the investment consists of rights under a regulated mortgage contract;

(i) the regulated activities of dealing in investments as agent, arranging deals in investments, managing investments or advising on investments, in so far as the investment consists of rights under, or any right to or interest in, a contract of insurance which is not a qualifying contract of insurance; or

(j) the Official Solicitor to the Supreme Court when acting as trustee in his official capacity.

(4) The following must be read with section 22 of the 2000 Act, any relevant order under that section and Schedule 2 to that Act –

---

15 1989 c40.

16 SI 1990/593 (NI 5).

17 1965 c12.

18 1969 c24 (NI).

19 1986 c60. This Act was repealed as from 1st December 2001 by SI 2001/3649, art 3(1)(c).

Appendix 2

(a) paragraphs (2)(a) and (3)(h) and (i);

(b) regulation 25 (authorised persons operating a bureau de change);

(c) references in these Regulations to a contract of long-term insurance.

(5) For the purposes of these Regulations, and subject to paragraph (6), 'satisfactory evidence of identity' is evidence which is reasonably capable of establishing (and does in fact establish to the satisfaction of the person who obtains it) that the applicant for business is the person he claims to be.

(6) Where the person who obtains the evidence mentioned in paragraph (5) knows or has reasonable grounds for believing that the applicant for business is a money service operator, satisfactory evidence of identity must also include the applicant's registered number (if any).

(7) For the purposes of these Regulations, each of the following is a supervisory authority –

(a) the Bank of England;

(b) the Authority;

(c) the Council of Lloyd's;

(d) the Office of Fair Trading;

(e) the Occupational Pensions Regulatory Authority;

(f) a body which is a designated professional body for the purposes of Part 20 of the 2000 Act;

(g) the Gaming Board for Great Britain.

(8) The Secretary of State and the Treasury are each a supervisory authority in the exercise, in relation to a person carrying on relevant business, of their respective functions under the enactments relating to companies or insolvency or under the 2000 Act.

(9) In these Regulations, references to amounts in euro include references to equivalent amounts in another currency.

(10) For the purpose of the application of these Regulations to Scotland, 'real property' means 'heritable property'.

PART II

OBLIGATIONS ON PERSONS WHO CARRY ON RELEVANT BUSINESS

Systems and training etc to prevent money laundering

3.-(1) Every person must in the course of relevant business carried on by him in the United Kingdom –

(a) comply with the requirements of regulations 4 (identification procedures), 6 (record-keeping procedures) and 7 (internal reporting procedures);

(b) establish such other procedures of internal control and communication as may be appropriate for the purposes of forestalling and preventing money laundering; and

(c) take appropriate measures so that relevant employees are –

(i) made aware of the provisions of these Regulations, Part 7 of the Proceeds of Crime Act 2002 (money laundering) and sections 18 and 21A of the Terrorism Act 2000[20]; and

(ii) given training in how to recognise and deal with transactions which may be related to money laundering.

(2) A person who contravenes this regulation is guilty of an offence and liable –

(a) on conviction on indictment, to imprisonment for a term not exceeding 2 years, to a fine or to both;

(b) on summary conviction, to a fine not exceeding the statutory maximum.

---

[20] Section 21A was inserted by the Anti-terrorism, Crime and Security Act 2001 (c 24), Schedule 2, Part 3, para 5.

(3) In deciding whether a person has committed an offence under this regulation, the court must consider whether he followed any relevant guidance which was at the time concerned –

   (a) issued by a supervisory authority or any other appropriate body;

   (b) approved by the Treasury; and

   (c) published in a manner approved by the Treasury as appropriate in their opinion to bring the guidance to the attention of persons likely to be affected by it.

(4) An appropriate body is any body which regulates or is representative of any trade, profession, business or employment carried on by the alleged offender.

(5) In proceedings against any person for an offence under this regulation, it is a defence for that person to show that he took all reasonable steps and exercised all due diligence to avoid committing the offence.

(6) Where a person is convicted of an offence under this regulation, he shall not also be liable to a penalty under regulation 20 (power to impose penalties).

Identification procedures

4-(1) In this regulation and in regulations 5 to 7 –

   (a) 'A' means a person who carries on relevant business in the United Kingdom; and

   (b) 'B' means an applicant for business.

(2) This regulation applies if –

   (a) A and B form, or agree to form, a business relationship;

   (b) in respect of any one-off transaction –

      (i) A knows or suspects that the transaction involves money laundering; or

      (ii) payment of 15,000 euro or more is to be made by or to B; or

   (c) in respect of two or more one-off transactions, it appears to A (whether at the outset or subsequently) that the transactions are linked and involve, in total, the payment of 15,000 euro or more by or to B.

(3) A must maintain identification procedures which –

   (a) require that as soon as is reasonably practicable after contact is first made between A and B –

      (i) B must produce satisfactory evidence of his identity; or

      (ii) such measures specified in the procedures must be taken in order to produce satisfactory evidence of B's identity;

   (b) take into account the greater potential for money laundering which arises when B is not physically present when being identified;

   (c) require that where satisfactory evidence of identity is not obtained, the business relationship or one-off transaction must not proceed any further; and

   (d) require that where B acts or appears to act for another person, reasonable measures must be taken for the purpose of establishing the identity of that person.

Exceptions

5-(1) Except in circumstances falling within regulation 4(2)(b)(i), identification procedures under regulation 4 do not require A to take steps to obtain evidence of any person's identity in any of the following circumstances.

(2) Where A has reasonable grounds for believing that B –

   (a) carries on in the United Kingdom relevant business falling within any of sub-paragraphs (a) to (e) of regulation 2(2), is not a money service operator and, if carrying on an activity falling within regulation 2(2)(a), is an authorised person with permission under the 2000 Act to carry on that activity;

   (b) does not carry on relevant business in the United Kingdom but does carry on comparable activities to those falling within sub-paragraph (a) and is covered by the

Appendix 2

Money Laundering Directive; or

(c) is regulated by an overseas regulatory authority (within the meaning given by section 82 of the Companies Act 1989) and is based or incorporated in a country (other than an EEA State) whose law contains comparable provisions to those contained in the Money Laundering Directive.

(3) Where –

(a) A carries out a one-off transaction with or for a third party pursuant to an introduction effected by a person who has provided a written assurance that evidence of the identity of all third parties introduced by him will have been obtained and recorded under procedures maintained by him;

(b) that person identifies the third party; and

(c) A has reasonable grounds for believing that that person falls within any of sub-paragraphs (a) to (c) of paragraph (2).

(4) In relation to a contract of long-term insurance –

(a) in connection with a pension scheme taken out by virtue of a person's contract of employment or occupation where the contract of long-term insurance –

(i) contains no surrender clause; and

(ii) may not be used as collateral for a loan; or

(b) in respect of which a premium is payable –

(i) in one instalment of an amount not exceeding 2,500 euro; or

(ii) periodically and where the total payable in respect of any calendar year does not exceed 1,000 euro.

(5) Where the proceeds of a one-off transaction are payable to B but are instead directly reinvested on his behalf in another transaction –

(a) of which a record is kept; and

(b) which can result only in another reinvestment made on B's behalf or in a payment made directly to B.

Record-keeping procedures

6-(1) A must maintain procedures which require the retention of the records prescribed in paragraph (2) for the period prescribed in paragraph (3).

(2) The records are –

(a) where evidence of identity has been obtained under the procedures stipulated by regulation 4 (identification procedures) or pursuant to regulation 8 (casinos) –

(i) a copy of that evidence;

(ii) information as to where a copy of that evidence may be obtained; or

(iii) information enabling the evidence of identity to be re-obtained, but only where it is not reasonably practicable for A to comply with paragraph (i) or (ii); and

(b) a record containing details relating to all transactions carried out by A in the course of relevant business.

(3) In relation to the records mentioned in paragraph (2)(a), the period is –

(a) where A and B have formed a business relationship, at least five years commencing with the date on which the relationship ends; or

(b) in the case of a one-off transaction (or a series of such transactions), at least five years commencing with the date of the completion of all activities taking place in the course of that transaction (or, as the case may be, the last of the transactions).

(4) In relation to the records mentioned in paragraph (2)(b), the period is at least five years commencing with the date on which all activities taking place in the course of the transaction in question were completed.

(5) Where A is an appointed representative, his principal must ensure that A complies with this regulation in respect of any relevant business carried out by A for which the principal has accepted responsibility pursuant to section 39(1) of the 2000 Act.

(6) Where the principal fails to do so, he is to be treated as having contravened regulation 3 and he, as well as A, is guilty of an offence.

(7) 'Appointed representative' has the meaning given by section 39(2) of the 2000 Act and 'principal' has the meaning given by section 39(1) of that Act.

Internal reporting procedures

7-(1) A must maintain internal reporting procedures which require that –

(a) a person in A's organisation is nominated to receive disclosures under this regulation ('the nominated officer');

(b) anyone in A's organisation to whom information or other matter comes in the course of relevant business as a result of which he knows or suspects or has reasonable grounds for knowing or suspecting that a person is engaged in money laundering must, as soon as is practicable after the information or other matter comes to him, disclose it to the nominated officer or a person authorised for the purposes of these Regulations by the Director General of the National Criminal Intelligence Service;

(c) where a disclosure is made to the nominated officer, he must consider it in the light of any relevant information which is available to A and determine whether it gives rise to such knowledge or suspicion or such reasonable grounds for knowledge or suspicion; and

(d) where the nominated officer does so determine, the information or other matter must be disclosed to a person authorised for the purposes of these Regulations by the Director General of the National Criminal Intelligence Service.

(2) Paragraph (1) does not apply where A is an individual who neither employs nor acts in association with any other person.

(3) Paragraph (1)(b) does not apply in relation to a professional legal adviser where the information or other matter comes to him in privileged circumstances.

(4) Information or other matter comes to a professional legal adviser in privileged circumstances if it is communicated or given to him –

(a) by (or by a representative of) a client of his in connection with the giving by the adviser of legal advice to the client;

(b) by (or by a representative of) a person seeking legal advice from the adviser; or

(c) by a person in connection with legal proceedings or contemplated legal proceedings.

(5) But paragraph (4) does not apply to information or other matter which is communicated or given with the intention of furthering a criminal purpose.

(6) 'Professional legal adviser' includes any person in whose hands information or other matter may come in privileged circumstances.

Casinos

8-(1) A person who operates a casino by way of business in the United Kingdom must obtain satisfactory evidence of identity of any person before allowing that person to use the casino's gaming facilities.

(2) A person who fails to do so is to be treated as having contravened regulation 3.

PART III

MONEY SERVICE OPERATORS AND HIGH VALUE DEALERS

Registration

Registers of money service operators and high value dealers

9-(1) The Commissioners must maintain a register of operators.

(2) The Commissioners must allocate to every registered operator a number, which is to be

Appendix 2

known as his registered number.

(3) The Commissioners must maintain a register of high value dealers.

(4) The Commissioners may keep the registers in any form they think fit.

Requirement to be registered

10-(1) A person who acts as an operator or as a high value dealer must first be registered by the Commissioners.

(2) An applicant for registration must –

(a) make an application to be registered in such manner as the Commissioners may direct; and

(b) furnish the following information to the Commissioners –

(i) his name and (if different) the name of the business;

(ii) his VAT registration number or, if he is not registered for VAT, any other reference number issued to him by the Commissioners;

(iii) the nature of the business;

(iv) the address of each of the premises at which he proposes to carry on the business;

(v) any agency or franchise agreement relating to the business, and the names and addresses of all relevant principals, agents, franchisors or franchisees;

(vi) the name of the nominated officer (if any); and

(vii) whether any person concerned (or proposed to be concerned) in the management, control or operation of the business has been convicted of money laundering or an offence under these Regulations.

(3) At any time after receiving an application for registration and before determining it, the Commissioners may require the applicant for registration to furnish them, within 21 days beginning with the date of being requested to do so, with such further information as they reasonably consider necessary to enable them to determine the application.

(4) Any information to be furnished to the Commissioners under this regulation must be in such form or verified in such manner as they may specify.

(5) In this regulation, 'the business' means money service business (or, in the case of a high value dealer, the business of dealing in goods) which the applicant for registration carries on or proposes to carry on.

(6) In paragraph (2)(b)(vii), the reference to 'money laundering or an offence under these Regulations' includes an offence referred to in regulation 2(3) of the Money Laundering Regulations 1993 or an offence under regulation 5 of those Regulations.

Supplementary information

11-(1) If at any time after a person has furnished the Commissioners with any information under regulation 10 –

(a) there is a change affecting any matter contained in that information; or

(b) it becomes apparent to that person that the information contains an inaccuracy;

he must supply the Commissioners with details of the change or, as the case may be, a correction of the inaccuracy (hereafter 'supplementary information') within 30 days beginning with the date of the occurrence of the change (or the discovery of the inaccuracy) or within such later time as may be agreed with the Commissioners.

(2) The supplementary information must be supplied in such manner as the Commissioners may direct.

(3) The obligation in paragraph (1) applies also to changes affecting any matter contained in any supplementary information supplied pursuant to this regulation.

Determination of application to register

12-(1) The Commissioners may refuse to register an applicant for registration if, and only if –

(a) any requirement of –

    (i) paragraphs (2) to (4) of regulation 10 (requirement to be registered);

    (ii) regulation 11 (supplementary information); or

    (iii) regulation 14 (fees);

has not been complied with; or

(b) it appears to them that any information furnished pursuant to regulation 10 or 11 is false or misleading in a material particular.

(2) The Commissioners must, by the end of the period of 45 days beginning with the date on which they receive the application or, where applicable, the date on which they receive any further information required under regulation 10(3), give notice in writing to the applicant for registration of –

(a) their decision to register him and, in the case of an applicant for registration as an operator, his registered number; or

(b) the following matters –

    (i) their decision not to register him;

    (ii) the reasons for their decision;

    (iii) the review procedure; and

    (iv) the right to appeal to a tribunal.

Cancellation of registration

13-(1) The Commissioners may cancel the registration of an operator or high value dealer if, at any time after registration, it appears to them that they would have had grounds to refuse registration under paragraph (1) of regulation 12 (determination of application to register).

(2) Where the Commissioners decide to cancel the registration of an operator or high value dealer, they must forthwith inform him, in writing, of –

(a) their decision and the date from which the cancellation takes effect;

(b) the reasons for their decision;

(c) the review procedure; and

(d) the right to appeal to a tribunal.

Fees

14-(1) The Commissioners may charge a fee –

(a) to an applicant for registration; and

(b) to an operator or high value dealer annually on the anniversary of his registration by them under these Regulations.

(2) The Commissioners may charge under paragraph (1) such fees as they consider will enable them to meet any expenses incurred by them in carrying out any of their functions under these Regulations or for any incidental purpose.

(3) Without prejudice to the generality of paragraph (2), a fee may be charged in respect of each of the premises at which the operator, high value dealer or applicant for registration carries on (or proposes to carry on) money service business or relevant business falling within regulation 2(2)(n).

Powers of the Commissioners

Entry, inspection etc

15-(1) Where an officer has reasonable cause to believe that any premises are used in connection with money service business or relevant business falling within regulation 2(2)(n), he may at any reasonable time enter and inspect the premises and inspect any recorded information or currency found on the premises.

(2) An operator or high value dealer must –

(a) furnish to an officer, within such time and in such form as the officer may reasonably require, such information relating to the business as the officer may reasonably specify; and

(b) upon demand made by the officer, produce or cause to be produced for inspection by the officer at such place, and at such time, as the officer may reasonably require, any recorded information relating to the business.

(3) An officer may take copies of, or make extracts from, any recorded information produced under paragraph (2).

Order for access to recorded information

16-(1) Where, on an application by an officer, a justice is satisfied that there are reasonable grounds for believing –

(a) that an offence under these Regulations is being, has been or is about to be committed by an operator or high value dealer; and

(b) that any recorded information which may be required as evidence for the purpose of any proceedings in respect of such an offence is in the possession of any person;

he may make an order under this regulation.

(2) An order under this regulation is an order that the person who appears to the justice to be in possession of the recorded information to which the application relates must –

(a) give an officer access to it;

(b) permit an officer to take copies of, or make extracts from, any information produced; or

(c) permit an officer to remove and take away any of it which he reasonably considers necessary;

not later than the end of the period of 7 days beginning with the date of the order or the end of such longer period as the order may specify.

(3) Where the recorded information consists of information stored in any electronic form, an order under this regulation has effect as an order to produce the information in a form in which it is visible and legible, or from which it can readily be produced in a visible and legible form, and, if the officer wishes to remove it, in a form in which it can be removed.

Procedure where recorded information is removed

17-(1) An officer who removes any recorded information in the exercise of a power conferred by regulation 16 must, if so requested by a person showing himself –

(a) to be the occupier of premises from which the information was removed; or

(b) to have had custody or control of the information immediately before the removal;

provide that person with a record of what he has removed.

(2) The officer must provide the record within a reasonable time from the making of the request for it.

(3) Subject to paragraph (7), if a request for permission to be granted access to anything which –

(a) has been removed by an officer; and

(b) is retained by the Commissioners for the purposes of investigating an offence;

is made to the officer in overall charge of the investigation by a person who had custody or control of the thing immediately before it was so removed or by someone acting on behalf of such a person, that officer must allow the person who made the request access to it under the supervision of an officer.

(4) Subject to paragraph (7), if a request for a photograph or copy of any such thing is made to the officer in overall charge of the investigation by a person who had custody or control of the thing immediately before it was so removed, or by someone acting on behalf of such a person, that officer must –

(a) allow the person who made the request access to it under the supervision of an officer for the purpose of photographing it or copying it; or

(b) photograph or copy it, or cause it to be photographed or copied.

(5) Where anything is photographed or copied under paragraph (4)(b), the photograph or copy must be supplied to the person who made the request.

(6) The photograph or copy must be supplied within a reasonable time from the making of the request.

(7) There is no duty under this regulation to grant access to, or supply a photograph or a copy of, anything if the officer in overall charge of the investigation for the purposes of which it was removed has reasonable grounds for believing that to do so would prejudice –

(a) that investigation;

(b) the investigation of an offence other than the offence for the purposes of the investigation of which the recorded information was removed; or

(c) any criminal proceedings which may be brought as a result of –

(i) the investigation of which he is in charge; or

(ii) any such investigation as is mentioned in sub-paragraph (b).

Failure to comply with requirements under regulation 17

18-(1) Where, on an application made as mentioned in paragraph (2), the appropriate judicial authority is satisfied that a person has failed to comply with a requirement imposed by regulation 17, the authority may order that person to comply with the requirement within such time and in such manner as may be specified in the order.

(2) An application under paragraph (1) may only be made –

(a) in the case of a failure to comply with any of the requirements imposed by regulation 17(1) and (2), by the occupier of the premises from which the thing in question was removed or by the person who had custody or control of it immediately before it was so removed;

(b) in any other case, by the person who had such custody or control.

(3) In England and Wales and Northern Ireland, an application for an order under this regulation is to be made by complaint; and sections 21 and 42(2) of the Interpretation Act (Northern Ireland) 1954[21] apply as if any reference in those provisions to any enactment included a reference to this regulation.

Entry, search etc

19-(1) Where a justice is satisfied on information on oath that there is reasonable ground for suspecting that an offence under these Regulations is being, has been or is about to be committed by an operator or high value dealer on any premises or that evidence of the commission of such an offence is to be found there, he may issue a warrant in writing authorising any officer to enter those premises, if necessary by force, at any time within one month from the time of the issue of the warrant and search them.

(2) A person who enters the premises under the authority of the warrant may –

(a) take with him such other persons as appear to him to be necessary;

(b) seize and remove any documents or other things whatsoever found on the premises which he has reasonable cause to believe may be required as evidence for the purpose of proceedings in respect of an offence under these Regulations; and

(c) search or cause to be searched any person found on the premises whom he has reasonable cause to believe to be in possession of any such documents or other things; but no woman or girl may be searched except by a woman.

(3) The powers conferred by a warrant under this regulation may not be exercised –

(a) outside such times of day as may be specified in the warrant; or

(b) if the warrant so provides, otherwise than in the presence of a constable in uniform.

---

21 1954 c 33 (NI).

Appendix 2

(4) An officer seeking to exercise the powers conferred by a warrant under this regulation or, if there is more than one such officer, that one of them who is in charge of the search must provide a copy of the warrant endorsed with his name as follows –

(a) if the occupier of the premises concerned is present at the time the search is to begin, the copy must be supplied to the occupier;

(b) if at that time the occupier is not present but a person who appears to the officer to be in charge of the premises is present, the copy must be supplied to that person;

(c) if neither sub-paragraph (a) nor (b) applies, the copy must be left in a prominent place on the premises.

Penalties, review and appeals

Power to impose penalties

20-(1) The Commissioners may impose a penalty of such amount as they consider appropriate, not exceeding £5,000, on a person to whom regulation 10 (requirement to be registered) applies, where that person fails to comply with any requirement in regulation 3 (systems and training etc to prevent money laundering), 10, 11 (supplementary information), 14 (fees) or 15 (entry, inspection etc).

(2) The Commissioners must not impose a penalty on a person where there are reasonable grounds for them to be satisfied that the person took all reasonable steps for securing that the requirement would be complied with.

(3) Where the Commissioners decide to impose a penalty under this regulation, they must forthwith inform the person, in writing, of –

(a) their decision to impose the penalty and its amount;

(b) their reasons for imposing the penalty;

(c) the review procedure; and

(d) the right to appeal to a tribunal.

(4) Where a person is liable to a penalty under this regulation, the Commissioners may reduce the penalty to such amount (including nil) as they think proper.

Review procedure

21-(1) This regulation applies to the following decisions of the Commissioners –

(a) a decision under regulation 12 to refuse to register an applicant;

(b) a decision under regulation 13 to cancel the registration of an operator or high value dealer;

(c) a decision under regulation 20 to impose a penalty.

(2) Any person who is the subject of a decision as mentioned in paragraph (1) may by notice in writing to the Commissioners require them to review that decision.

(3) The Commissioners need not review any decision unless the notice requiring the review is given before the end of the period of 45 days beginning with the date on which written notification of the decision was first given to the person requiring the review.

(4) A person may give a notice under this regulation to require a decision to be reviewed for a second or subsequent time only if –

(a) the grounds on which he requires the further review are that the Commissioners did not, on any previous review, have the opportunity to consider certain facts or other matters; and

(b) he does not, on the further review, require the Commissioners to consider any facts or matters which were considered on a previous review except in so far as they are relevant to any issue to which the facts or matters not previously considered relate.

(5) Where the Commissioners are required under this regulation to review any decision they must either –

(a) confirm the decision; or

(b) withdraw or vary the decision and take such further steps (if any) in consequence of the withdrawal or variation as they consider appropriate.

(6) Where the Commissioners do not, within 45 days beginning with the date on which the review was required by a person, give notice to that person of their determination of the review, they are to be assumed for the purposes of these Regulations to have confirmed the decision.

Appeals to a VAT and duties tribunal

22 On an appeal from any decision by the Commissioners on a review under regulation 21, the tribunal have the power to –

(a) quash or vary any decision of the Commissioners, including the power to reduce any penalty to such amount (including nil) as they think proper; and

(b) substitute their own decision for any decision quashed on appeal.

Miscellaneous

Prosecution of offences by the Commissioners

23-(1) Proceedings for an offence under these Regulations may be instituted by order of the Commissioners.

(2) Such proceedings may be instituted only against an operator or high value dealer or, where such a person is a body corporate, a partnership or an unincorporated association, against any person who is liable to be proceeded against under regulation 27 (offences by bodies corporate etc).

(3) Any such proceedings which are so instituted must be commenced in the name of an officer.

(4) In the case of the death, removal, discharge or absence of the officer in whose name any such proceedings were commenced, those proceedings may be continued by another officer.

(5) Where the Commissioners investigate, or propose to investigate, any matter with a view to determining –

(a) whether there are grounds for believing that an offence under these Regulations has been committed by any person mentioned in paragraph (2); or

(b) whether such a person should be prosecuted for such an offence;

that matter is to be treated as an assigned matter within the meaning of the Customs and Excise Management Act 1979.

(6) In exercising their power to institute proceedings for an offence under these Regulations, the Commissioners must comply with any conditions or restrictions imposed in writing by the Treasury.

(7) Conditions or restrictions may be imposed under paragraph (6) in relation to –

(a) proceedings generally; or

(b) such proceedings, or categories of proceedings, as the Treasury may direct.

Recovery of fees and penalties through the court

24 Where any fee is charged, or any penalty is imposed, by virtue of these Regulations –

(a) if the person from whom it is recoverable resides in England and Wales or Northern Ireland, it is recoverable as a civil debt; and

(b) if that person resides in Scotland, it may be enforced in the same manner as an extract registered decree arbitral bearing a warrant for execution issued by the sheriff court of any sheriffdom in Scotland.

Authorised persons operating a bureau de change

25-(1) No authorised person may, as from 1st April 2004, carry on the business of operating a bureau de change unless he has first informed the Authority that he proposes to do so.

(2) Where an authorised person ceases to carry on that business, he must inform the Authority forthwith.

Appendix 2

(3) Any information to be supplied to the Authority under this regulation must be in such form or verified in such manner as the Authority may specify.

(4) Any requirement imposed by this regulation is to be treated as if it were a requirement imposed by or under the 2000 Act.

(5) Any function of the Authority under this regulation is to be treated as if it were a function of the Authority under the 2000 Act.

PART IV

MISCELLANEOUS

Supervisory authorities etc to report evidence of money laundering

26-(1) Where a supervisory authority, in the light of any information obtained by it, knows or suspects, or has reasonable grounds for knowing or suspecting, that someone has or may have been engaged in money laundering, the supervisory authority must disclose the information to a constable as soon as is reasonably practicable.

(2) Where a supervisory authority passes the information to any other person who has such knowledge or suspicion or such reasonable grounds for knowledge or suspicion as is mentioned in paragraph (1), he may disclose the information to a constable.

(3) Where any person within paragraph (6), in the light of any information obtained by him, knows or suspects or has reasonable grounds for knowing or suspecting that someone has or may have been engaged in money laundering, he must, as soon as is reasonably practicable, disclose that information either to a constable or to the supervisory authority by whom he was appointed or authorised.

(4) Where information has been disclosed to a constable under this regulation, he (or any person obtaining the information from him) may disclose it in connection with the investigation of any criminal offence or for the purpose of any criminal proceedings, but not otherwise.

(5) A disclosure made under this regulation is not to be taken to breach any restriction on the disclosure of information (however imposed).

(6) Persons within this paragraph are –

(a) a person or inspector appointed under section 65 or 66 of the Friendly Societies Act 1992[22];

(b) an inspector appointed under section 49 of the Industrial and Provident Societies Act 1965 or section 18 of the Credit Unions Act 1979[23];

(c) an inspector appointed under section 431, 432, 442 or 446 of the Companies Act 1985[24] or under Article 424, 425, 435 or 439 of the Companies (Northern Ireland) Order 1986[25];

(d) a person or inspector appointed under section 55 or 56 of the Building Societies Act 1986[26];

(e) a person appointed under section 167, 168(3) or (5), 169(1)(b) or 284 of the 2000 Act, or under regulations made as a result of section 262(2)(k) of that Act, to conduct an investigation; and

(f) a person authorised to require the production of documents under section 447 of the Companies Act 1985, Article 440 of the Companies (Northern Ireland) Order 1986 or section 84 of the Companies Act 1989.

Offences by bodies corporate etc

27-(1) If an offence under regulation 3 committed by a body corporate is shown –

---

22 1992 c40.

23 1979 c34.

24 1985 c6.

25 SI 1986/1032 (NI 6).

26 1986 c53.

(a) to have been committed with the consent or the connivance of an officer; or

(b) to be attributable to any neglect on his part;

the officer as well as the body corporate is guilty of an offence and liable to be proceeded against and punished accordingly.

(2) If an offence under regulation 3 committed by a partnership is shown –

(a) to have been committed with the consent or the connivance of a partner; or

(b) to be attributable to any neglect on his part;

the partner as well as the partnership is guilty of an offence and liable to be proceeded against and punished accordingly.

(3) If an offence under regulation 3 committed by an unincorporated association (other than a partnership) is shown –

(a) to have been committed with the consent or the connivance of an officer of the association or a member of its governing body; or

(b) to be attributable to any neglect on the part of such an officer or member;

that officer or member as well as the association is guilty of an offence and liable to be proceeded against and punished accordingly.

(4) If the affairs of a body corporate are managed by its members, paragraph (1) applies in relation to the acts and defaults of a member in connection with his functions of management as if he were a director of the body.

(5) In this regulation –

(a) 'partner' includes a person purporting to act as a partner; and

(b) 'officer', in relation to a body corporate, means a director, manager, secretary, chief executive, member of the committee of management, or a person purporting to act in such a capacity.

Prohibitions in relation to certain countries

28-(1) The Treasury may direct any person who carries on relevant business –

(a) not to enter a business relationship;

(b) not to carry out any one-off transaction; or

(c) not to proceed any further with a business relationship or one-off transaction;

in relation to a person who is based or incorporated in a country (other than an EEA State) to which the Financial Action Task Force has decided to apply counter-measures.

(2) A person who fails to comply with a Treasury direction is to be treated as having contravened regulation 3.

Minor and consequential amendments

29 The provisions mentioned in Schedule 2 to these Regulations have effect subject to the amendments there specified, being minor amendments and amendments consequential on the provisions of these Regulations.

Transitional provisions

30-(1) Nothing in these Regulations obliges any person who carries on relevant business falling within any of sub-paragraphs (a) to (e) of regulation 2(2) to maintain identification procedures which require evidence to be obtained in respect of any business relationship formed by him before 1st April 1994.

(2) Nothing in these Regulations obliges any person who carries on relevant business falling within any of sub-paragraphs (f) to (n) of regulation 2(2) –

(a) to maintain identification procedures which require evidence to be obtained in respect of any business relationship formed by him before 1st March 2004; or

(b) to maintain internal reporting procedures which require any action to be taken in respect of any knowledge, suspicion or reasonable grounds for knowledge or suspicion

Appendix 2

which came to that person before 1st March 2004.

John Heppell

Nick Ainger

Two of the Lords Commissioners of Her Majesty's Treasury

28th November 2003

SCHEDULE 1

Regulation 2(2)(e)

ACTIVITIES LISTED IN ANNEX 1 TO THE BANKING CONSOLIDATION DIRECTIVE

1 Acceptance of deposits and other repayable funds.

2 Lending.

3 Financial leasing.

4 Money transmission services.

5 Issuing and administering means of payment (eg credit cards, travellers' cheques and bankers' drafts).

6 Guarantees and commitments.

7 Trading for own account or for account of customers in –

(a) money market instruments (cheques, bills, certificates of deposit, etc);

(b) foreign exchange;

(c) financial futures and options;

(d) exchange and interest-rate instruments;

(e) transferable securities.

8 Participation in securities issues and the provision of services related to such issues.

9 Advice to undertakings on capital structure, industrial strategy and related questions and advice as well as services relating to mergers and the purchase of undertakings.

10 Money broking.

11 Portfolio management and advice.

12 Safekeeping and administration of securities.

13 Credit reference services.

14 Safe custody services.

SCHEDULE 2

Regulation 29

MINOR AND CONSEQUENTIAL AMENDMENTS

PART I

Primary Legislation

Value Added Tax Act 1994 (c 23)

1-(1) Section 83 of the Value Added Tax Act 1994 is amended as follows.

(2) In paragraph (zz), for 'regulation 16 of the Money Laundering Regulations 2001', substitute 'regulation 21 of the Money Laundering Regulations 2003'.

Appendix 2

Northern Ireland Act 1998 (c 47)

2-(1) Paragraph 25 of Schedule 3 (reserved matters) to the Northern Ireland Act 1998 is amended as follows.

(2) For '1993' substitute '2003'.

PART II
Secondary Legislation
The Cross-Border Credit Transfers Regulations 1999 (SI 1999/1876)

3-(1) Regulation 12 of the Cross-Border Credit Transfers Regulations 1999 is amended as follows.

(2) For paragraph (2) substitute –

' (2) In this regulation 'enactments relating to money laundering' means section 18 of the Terrorism Act 2000, section 340(11) of the Proceeds of Crime Act 2002 and the Money Laundering Regulations 2003.'.

The Terrorism Act 2000 (Crown Servants and Regulators)
Regulations 2001 (SI 2001/192)

4-(1) The Terrorism Act 2000 (Crown Servants and Regulators) Regulations 2001 are amended as follows.

(2) In regulation 2, for the definition of 'relevant financial business' substitute –

' 'relevant business' has the meaning given by regulation 2(2) of the Money Laundering Regulations 2003.'.

(3) In regulation 3, for 'relevant financial business' substitute 'relevant business'.

The Representation of the People (England and Wales)
Regulations 2001 (SI 2001/341)

5-(1) The Representation of the People (England and Wales) Regulations 2001 are amended as follows.

(2) In regulation 114(3)(b)[27] –

(i) for '1993' substitute '2003'; and

(ii) omit ', the Money Laundering Regulations 2001'.

The Representation of the People (Northern Ireland)
Regulations 2001 (SI 2001/400)

6-(1) The Representation of the People (Northern Ireland) Regulations 2001 are amended as follows.

(2) In regulation 107(3)(b)[28] –

(i) in paragraph (i), for '1993' substitute '2003';

(ii) omit paragraph (ii); and

(iii) in paragraph (iii), omit the words 'either of' and 'sets of'.

---

[27] Inserted by regulation 15 of the Representation of the People (England and Wales) (Amendment) Regulations 2002 (SI 2002/1871).

[28] Inserted by regulation 21 of the Representation of the People (Northern Ireland) (Amendment) Regulations 2002 (SI 2002/1873).

Appendix 2

*The Representation of the People (Scotland)
Regulations 2001 (SI 2001/497)*

7-(1) The Representation of the People (Scotland) Regulations 2001 are amended as follows.

(2) In regulation 113(3)(b)[29] –

(i) for '1993' substitute '2003'; and

(ii) omit ', the Money Laundering Regulations 2001'.

*The Proceeds of Crime Act 2002 (Failure to Disclose Money Laundering:
Specified Training)Order 2003 (SI 2003/171)*

8-(1) The Proceeds of Crime Act 2002 (Failure to Disclose Money Laundering: Specified Training) Order 2003 is amended as follows.

(2) In article 2, for 'regulation 5(1)(c) of the Money Laundering Regulations 1993' substitute 'regulation 3(1)(c)(ii) of the Money Laundering Regulations 2003'.

---

29 Inserted by regulation 14 of the Representation of the People (Scotland) (Amendment) Regulations 2002 (SI 2002/1872).

Appendix 3: Terrorism Act 2000, ss15-18 and 21A

Fund-raising

15-(1) A person commits an offence if he –

(a) invites another to provide money or other property, and

(b) intends that it should be used, or has reasonable cause to suspect that it may be used, for the purposes of terrorism.

(2) A person commits an offence if he –

(a) receives money or other property, and

(b) intends that it should be used, or has reasonable cause to suspect that it may be used, for the purposes of terrorism.

(3) A person commits an offence if he –

(a) provides money or other property, and

(b) knows or has reasonable cause to suspect that it will or may be used for the purposes of terrorism.

(4) In this section a reference to the provision of money or other property is a reference to its being given, lent or otherwise made available, whether or not for consideration.

Use and possession

16-(1) A person commits an offence if he uses money or other property for the purposes of terrorism.

(2) A person commits an offence if he –

(a) possesses money or other property, and

(b) intends that it should be used, or has reasonable cause to suspect that it may be used, for the purposes of terrorism.

Funding arrangements

17 A person commits an offence if –

(a) he enters into or becomes concerned in an arrangement as a result of which money or other property is made available or is to be made available to another, and

(b) he knows or has reasonable cause to suspect that it will or may be used for the purposes of terrorism.

Money laundering

18-(1) A person commits an offence if he enters into or becomes concerned in an arrangement which facilitates the retention or control by or on behalf of another person of terrorist property –

(a) by concealment,

(b) by removal from the jurisdiction,

(c) by transfer to nominees, or

(d) in any other way.

(2) It is a defence for a person charged with an offence under subsection (1) to prove that

Appendix 3

he did not know and had no reasonable cause to suspect that the arrangement related to terrorist property.

21A Failure to disclose: regulated sector

(1) A person commits an offence if each of the following three conditions is satisfied.

(2) The first condition is that he –

    (a) knows or suspects, or

    (b) has reasonable grounds for knowing or suspecting, that another person has committed an offence under any of sections 15 to 18.

(3) The second condition is that the information or other matter –

    (a) on which his knowledge or suspicion is based, or

    (b) which gives reasonable grounds for such knowledge or suspicion, came to him in the course of a business in the regulated sector.

(4) The third condition is that he does not disclose the information or other matter to a constable or a nominated officer as soon as is practicable after it comes to him.

(5) But a person does not commit an offence under this section if –

    (a) he has a reasonable excuse for not disclosing the information or other matter;

    (b) he is a professional legal adviser and the information or other matter came to him in privileged circumstances.

(6) In deciding whether a person committed an offence under this section the court must consider whether he followed any relevant guidance which was at the time concerned –

    (a) issued by a supervisory authority or any other appropriate body,

    (b) approved by the Treasury, and

    (c) published in a manner it approved as appropriate in its opinion to bring the guidance to the attention of persons likely to be affected by it.

(7) A disclosure to a nominated officer is a disclosure which –

    (a) is made to a person nominated by the alleged offender's employer to receive disclosures under this section, and

    (b) is made in the course of the alleged offender's employment and in accordance with the procedure established by the employer for the purpose.

(8) Information or other matter comes to a professional legal adviser in privileged circumstances if it is communicated or given to him –

    (a) by (or by a representative of) a client of his in connection with the giving by the adviser of legal advice to the client,

    (b) by (or by a representative of) a person seeking legal advice from the adviser, or

    (c) by a person in connection with legal proceedings or contemplated legal proceedings.

(9) But subsection (8) does not apply to information or other matter which is communicated or given with a view to furthering a criminal purpose.

(10) Schedule 3A has effect for the purpose of determining what is –

    (a) a business in the regulated sector;

    (b) a supervisory authority.

(11) For the purposes of subsection (2) a person is to be taken to have committed an offence there mentioned if –

    (a) he has taken an action or been in possession of a thing, and

    (b) he would have committed the offence if he had been in the United Kingdom at the time when he took the action or was in possession of the thing.

(12) A person guilty of an offence under this section is liable –

Appendix 3

(a) on conviction on indictment, to imprisonment for a term not exceeding five years or to a fine or to both;

(b) on summary conviction, to imprisonment for a term not exceeding six months or to a fine not exceeding the statutory maximum or to both.

(13) An appropriate body is any body which regulates or is representative of any trade, profession, business or employment carried on by the alleged offender.

(14) The reference to a constable includes a reference to a person authorised for the purposes of this section by the Director General of the National Criminal Intelligence Service.

Appendix 4: NCIS Source Registration Document[1]

Version 2.0 - Appendix 1

NCIS — National Criminal Intelligence Service

PO Box 8000
London
SE11 5EN
Tel: 020 7238 8282
Fax: 020 7238 8286

SOURCE REGISTRATION DOCUMENT

IMPORTANT - THE DETAILS IN THIS FORM MUST BE PROVIDED WITH YOUR FIRST DISCLOSURE TO NCIS OR FOLLOWING ANY SUBSEQUENT CHANGE TO THOSE DETAILS.

Institution Name:

Institution Type:

Regulator:

Regulator ID:

Contact Details (1): Forename:

Surname:

Position:

Address:

Telephone Details:

Facsimile Details:

E-mail Address:

Contact Details (2): Forename:
(where applicable)

Surname:

Position:

Address:

Telephone Details:

Facsimile Details:

E-mail Address:

---

1. This form is reproduced for information purposes only. NCIS forms and guidance are subject to regular change and readers should refer to www.ncis.co.uk for the latest versions. © NCIS 2004. All rights reserved.

APPENDIX 5: NCIS STANDARD REPORT FORM[1]

Version 2.0 - Appendix 2

NCIS
NATIONAL CRIMINAL INTELLIGENCE SERVICE

PO Box 8000
London
SE11 5EN
Tel: 020 7238 8282
Fax: 020 7238 8286

DISCLOSURE REPORT DETAILS: STANDARD REPORT:

Reporting Institution:

Your Ref:

Branch/Office:

Disclosure Reason:
PoCA 2002: ○   Terrorism Act 2000: ○
Consent Required: ☐

Disclosure Date: D D - M M M - Y Y Y Y   Type: New ○   OR   Update ○

Existing Disclosure ID/s: (where applicable)

Please use whichever sheets you feel are necessary and indicate below how many of each you are submitting.

REPORT SUMMARY:

Number of 'Subject Details' sheet appended relating to a Main Subject:

Number of 'Additional Details' sheets appended relating to Main Subject:

Number of 'Subjects Details' sheets appended relating to Associated Subject/s:

Number of 'Additional Details' sheets' appended relating to Associated Subject/s:

Number of 'Transaction Detail' sheet/s appended:

Number of 'Reason For Disclosure Sheets' appended:

Once completed please collate your sheets in the above mentioned order and then sequentially number your sheets at the bottom of each page. This will ensure that the information is processed in the correct sequence.

Total number of pages submitted including this Header:

Page 1 of

---

[1]. This form is reproduced for information purposes only. NCIS forms and guidance are subject to regular change and readers should refer to www.ncis.co.uk for the latest versions. © NCIS 2004. All rights reserved.

Appendix 5

SUBJECT DETAILS: Version 2.0 - Appendix 3

Subject Type: Main Subject: ☐   **OR**   Associated Subject: ☐ (number ☐ of ☐)

Individual's Details:

Subject Status: Suspect : ○   **OR**   Victim: ○

Surname: _____

Forename 1: _____

Forename 2: _____

Occupation: _____

DoB: [DD] - [MM M] - [Y Y Y Y]   Gender: Male ○   Female ○

Title: Mr ○   Mrs ○   Miss ○   Ms ○   Other _____

Reason for Association of this subject to the Main Subject (for use only with Associated Subject details)

_____

OR

Legal Entity's Details

Subject Status: Suspect : ○   **OR**   Victim: ○

Legal Entity Name: _____

Legal Entity No: _____   VAT No: _____

Country of Reg: _____

Type of Business: _____

Reason for Association of this subject to the Main Subject (for use only with Associated Subject details)

_____

Page ☐ of ☐

Appendix 5

ADDITIONAL DETAILS:	Version 2.0 - Appendix 4
Do these details refer to the Main Subject: ☐ OR to an Associated Subject ☐ (Please indicate the Associate's number where applicable)	

Subject Name:

Premise No/Name: Current: ☐   Type:

Street:
City/Town:
County: Post Code:
Country:

Premise No/Name: Current: ☐   Type:

Street:
City/Town:
County: Post Code:
Country:

Premise No/Name: Current: ☐   Type:

Street:
City/Town:
County: Post Code:
Country:

Information Type: Unique Information Identifier:

Extra Information / Description

Information Type: Unique Information Identifier:

Extra Information / Description

Page ☐ of ☐

Appendix 5

TRANSACTION DETAILS: (Complete if applicable)

Version 2.0 - Appendix 5

MAIN SUBJECT ACCOUNT SUMMARY

- Institution Name:
- Account Name:
- Sort Code:
- Account No /Identifier:
- Business Relationship Commenced: (DD-MMM-YYYY)
- Business Relationship Finished: (DD-MMM-YYYY)
- Acct Bal:
- Bal Date: (DD-MMM-YYYY)
- Turnover Period:
- Credit Turnover:
- Debit Turnover:

TRANSACTION/S

Transaction 1
- Activity Type:
- Activity Date: (DD-MMM-YYYY)
- Amount:
- Currency:
- Credit: ○ or Debit: ○
- Other party name:
- Account No/Identifier:
- Institution Name or Sort Code:

Transaction 2
- Activity Type:
- Activity Date: (DD-MMM-YYYY)
- Amount:
- Currency:
- Credit: ○ or Debit: ○
- Other party name:
- Account No/Identifier:
- Institution Name or Sort Code:

Transaction 3
- Activity Type:
- Activity Date: (DD-MMM-YYYY)
- Amount:
- Currency:
- Credit: ○ or Debit: ○
- Other party name:
- Account No/Identifier:
- Institution Name or Sort Code:

Transaction 4
- Activity Type:
- Activity Date: (DD-MMM-YYYY)
- Amount:
- Currency:
- Credit: ○ or Debit: ○
- Other party name:
- Account No/Identifier:
- Institution Name or Sort Code:

Page ☐ of ☐

Appendix 5

REASON FOR DISCLOSURE: Version 2.0 - Appendix 6

Main Subject Name:
(cross reference purposes)

Report Activity Assessment
(Please use only where you know or suspect what the offence behind the reported activity may be)

Drugs: ☐   Missing Trader, Inter Community (VAT) Fraud ☐   Immigration: ☐   Tobacco/Alcohol Excise Fraud: ☐

Personal Tax Fraud: ☐   Corporate Tax Fraud: ☐   Other Offences: _____

Reason for Disclosure:

Page ☐ of ☐

Appendix 5

REASON FOR DISCLOSURE CONTINUATION:　　　Version 2.0 - Appendix 8

Main Subject Name:
(cross reference purposes)

Reason for Disclosure Continuation:

Page ☐ of ☐

Appendix 6: NCIS Limited Intelligence Value Report form[1]

NCIS
National Criminal Intelligence Service

Version 2.1 - Appendix 7

PO Box 8000
London
SE11 5EN
Tel: 020 7238 8282
Fax: 020 7238 8286

PROCEEDS OF CRIME ACT 2002 - LIMITED INTELLIGENCE VALUE REPORT

Reporting Institution:
Your Ref:
Branch/Office:

Disclosure Date:
DD - MMM - YYYY

SUBJECT DETAILS:

Individual's Details: Subject Status: Suspect: ○   **OR**   Victim: ○

Surname:
Forename:
DoB: D D - M M M - Y Y Y Y   Gender: Male ○   Female ○
Title: Mr ○   Mrs ○   Miss ○   Ms ○   Other

Legal Entity Details: Subject Status: Suspect: ○   **OR**   Victim: ○

Legal Entity Name:
Legal entity No: VAT No:

REASON FOR DISCLOSURE:

APPENDIX SEVEN

---

[1]. This form is reproduced for information purposes only. NCIS forms and guidance are subject to regular change and readers should refer to www.ncis.co.uk for the latest versions. © NCIS 2004. All rights reserved.

Appendix 7: Guidance Notes for the NCIS Regulated Sector Disclosure Report, Proceeds Of Crime Act 2002 & Terrorism Act 2000 – Standard Report[1]

Content

Page [228-229]	Scope and Purpose Statement
Page [229-231]	Completion Instructions:-
	Source Registration Document (Module/*Appendix* 1)
Page [231-232]	Completion Instructions:-
	Disclosure Report Details Sheet (Module/*Appendix* 2)
	(Disclosure Report Details and Report Summary)
Page [232-234]	Completion Instructions:-
	Subject Details Sheet (Module/*Appendix* 3)
	(Subject Type, Individual's Details and Legal Entities Details)
Page [234-235]	Completion Instructions:-
	Additional Details Sheet (Module/*Appendix* 4)
	(Type, Address Details and Additional Information Details)
Page [235-236]	Completion Instructions:-
	Transaction Details Sheet (Module/*Appendix* 5)
	(Account/Customer Summary and Transaction/s)
Page [236]	Completion Instructions:-
	Reason for Disclosure Sheet (Module/*Appendix* 6)
	(Report Activity Assessment and Reason For Disclosure)
Page [236]	Completion Instructions:-
	Reason for Disclosure Continuation Sheet (Module/*Appendix* 8)
	(Reason for Disclosure Continuation)Scope and Purpose

Scope and Purpose

This document provides guidance for the completion of protected and authorised disclosures, under sections 337 and 338 of the Proceeds of Crime Act (2002). This guidance should be read alongside the preferred Standard forms (the Forms) which have been issued by NCIS

---

1. This guidance is reproduced for information purposes only. NCIS forms and guidance are subject to regular change and readers should refer to www.ncis.co.uk for the latest versions.
© NCIS 2004. All rights reserved.

for the completion of disclosures. Both the Forms and Guidance have been prepared by NCIS following consultation with a number of organisations representing the Regulated Sector.

The Form has not been prescribed by the Secretary of State under section 339 of the Proceeds of Crime Act 2002 and, therefore, use of the form as a method for reporting money laundering is not mandatory. However, these Forms are the preferred format by NCIS as they have been designed to:-

- accommodate the needs of different Regulated Sector businesses and
- facilitate the efficient and effective handling of disclosures by NCIS

Although none of the fields in the form is mandatory, since the format is not prescribed, those submitting disclosures should take account of regulatory and sector approved guidance. NCIS' feedback to reporting institutions will assess the quality of reporting against relevant guidance.

How to obtain the new Forms and Guidance

Those organisations which currently use the Money.web system or Bulk File submission should continue to submit reports electronically, using the existing input screens or reporting format.

Organisations **not** using the money.web system or Bulk File Submission, are advised to obtain a copy of the preferred Forms. Those reporters who wish to complete reports on their own computer should download the Form(s) from the NCIS website. Alternatively, please send a request for the Form(s) and Guidance to ECBDutyDesk@ncis.co.uk.

If you wish to **complete a report by hand** you will need to request a special version of the Form by telephoning 020 7238 8282. **Please do not complete the version of the Form downloaded from the Internet by hand.**

Sending your report to NCIS

Those organisations which currently use the money.web system or Bulk File submission method should continue to submit reports in the same way. Please do not email completed disclosures to NCIS without encryption.

Other organisations should submit reports by fax to 0207 238 8286 or by post to PO Box 8000, London SE11 5EN. Note, if you complete a Form on your computer, you will need to print it off and submit it by fax or post.

Types of Report

Specific forms have been designed to support the submission of both 'Standard Reports' and 'Limited Intelligence Value Reports'. Further details of what constitutes a Limited Intelligence Value Report and the format of such a report can be found within the **Guidance Notes for the NCIS Regulated Sector Disclosure Report** – Proceeds of Crime Act 2002 - Limited Intelligence Value Report. Please refer to the NCIS' Internet site (www.NCIS.gov.uk)

Structure of the Standard Form

The Standard Report is the default version which reporting institutions should complete unless the disclosure fits the criteria for a Limited Intelligence Value report (Please see **Guidance Notes for the NCIS Regulated Sector Disclosure Report - Proceeds of Crime Act 2002 – Limited Intelligence Value Report** for further information concerning this method of disclosure).

The Standard Form comprises five separate sheets, or modules, (Modules/*Appendices 2-6*). In addition, the Source Registration Document (Module/*Appendix 1*) should be completed when an organisation makes its first disclosure to NCIS or when its contact details change.

The five modules which comprise the Form may be submitted in different combinations depending on the amount and type of information the author of the report has available to disclose. Multiple copies of a particular sheet may be required and in some circumstances it

Appendix 7

may be appropriate for particular sheets to be omitted. It is essential that the Summary Section of Module/*Appendix 2* is clearly completed thereby enabling NCIS to check whether it has received the correct number of sheets and in the correct order.

An additional module (Appendix 8) has been created to allow for lengthier Reason for Disclosure information, where applicable, to be provided rather than to constrain the user to the size of the space provided on Appendix 6.

The Form has been designed to be read by Image Character Recognition (ICR) technology. Therefore any amendments or additions outside the structure of the Form will significantly hamper NCIS' capability to process the disclosure efficiently.

A document entitled 'Field Values List' is available through the NCIS website under the heading 'additional information'. It contains various options for completing particular fields in the Form. The relevant fields are highlighted throughout the 'Completion Instructions' which follow.

Completion Instructions

Source Registration Document (Module/*Appendix* 1)

In order to record disclosures and correspond accurately in a timely manner with the regulated sector, NCIS needs accurate contact details of each reporting organisation. A **Source Registration Document** has been constructed to capture this information as concisely as possible. NCIS already holds such details for organisations which have previously disclosed, therefore **this form should only be used by organisations that have never previously reported and then only when making their first report**. It will not be required for each subsequent disclosure. **However, all organisations should use the source registration document to update NCIS about any changes to their contact details in order that NCIS' records can be accurately maintained.**

Institution Name	Please provide details of the Registered and/or Trading name of the company or individual making the report.
Institution Type	Please provide details of the type of company or individual making the report, eg Money Transmission agent, Bank, Bureau de Change, Estate Agent etc
Regulator	Please provide details of your regulator, where applicable, (eg FSA, Gaming Board of Great Britain etc)
Regulator ID	Please provide details of your regulator's Identity Number, where known to you (eg FSA's register number).
Contact Details (1)	This will be NCIS' primary point of contact with you.
Forename	Please provide full details of your Forename/s.
Surname	Please provide full details of your Surname.
Position	Please provide details as to the position you hold within your employing organisation where applicable.
Address	Please provide your full postal address details (inc Post Code).
Telephone Details	Please provide details of your principal contact number.
Facsimile Details	Please provide details of your principal contact number.
E-mail Address	Please provide details where applicable. The use of this medium will speed up the delivery of correspondence to you.
Contact Details (2) (where applicable)	This will be NCIS' point of contact with you in the absence of the above detailed individual, if applicable.
Forename	As above.
Surname	As above.
Position	As above.
Address	As above.

Appendix 7

Telephone Details	As above.
Facsimile Details	Please provide details of your principal contact number.
E-mail Address	As above.

Disclosure Reports Details Sheet (Module/Appendix 2)

Reporting Institution	Please provide details of the company or individual **making** the report. If a Money Laundering Reporting Officer (MLRO) is completing the form it is not essential at any point to mention by name the person making the initial disclosure.
Your Reference	Please provide details of <u>your</u> own reference number relevant to the disclosure in question. **This is an important field as the information supplied will be quoted by NCIS in any correspondence with you relating to this disclosure.** We are shortly to explore a system change so that our automated response letters will quote **only** your reference number (alongside our own Intelligence Reference Number).
Branch/Office	This information will enable NCIS to ascertain which of your outlets is reporting the activity, assisting NCIS decide which law enforcement agency to allocate the disclosure to.
Disclosure Date	The date upon which you submit your report to NCIS. The format DD/MMM/YYYY has been used to prevent any transposition of Day and Month. Please insert two digits in the DD field to state the day, three letters in the MMM field (for example, JAN for January) and four digits to show the year in the YYYY field.
Disclosure Reason	Confirmation of under which piece of Legislation your report is being made. **Only one piece of legislation should be indicated.**
Consent Required	If you require Consent to undertake a prohibited act, under s336 of the **Proceeds of Crime Act** 2002, please ensure that this field is clearly indicated. This will help NCIS to respond to you as speedily as possible.
Type	Please indicate into which category your report falls.
	A **New** disclosure concerns a person, legal entity or criminal property upon whom/which you have never previously disclosed. Alternatively you may have previously submitted a disclosure, in respect of the person or legal entity, but have now received information causing you to formulate a new suspicion or acquire new knowledge of money laundering.
	An **Update** is classified as revised or additional information that has come to light about a subject or legal entity whom/which you have already reported in a disclosure, e.g. Identification details or a change to an address. **New transactions which you regard as suspicious should be reported in a new disclosure.**
Existing Disclosure IDs	
	When you submit a **new** disclosure about an entity or individual whom you have previously reported, please state the original Intelligence Reference Number(s) supplied by NCIS here.

Report Summary Sheet (Module/Appendix 2 continued)

This part of the form should be used to summarise the number of sheets used by you in the completion of your report and should be filled out once your report has been completed. This summary will ensure that all the sheets are correctly ordered and accounted for by NCIS.

Appendix 7

Number of Subject Details' sheets appended relating to a Main Subject:
This is the person who the report is about. Normally, there will be such a person, although in some circumstances this is not the case, for example you may be reporting a fraud where the perpetrator is unknown.

Number of 'Additional Details' sheets appended relating to Main Subject:
Multiple sheets are acceptable. *However they must be ordered to ensure the correct details are connected to the correct subject (especially important if there is more than one subject).*

Number of 'Subject Details' sheets appended relating to Associated Subject/s:
This is anyone linked to the Main Subject through the reported activity. There may be any number of Associated Subjects. Please complete a separate sheet for each Associated Subject.

Number of 'Additional Details' sheets appended relating to Associated Subject/s:
Please complete, if applicable, as many sheets as is necessary for each Associated Subject. These sheets should be placed immediately behind the Associated Subject to which they refer and numbered accordingly.

Number of 'Transaction Detail' sheets appended:
This sheet will not be relevant for every disclosure since it is largely designed to capture information relating to financial transactions. However, reporters outside the banking sector may be able to complete some of the fields on this sheet, in particular the date that a business relationship commenced and finished.

Number of 'Reason for Disclosure' sheets appended:
Please provide details of the reason(s) why you have knowledge or suspicion or reasonable grounds for knowing or suspecting that another person is engaged in money laundering. This is essential to enable law enforcement to decide whether to commence a money laundering investigation.

Total Number of Pages Submitted:
This field should summarise the total amount of all sheet types being submitted. The information will be used by NCIS to ensure that all the information you consider you provided was received.

Subject Details Sheet (Module/Appendix 3)

Subject Type
This indicates the category of the subject about whom you are reporting. This sheet has dual purpose and can be completed when referring to either a 'Main Subject' or an 'Associated Subject' (an individual linked to the Main Subject). However do not provide the details of a 'Main Subject' and 'Associated Subject' on the same sheet.

(Please note that normally, there will be either a Main Subject or an Associated Subject although in some circumstances this is not the case. For example, you may be reporting a fraud where the perpetrator is unknown).

If you have more than one subject you should consider which one you feel to be the Main Subject or the focus of your report, completing his/her details accordingly. All other subjects should be noted as 'Associated Subjects' on separate 'Subject Details Sheets'. If your disclosure refers only to one subject then they should be notified to NCIS as the Main Subject.

Appendix 7

	If you are providing details of more than one Associated Subject then please use additional copies of this sheet but remember to number them accordingly (e.g. 1 of 3, 2 of 3 etc). This becomes particularly important if you are providing 'Additional Details', enabling you and NCIS to cross-refer any 'Additional Details' forms to the appropriate 'Associated Subject'.
IMPORTANT NOTICE – For any one Subject, only one, of either the 'Individual's Details' Section (top half of sheet) or the 'Legal Entity Details Section' (lower half of sheet), should be completed irrespective of whether the sheet is being used to report a 'Main Subject' or an 'Associated Subject'. Please do not complete both sections.	
Subject Status	Please indicate **only one** box from 'Suspect' or 'Victim'
	Suspect should be ticked if you know or suspect or have reasonable grounds for knowing or suspecting that this individual is engaged in money laundering.
	Victim is the person or entity who/which is harmed by or loses as a result of the criminal activity which you are reporting. To ensure that any intrusion against a victim's privacy is minimised, the victim's details should not, ideally, be included in subject fields. The personal details of victims should only be included if, in the judgement of the nominated officer, the details are essential to understanding the activity being reported.
Surname	Please provide details as appropriate
Forename 1	Please provide details as appropriate of primary forename
Forename 2	Please provide details as appropriate of secondary forename.
Occupation	Please provide details as appropriate. If this information is not known to you please quote 'Unknown'.
Date of birth (DoB)	This is an important field. Date of birth information helps law enforcement to positively identify individuals when cross-matching personal data. The format DD/MMM/YYYY has been used to prevent any transposition of Day and Month. Please insert two digits in the DD field to state the day, three letters in the MMM field (for example, JAN for January) and four digits to show the year in the YYYY field.
Title	Please provide details as appropriate. Common options are provided as tick boxes. If the correct title is not shown, please specify the relevant title in the 'Other' field. Existing options are available from the Field Values List.
Gender	Please select from 'Male' or 'Female' options. If your records do not provide such details please leave both blank
Reason for Association	
	This field should only be completed if using the sheet to report 'Associated Subject' details. The information required would be the reason that links the Associated Subject to the Main Subject. *Appropriate options are provided in the Field Values List.*
Subject Status	Please indicate **only one** box from 'Suspect' or 'Victim'.
	Suspect should be ticked if this entity is central to any know or suspected money laundering which your report outlines.
	Victim is the person or entity who/which is harmed by or loses as a result of the criminal activity which you are reporting. To ensure that any intrusion against a victim's privacy is minimised, the victim's details should not, ideally, be included in subject fields. The personal details of victims should only be included if, in the judgement of the nominated officer, the details are essential to understanding the activity being reported.

Appendix 7

Legal Entity Name	Please provide details as appropriate, eg a Company Name or Charity.
Legal Entity Number	Please provide details as appropriate, eg a Company Number.
VAT no	Please complete as appropriate.
Country of Registration	
	Please provide details as appropriate, eg the country where the legal entity is registered. *Appropriate options are provided in the Field Values List.*
Type of Business	Please provide details as appropriate.
Reason for Association	
	This field should only be completed if you are using the sheet to provide 'Associated Subject' details. The information required is the reason that links the Associated Subject to the Main Subject. *Appropriate options are provided in the Field Values List.*

Additional Details Sheet (Module/Appendix 4)

This sheet should be used to provide Address/es, Identification or any other appropriate details as known to you relating to either the Main or Associated Subject/s. When completed, each of these sheets should be placed immediately behind the relevant Main or Associated Subject sheet to which it refers.

'Details refer to'	Please select either Main Subject or Associated Subject. **Important** When providing Additional Details in which you report more than one Associated Subject, please number each Associate concurrently (e.g. 1 of 2; 2 of 2). This will enable you to cross-refer any additional details to the appropriate Associate Subject.
Subject Name	Please provide details as appropriate
Premise No/Name	Please provide details as appropriate
Current	Please indicate with a tick if this is known to be the subject's present address.
Street	Please provide details as appropriate
City/Town	Please provide details as appropriate
County	Please provide details as appropriate
Country	Please provide details as appropriate
Post Code	Please provide details as appropriate
Type	Please state the type of address (ie home, previous, registered). *Appropriate options are provided in the Field Values List.*

Note	

Up to three addresses can be provided on each sheet. If you wish to provide additional addresses please use another copy of the 'Additional Details' sheet. For each Main or Associated Subject, please match the numbering that you state within the **'Details refer to'** box of the 'Subject Details' sheet to the relevant Additional Details sheet; (eg the additional details for the Associate who was numbered '3 of 5' should also be numbered '3 of 5').

Information Type	This field is intended to assist law enforcement identify a main or associated subject reported in your disclosure. The field may comprise details of Identification taken for the Subject (eg National Insurance Number, Passport or Drivers Licence, MSB Number, Company Number etc) or any other details you may hold such as telephone numbers or Car registration details which you feel will assist any investigation. *Appropriate options are provided in the Field Values List.*

Appendix 7

Unique Information Identifier
    This field refers to the unique information relevant to the Information Type field (eg a Passport Number, National Insurance Number or Drivers Licence Number)

Extra information/Description
    This field refers to additional relevant details (eg British Passport or Full/Provisional Licence)

Note
Up to two pieces of identification can be recorded on one sheet. If you wish to provide additional identification details, please use another copy of the 'Additional Details' sheet. For each Main or Associated Subject about whom you provide additional identification details, please match the number that you state within the **'Details refer to'** box of the 'Subject Details' sheet to the relevant Additional Details sheet; (eg the additional details for the Associate who was numbered '3 of 5' should also be numbered '3 of 5').

Transaction Details Sheet (Module/Appendix 5)

The completion of this sheet depends on the nature of the activity that you are reporting and your sector. For some sectors this sheet may not be applicable, although reporters should note that they may be able to complete the date that a business relationship commenced and finished, even if most or all of the transaction fields are irrelevant. A separate sheet should be completed for each different account which is relevant to the disclosure. Note, there is no general requirement to provide a lengthy list of transactions. Only provide detail if you think it will add to law enforcement's understanding of the criminality that you are knowledgeable or suspicious about.

Main Subject Account Summary

Institution Name	Please provide details as appropriate of the asset holding institution.
Account Name	Please provide details as appropriate
Sort Code	Please provide details as appropriate
Account Number/Identifier	
	Please provide details as appropriate
Business Relationship Commenced/Account Opened	
	Please provide details as appropriate. Note that this field is more widely applicable than the banking sector alone.
Business Relationship Finished/Account Closed	
	Please provide details as appropriate. Note that this field is more widely applicable than the banking sector alone.
Account Balance	Please provide details as appropriate.
Balance Date	Please provide details as appropriate.
Turnover Period	Please provide details, as appropriate *Appropriate options are provided with the Field Values List.*
Credit Turnover	Please provide details as appropriate.
Debit Turnover	Please provide details as appropriate.

TRANSACTION/S

Activity Type	Please provide details, as appropriate. *Appropriate options are provided in the Field Values List.*
Activity Date	Please provide details as appropriate
Amount	Please provide details as appropriate.
Currency	Please provide details as appropriate. *Appropriate options are provided in the Field Values List.*

Appendix 7

Credit or Debit Please provide details as appropriate

Other Party Name Please provide details, as appropriate, of the counterparty to the transaction/activity reported.

Institution Name or Sort Code

Please provide details as appropriate of the counterparty institution to the transaction/activity reported.

Account No/Identifier

Please provide details as appropriate of the counterparty institution to the transaction/activity reported.

Note

Up to four separate transactions can be provided on this sheet. If you need to provide additional transactions please use additional copies of the 'Transaction Details' sheet as appropriate.

Reason for Disclosure Sheet (Module/Appendix 6)

In this section please provide your reasons for knowledge or suspicion, or reasonable grounds for knowledge or suspicion, that another person is engaged in money laundering. This will help law enforcement judge whether to launch a money laundering investigation.

Report Activity Assessment

Where you are aware of an underlying criminal offence (ie the criminal activity which generated the criminal proceeds in question) please indicate it by ticking the relevant box. This will help NCIS to prioritise and allocate your disclosure to the relevant agency. **Please do not complete any of these tick boxes if you have to guess.**

Reason for Disclosure

This area is free text and should include any information not already provided which you feel is relevant to your disclosure. It should provide details of the reason(s) why you have knowledge or suspicion, or reasonable grounds to know or suspect, that another person is engaged in money laundering. You may wish to give consideration to the following prompts to assist you with the content:

- The dates/period over which the suspicious activity in question has occurred;
- The knowledge you have about the origin of the assets;
- Knowledge of the destination / intended beneficiary of assets (this might be an institution, individual or company);
- If the activity is planned for a future date, knowledge of the schedule and intention behind the activity and any specified deadlines which you are normally required to meet;
- Please indicate in your initial comments whether you regard any aspect of your report to be particularly urgent or interesting (for example if you are reporting activity which matches a particular money laundering typology that you are aware of);
- Reporters should indicate where they do not trust or cannot confirm 'know your customer information', such as a date of birth.

Reason for Disclosure Continuation Sheet (Module/Appendix 8)

Where required, please use this section to continue your reasons for knowledge or suspicion, where the space provided within Appendix 6 is insufficient. Multiples of this module can be utilised as required.

Please ensure that you complete the Main Subject Name at the top of any of these modules completed in order that we may cross reference this module to the rest of your report.

Appendix 8: Guidance Notes for the NCIS Regulated Sector Disclosure Report, Proceeds Of Crime Act 2002 – Limited Intelligence Value Report[1]

Content

Page [237]	Scope and Purpose Statement
Page [238-240]	Limited Intelligence Value Report
	Examples of relevant circumstances suitable for such reports
Page [241]	Completion Instructions:-
	'Source Registration Document' (Module/*Appendix* 1)
Page [241-243]	Completion Instructions:-
	'Limited Intelligence Value Report' (Module/*Appendix* 7)
	(Reporting Institution Details and Subject Details)
Page [243]	Completion Instructions:-
	Reason for Disclosure Continuation Sheet (Module/*Appendix* 8)
	(Reason for Disclosure Continuation)

Scope and Purpose

This document provides guidance for the completion of authorised and protected disclosures, under sections 337 and 338 of the Proceeds of Crime Act (2002), categorised as 'Limited Intelligence Value Reports'. This guidance should be read alongside the Limited Intelligence Value Report (Appendix 7) which has been issued by NCIS. Both the Form and Guidance have been completed following consultation with organisations representing the Regulated Sector. **Please note that Limited Intelligence Value Reports should only be made under the Proceeds of Crime Act (PoCA). Any reports being made under the Terrorism Act (2000) should be Standard Reports.**

The Form has not been prescribed by the Secretary of State and therefore is not mandatory. However the Form has been agreed by NCIS and organisations representing the Regulated Sector as the preferred format for all reports. The Form has been designed to reflect the different needs of the sectors as well as NCIS' requirement to handle the disclosures as efficiently and effectively as possible.

Although none of the fields in the form is mandatory, since the format is not prescribed, those submitting disclosures should take account of regulatory and sectoral approved guidance. NCIS' feedback to reporting institutions will assess the quality of reporting against relevant guidance.

---

[1]. This guidance is reproduced for information purposes only. NCIS forms and guidance are subject to regular change and readers should refer to www.ncis.co.uk for the latest versions.
© NCIS 2004. All rights reserved.

Appendix 8

How to obtain the new Forms and Guidance

Those organisations which currently use the Money.web system or Bulk File submission should continue to submit reports electronically, using the existing input screens or reporting format.

Organisations **not** using the money.web system or Bulk File Submission, are advised to obtain a copy of the preferred Forms. Those reporters who wish to complete reports on their own computer should download the Form(s) from the NCIS website. Alternatively, please send a request for the Form(s) and Guidance to ECBDutyDesk@ncis.co.uk.

If you wish **to complete a report by hand** you will need to request a special version of the Form by telephoning 020 7238 8282. **Please do not complete the version of the Form downloaded from the Internet by hand.**

Sending your report to NCIS

Those organisations which currently use the money.web system or Bulk File submission method, should continue to submit reports in the same way. Please do not email completed disclosures to NCIS without encryption.

Other organisations will need to submit reports by fax to 0207 238 8286 or by post to PO Box 8000, London SE11 5EN. Note, if you complete a Form on your computer, you will need to print it off and submit it by fax or post.

Report Structure

These Guidance Notes are provided to explain the various fields within the Report and assist you in its completion and should be read alongside the Report Forms themselves. The Form has been designed to be read by Image Character Recognition (ICR) technology. Therefore any amendments or additions outside the structure of the Form will significantly hamper NCIS's capability to process the disclosure efficiently.

Limited Intelligence Value Reports

NCIS recognises that POCA results in reports being required in some circumstances where, individually, there is likely to be limited intelligence value to law enforcement, although wider analysis of such reports may provide useful data. The table below provides guidance on the types of circumstance that are appropriate for abbreviated information to be provided in the form of a Limited Intelligence Value report. NCIS reserves the right, in all cases, to ask for the Standard Report format to be used and will monitor disclosures submitted to ensure that Limited Intelligence Value reporting is not exploited as a 'short cut' where its use is not justified.

Type	Detail	Comments
1 Certain classes of crimes committed overseas	This is intended to apply where the suspicious activity takes place outside the UK and:- • Is not a criminal offence in the jurisdiction where committed, and • Relates either to local differences in regulation or social and cultural practices	A Limited Intelligence Value Report is **not** appropriate to report money laundering relating to serious tax evasion or occasions where the underlying offence is a serious crime such as terrorism, offences relating to drugs, paedophilia etc. In these circumstances, a full report is appropriate.

Appendix 8

Type	Detail	Comments
2 Minor irregularities where there is nothing to suggest that these are the result of dishonest behaviour.	Balance discrepancies and minor credit balances not returned because of the administrative costs involved, or other small discrepancies which are judged to have resulted from a mistake rather than dishonest behaviour.	If reporting institutions are satisfied that no criminal property is involved (as defined by s340 (3) of the Proceeds of Crime Act, 2002), they may conclude that a report is not required. However where reporting institutions feel obliged to make a disclosure, a Limited Intelligence Value report is appropriate.
3 The subject of the report cannot be deduced from the information to hand and the proceeds have disappeared without trace.	This would include bank raids, driving away from a petrol station without paying, shoplifting, retail shrinkage and various cheque and credit card frauds.	None.
4 Accountants, auditors and tax advisers. Multiple instances of suspicion arising during one audit: 'Aggregation of incidents to form one report'	Multiple incidents may be aggregated within a single Limited Intelligence Value Report provided that:- • One or more of the other categories in this table for limited intelligence value reporting is met, for example number three (above): bank raids, driving away from a petrol station without paying, shoplifting, retail shrinkage and various cheque and credit card frauds; • The reason for the aggregate report is summarised; • Aggregate reports relate to a single audit only.	The Act refers to reports being made 'as soon as practicable'. NCIS accepts that this will not always mean 'immediately' and is content to receive aggregate Limited Intelligence Value Reports within one month of the completion of an audit, provided that during the assignment no time sensitive information is discovered (that may, for example, allow the recovery of proceeds of crime if communicated immediately). Reporters should note that a Standard Report is appropriate should the issue of a Hansard (CoP9) letter by the Inland Revenue, taken with such other information as may be available, cause (or provide reasonable grounds for) knowledge or suspicion of money laundering.

Appendix 8

5 Duplicate reports to NCIS, or a prosecuting authority (including regulators with powers of prosecution)	Where the institution considering whether to disclose knows (as opposed to assumes) that a report has been made to NCIS, another prosecuting authority or to another person authorised by NCIS to receive reports, and a further report would provide no additional information. An example is where a client in the regulated sector has filed a report and an auditor or accountant knows this.	Provided the caveat of 'no additional information' is adhered to, a Limited intelligence Value report is appropriate. Note that the Inland Revenue is not authorised to receive disclosures direct from the regulated sector under POCA.
6 Law enforcement prosecutor, regulator or other Government agency already aware of an offence that also happens to be an instance of suspected money laundering	This category is intended to capture a range of regulatory/procedural offences. Examples include health and safety offences, environmental offences, and failure to file annual returns with the Companies Registrar.	Provided the caveat of "no additional information" is adhered to, a Limited Intelligence Value report is appropriate. However, any knowledge or suspicion of money laundering relating to serious tax evasion, including cases covered by the Hansard procedure, should be reported in a Standard Report.
7 Section 167 (3) Customs and Excise Management Act 1979	This makes the submission of an incorrect VAT or Customs return, however innocent, a criminal offence.	It is the position of NCIS that a disclosure is not required for innocent error in these circumstances. Where the person knows of the omission and does not rectify the situation there will be a duty to report. Where reporting institutions feel obliged to make a disclosure, a Limited Intelligence Value report is appropriate.
8 Reporting institution served with a Court Order, which prompts suspicion		A Limited Intelligence Value report is appropriate except where the suspicion and report relate to matters not covered by the Court Order letter, in which case a report on the Standard Form should be submitted.
9 Where the benefit from criminal conduct is in the form of cost savings, such as breaches of employment law and the illegal copying or distribution of software licences within a company.		

Appendix 8

Completion Instructions
Source Registration Document (*Module* 1)

In order to record disclosures and correspond accurately and in a timely manner with the regulated sector, NCIS needs accurate contact details of each reporting organisation. A **Source Registration Document** has been constructed to capture this information as concisely as possible. NCIS already holds such details for organisations which have previously disclosed, therefore **this sheet should only be used by organisations that have never previously reported and then only when making their first report**. It will not be required for each subsequent disclosure. **However, all organisations should use the source registration document to update NCIS about any changes to their contact details in order that NCIS' records can be accurately maintained.**

Institution Name	Please provide details of the Registered and/or Trading name of the company or individual making the report.
Institution Type	Please provide details of the type of company or individual making the report, eg Money Transmission Agent, Bank, Estate Agent etc
Regulator	Please provide details of your regulator, where applicable, (eg FSA, Gaming Board of Great Britain etc)
Regulator ID	Please provide details of your regulator's Identity Number, where known to you.
Contact Details (1)	This will be NCIS' primary point of contact with you.
Forename	Please provide full details of your Forename/s.
Surname	Please provide full details of your Surname.
Position	Please provide details as to the position you hold within your employer, where applicable.
Address	Please provide your full postal address details (inc Post Code).
Telephone Details	Please provide details of your principal contact number.
E-mail Address	Please provide details where applicable. The ability to use this medium will enhance the speed of delivery of our correspondence with you.
Contact Details (2) (where applicable)	This will be NCIS' point of contact with you in the absence of the above detailed individual, if applicable.
Name	As above.
Position	As above.
Address	As above.
Telephone Details	As above.
E-mail Address	As above.

Limited intelligence Value Report (*Module* 7)

Reporting Institution	Please provide details of the company or individual **making** the report. If a Money Laundering Reporting Officer (MLRO) is completing the form it is not essential at any point to mention by name the person making the initial disclosure.
Your Reference	Please provide details of your own reference number relevant to the disclosure in question. **This is an important field as the information supplied will be quoted by us NCIS in any correspondence with you relating to this disclosure.** We are shortly to explore a system change so that our automated response letters will quote **only** your reference number (alongside our own Intelligence Reference Number).

Appendix 8

Branch/Office	This information will enable NCIS to ascertain which of your outlets is reporting the activity, assisting NCIS decide which law enforcement agency to allocate the disclosure to.
Disclosure Date	The date upon which you submit your report to NCIS. The format DD/MMM/YYYY has been used to prevent any transposition of Day and Month. Please insert two digits in the DD field to state the day, three letters in the MMM field (for example, JAN for January) and four digits to show the year in the YYYY field.

Subject Details

This is the Person/Legal Entity about whom/which the report is being made. Normally, reporters will be in a position to complete one of these fields, although in some circumstances this is not the case. For example you may be reporting a fraud where the perpetrator is unknown

This section of the sheet can be used to refer to an Individual or a Legal Entity. **However only one of these sections should be completed.** This sheet should not be used for both an individual and a Legal Entity at the same time.

Subject Status	Please indicate **only one** box from 'Suspect' or 'Victim'.
	Suspect should be ticked if you know or suspect or have reasonable grounds for knowing or suspecting that this person is engaged in money laundering.
	Victim is the person or entity who/which is harmed by or loses as a result of the criminal activity which you are reporting. To ensure that any intrusion against a victim's privacy is minimised, the victim's details should not, ideally, be included in subject fields. The personal details of victims should only be included if, in the judgement of the nominated officer, the details are essential to understanding the activity being reported.

PLEASE COMPLETE EITHER THE INDIVIDUAL'S DETAILS SECTION OF THE SHEET OR THE LEGAL ENTITY SECTION. PLEASE DO NOT COMPLETE BOTH.

Surname	Please provide details, as appropriate.
Forename 1	Please provide details, as appropriate.
Date of Birth	This is an important field. Date of birth information helps law enforcement to positively identify individuals when cross-matching personal data. The format DD/MMM/YYYY has been used to prevent any transposition of Day and Month. Please insert two digits in the DD field to state the day, three letters in the MMM field (for example, JAN for January) and four digits to show the year in the YYYY field.
Gender	Please select from options provided.
Title	Please select from options provided. If the correct title is not shown, please specify the relevant title within the 'Other' field.
	Appropriate options are provided with the Field Values List.
OR	
Legal Entity Name	Please provide details as appropriate, eg a Company or Charity Name.
Legal Entity Number	Please provide details as appropriate, eg a Company or charity Number.
VAT Number	Please provide details as appropriate.

Reason for Disclosure

This area is free text and should include any information not already provided which you feel is relevant to your Report. It should provide details of the reason(s) why you have knowledge or suspicion or reasonable grounds for knowledge or suspicion that

Appendix 8

another person is engaged in money laundering and why you feel that a Limited Value Report is suitable.

Reason for Disclosure Continuation Sheet (Module/Appendix 8)

Where required, please use this section to continue your reasons for knowledge or suspicion, where the space provided within Appendix 7 is insufficient. Multiples of this module can be utilised as required.

Please ensure that you complete the Main Subject Name at the top of any of these modules completed in order that we may cross reference this module to the rest of your report.

Appendix 9: NCIS guidance in relation to disclosures by the legal profession[1]

1 In the view of the NCIS the following constitutes good practice on the part of a legal advisor who is advising a client in relation to a matter that might involve a suspicious financial arrangement.

2 There is no need to seek the consent of the NCIS to act – that is to take instructions and learn what a case is about. The NCIS will not accept such requests for consent.

3 Should a concern arise in relation to a prospective financial arrangement then the legal advisor should learn sufficient about the client and the source (or final destination) of any funds involved in the arrangement, including as necessary seeking information from the legal advisors, if any, on the other side.

4 Should the legal advisor then have a suspicion at the stage that there is a step to be taken in the case that would involve the legal advisor or their client becoming involved in an arrangement which he knows or suspects facilitates by whatever means the acquisition, retention, use or control of criminal property by or on behalf of another person or there is the possibility of offences under s327 or s329 of Proceeds of Crime Act 2002, a written report (a template is available at www.ncis.gov.uk) setting out all relevant details including the grounds for any suspicion should be submitted to the NCIS.

5 In the event that a solicitor makes a disclosure before instructing counsel there would be no requirement for counsel to make a further disclosure if the facts upon which he would otherwise have disclosed remain as they were when the solicitor made the original disclosure.

6 Legal advisors must not assume that 'the other side' in any matter has reported a suspicion to the NCIS and such enquiries should not be made of the NCIS.

7 Where the client of the legal advisor has joined in the disclosure that has been made the client would, from the point in time when a disclosure is made to the NCIS, not be regarded as having committed an offence under s327-329. Where a legal advisor makes a disclosure without the knowledge of their client then plainly and necessarily such protection for the client would not apply.

8 Where consent is sought to enter into or be concerned in an arrangement that is time sensitive this fact should be explicitly stated and highlighted in the written report faxed to the NCIS Consent Desk (formerly the Duty Desk).

9 For there to be a disclosure there is no necessity at all for any funds to be contemplated as having to pass through the legal advisors client account or actually to pass through such an account. The test for the legal advisor would simply be whether he had become concerned in an arrangement.

10 Following a disclosure the NCIS will follow the procedure in accordance with s335 either giving or with holding consent as the case may be. That is that they will give or refuse consent within seven days; if after seven days there has been no response from the NCIS consent to proceed on the basis of the information disclosed will be deemed to have occurred. If the NCIS refuse to give consent then there would follow a 31-day period from the date of the refusal

---

1. This guidance is reproduced for information purposes only. NCIS forms and guidance are subject to regular change and readers should refer to www.ncis.co.uk for the latest versions.

© NCIS 2003. All rights reserved.

Appendix 9

during which the legal advisor could not proceed with the arrangement, without risking the commission of a money laundering offence.

11 Once a disclosure has been made to the NCIS then the solicitor is free to continue with the arrangement (as reported to NCIS) if consent is given, or at the end of the moratorium period if consent is withheld.

12 The NCIS would wish the legal profession to note that subject to s333(4), under s333(3) POCA there is no restriction on the legal advisor informing any person of the fact that they have made a report to the NCIS if such a disclosure is to a client or his representative in connection with the giving of legal advice to the client or the disclosure is made in connection with legal proceedings or contemplated legal proceedings.

Part 8 Proceeds of Crime Act 2002

13 However, if a legal advisor takes the view that he should inform his client (or any other person) of a disclosure to the NCIS, then he must also have regard to s342. The section provides that if a person including a legal advisor at least suspecting that a person responsible for investigation under the Act is acting or proposing to act in connection with a confiscation, money laundering or civil recovery investigation which is being or is about to be conducted the offence of prejudicing an investigation is made out if a disclosure is made which is likely to prejudice such an investigation, whether or not there has been a disclosure to the NCIS. The legal advisor will note the defence contained in s342(3) which permits disclosures to a client or to any person in connection with legal proceedings or the giving of legal advice. This would have to be born in mind when considering whether or not it was necessary to inform a client or another person of a disclosure whether actual or contemplated.

The NCIS preferred approach post-disclosure

14 Where the legal advisor has made a disclosure to the NCIS, the NCIS would prefer as a matter of practise the legal advisor not to make any reference to that fact during the seven days following the disclosure or during the period of 31 days following a refusal to consent to an arrangement, unless not to do so would be in breach of a disclosure obligation imposed by the particular proceedings.

15 In the event that the legal advisor considers that a requirement of the legal proceedings is to require disclosure of the fact of the disclosure to the NCIS, but there has been no consent from NCIS within seven days or the moratorium period is applicable, then the legal advisor should firstly inform the NCIS and try to seek agreement on the way ahead. In the absence of such agreement the legal advisor should consider making a without notice application to the Court for directions giving the NCIS an opportunity to make representations. (See *C v S and others (Money Laundering: Discovery of Documents)* [1999] 1 WLR 1551 and *Bank of Scotland v A Limited* [2001] 1 WLR 752).

(NCIS October 2003)

Appendix 10: *P v P* – Law Society Guidance

Introduction

The judgment in this case arose out of ancillary relief proceedings in which a party's legal adviser had reported the other side to the National Criminal Intelligence Service (NCIS) for apparent tax evasion. The report had been made, and appropriate consent sought, in order to obtain a defence to the s328 arrangement offence under the Proceeds of Crime Act 2002 (POC). The matter was brought to the Court's attention because the legal advisers were unsure how to proceed, particularly in the light of the fact that the advice from NCIS appeared to conflict with the professional obligations of the legal advisers.

The Law Society's Money Laundering Task Force, in consultation with family lawyers, has, on behalf of the Law Society, prepared the following guidance for family solicitors on the effect of the judgment. However, solicitors should be aware that this is a new and developing area of law. This should therefore be regarded as interim guidance: further guidance will be published as necessary.

Guidance

The arrangement offence under POCA

1. It is an offence under s328 POCA to enter into an arrangement that a person knows or suspects facilitates (by whatever means) the acquisition, retention, use or control of criminal property by or on behalf of another person.

2. An arrangement offence under s328 POCA can be committed even if no money passes through the solicitor's client account.

3. It does not matter how small the financial benefit gained from the criminal conduct may be; nor when or where the criminal conduct took place, as long as it would be a criminal offence if committed in this country.

4. All criminal offences amount to 'criminal conduct' from which criminal property can arise, including tax evasion and social security fraud.

5. When solicitors act in ancillary relief proceedings (or proposed proceedings), from the moment they know or suspect that assets that include the proceeds of criminal conduct ('criminal property') are involved they risk committing the arrangement offence.

Withdrawing

6. If the solicitor does not wish to continue to act, they may at that stage withdraw.

7. It is necessary and appropriate for solicitors, in giving legal advice to the client or in acting in connection with the legal proceedings, to advise their client that, in the light of their knowledge or suspicion, if they continue to act for the client, both they and their client will commit a money-laundering offence unless an authorised disclosure is made to NCIS and the appropriate consent is received from NCIS to continue (see below at paragraph 15). In so doing, however, solicitors must be careful to avoid committing the offences of tipping off or prejudicing an investigation and should carefully consider the advice given below at paragraphs 19 onwards. In the event the client does not consent to the solicitor making an authorised disclosure, the solicitor should withdraw.

8. Once solicitors have withdrawn, whether or not they should report their knowledge or suspicion to NCIS will depend upon the circumstances in which they came by that knowledge or suspicion.

Appendix 10

9. If a solicitor's knowledge or suspicion arises from a confidential communication received by the solicitor for the sole or dominant purpose of the proceedings, it is likely that such a communication takes place in privileged circumstances. This of course will not be the case if the purpose of the communication is a criminal one whether on the part of the client or another.

10. Solicitors in the regulated sector, commit an offence under s330 POCA if they fail to make the required disclosure when in the course of business they acquire knowledge, suspicion or reasonable grounds for knowledge or suspicion that another person is engaged in money laundering unless the information came to them in privileged circumstances. Therefore solicitors in the regulated sector must carefully consider upon withdrawal whether their knowledge or suspicion arises in privileged circumstances. If it does, they commit no offence under s330 by failing to report; if it does not, then they commit an offence under s330.

11. It is crucial that solicitors should realise that legal professional privilege (as opposed to without prejudice privilege) does not attach to communications between opposing parties in litigation. Therefore if the solicitor's knowledge or suspicion arises from a communication from their opponent in the proceedings, it will not have come to them in privileged circumstances.

12. One of the effects of the Money Laundering Regulations 2003 is that from 1 March 2004, those involved in providing 'legal services... which involve participation in a financial or real property transaction' will be in the regulated sector. It is likely that this will include solicitors who provide ancillary relief advice.

13. If the solicitor is in the non-regulated sector then upon withdrawal they commit no offence of failure to report under s330 whether or not their knowledge or suspicion arose in privileged circumstances. The solicitor may of course make a 'protected disclosure' under s337 POCA. This is clearly of limited application and is likely to cease to be relevant to those providing ancillary relief services after 1 March 2004.

14. It seems unlikely that by failing to make a disclosure in such circumstances the solicitor commits an offence of concealment under s327 POCA. If this were so, then the protection from prosecution given to a solicitor in the regulated sector who fails to disclose knowledge or suspicion gained in privileged circumstances would be made redundant, for that solicitor could still be liable to prosecution for concealment under s327.

Continuing to act

15. Solicitors wishing to continue to act, to avoid prosecution for an arrangement offence, should make a report to NCIS and obtain appropriate consent before any substantive steps in the case are taken, that is to say further negotiations take place or the proceedings are progressed in any other way (although taking instructions, or seeking clarification from the other side as to issues, especially those that may affect whether a report needs to be made, may be acceptable).

16. Once the disclosure has been made to NCIS, it can give or withhold consent within seven working days; if no response is received in this period, consent to proceed is deemed to have been given. If NCIS refuses consent, solicitors risk committing a money-laundering offence if they take any step within the proceedings in the 31 day period following the date of refusal.

17. The arrangement offence, and reporting defence, apply regardless of whether it is the solicitor's own client who is the suspected party, or the other side;

18. From 1 March 2004 most solicitors will be in the regulated sector that will impose criminal penalties for non disclosure. Solicitors should be also bear in mind the specific offences which apply to nominated officers (MLROs) both in the regulated sector (s331) and outside the regulated sector (s332). In the event that an MLRO receives a report as nominated officer that is based upon information that has been received by a professional legal adviser in his firm in privileged circumstances, it is the Law Society's view that the MLRO has a reasonable excuse for not reporting that privileged information to NCIS.

Tipping off and prejudicing an investigation

Informing the client

19. Can the solicitor tell their client that they intend to make, or have made, a report to NCIS? The answer will depend upon the circumstances.

Appendix 10

20. It is an offence of tipping off (s333) to make a disclosure which is likely to prejudice any investigation that might be conducted, following a report that the solicitor knows, (or suspects) has been made.

21. It is also an offence of prejudicing an investigation (s342) if the solicitor knows that an appropriate officer is acting or proposing to act in connection with a confiscation, money laundering or civil recovery investigation that is being or about to be conducted, and he makes a disclosure that is likely to prejudice that investigation.

22. There is a defence to both of these offences for the professional legal adviser who makes a disclosure (most probably, to his client) in privileged circumstances, that is, in connection with the giving by the adviser of legal advice to the client, or to any person in connection with legal proceedings or contemplated legal proceedings (ss333(3) and 342(4)). The president of the Family Division held that a central element of advising and representing a client must be, in my view, the duty to keep one's client informed and not to withhold information from them.

23. However, if the solicitor's purpose in informing his client falls outside this strict exception, he may commit either or both offences; this is the position whether or not the solicitor's intention is criminal.

24. In circumstances when the exception does apply, there is no absolute duty on solicitors to tell their clients, that they have, or intend to, make a report to NCIS. An important factor that a solicitor should bear in mind when deciding whether to discuss reporting with a client is whether either they or their staff may be put in danger as a result, perhaps because the underlying crime is serious, eg drugs trafficking.

25. Once the POCA provisions are explained to them, clients may wish to make their own report, or to make a joint report with their legal representatives. Doing so may, by obtaining consent, also give the client protection from commission of the s328 arrangement offence, even if the report is made by, or on behalf of, the suspected parties themselves.

26. If a solicitor discusses reporting with his client, but the client does not agree with an NCIS report being made, the solicitor should withdraw from the case. The solicitor should consider carefully in accordance with the guidelines set out above, whether they should themselves make a report to NCIS after withdrawing.

Informing the other side

27. The president recognised in *P v P* that in family proceedings (and particularly in ancillary relief) there is an enhanced duty on lawyers of full and frank disclosure, to enable a court to have the true facts and to enable the parties to negotiate a genuine settlement. She concluded these enhanced duties in family proceedings appeared to attract protection under ss333(3) and 343(4), which permitted a legal adviser to communicate such information to their client or opponent as is necessary and appropriate in connection with the giving of legal advice or acting in connection with actual or contemplated legal proceedings.

Timing – when to tell the client/opponent

28. If it is necessary and appropriate to inform the client/opponent, neither s333 nor s342 impose a time limit in which solicitors may inform their clients of a disclosure to NCIS.

29. The Court in *P v P* suggested guidelines for good practice (rather than statutory obligation) –

- in most cases a seven-day delay before telling the client would not cause particular difficulty to the solicitor's obligation to their client and opponent;
- in the event that consent was refused by NCIS and a 31 day moratorium imposed, the solicitor and NCIS should seek to agree the degree of information to be disclosed;
- in the absence of agreement or in urgent cases where delay in disclosure to the client would be unacceptable, the court's guidance may be sought.

NCIS guidance

30. In the light of the *P v P* judgment NCIS have published guidance about disclosures by the legal profession, which can be found at [www.ncis.co.uk]. This has recently been changed to incorporate a number of important amendments to its previous version:

(i) there is no requirement for Counsel to make separate reports if their solicitors have made reports relating all relevant facts known to Counsel. There will usually not be a danger of tipping off in solicitors and Counsel discussing reports as there will be little likelihood of prejudice being caused to an investigation for the purposes of the tipping-off offences;

(ii) on the other hand legal advisers must not presume that the other side in any matter has reported; and

(iii) where the client or legal adviser have made a joint report the client may be protected from commission of any of the offences under ss327 and 329.

Application of the *P v P* judgment in other areas of law

This judgment arose in an ancillary relief case, and is particularly relevant to family proceedings. Solicitors must be extremely cautious however in seeking to extend its findings to general areas of practice.

The Law Society considers that whilst it does give the following general guidance on the interpretation of the statutory provisions dealing with tipping off (s333) and prejudicing an investigation (s342), solicitors must exercise the greatest caution when advising in such circumstances –

- a solicitor commits neither offence in properly advising their client that they have made, or will make, an 'authorised report' to NCIS when it is necessary and appropriate to do so in connection with the giving of legal advice or acting in connection with actual or contemplated legal proceedings;

- no such protection is available to solicitors if their intention in making such a disclosure to the client is the furtherance of a criminal purpose.

© The Law Society 2004. All rights reserved.

Appendix 11: Law Society 'Green Card' warning on property fraud

Could you be involved or implicated?

Could you be unwittingly assisting in a fraud? The general assumption is that if there has been a property fraud a solicitor must have been involved. Solicitors should therefore be vigilant to protect both their clients and themselves. Steps can be taken to minimise the risk of being involved or implicated in a fraud (see below).

Could you spot a property fraud?

The signs to watch for include the following (but this list is not exhaustive):

- Fraudulent buyer or fictitious solicitors especially if the buyer is introduced to your practice by a third party (for example a broker or estate agent) who is not well known to you. Beware of clients whom you never meet and solicitors not known to you.
- Unusual instructions, for example a solicitor being instructed by the seller to remit the net proceeds of sale to anyone other than the seller.
- Misrepresentation of the purchase price ensure that the true cash price actually to be paid is stated as the consideration in the contract and transfer and is identical to the price shown in the mortgage instructions and in the report on title to the lender.
- A deposit or any part of purchase price paid direct, a deposit or the difference between the mortgage advance and the price, paid direct, or said to be paid direct, to the seller.
- Incomplete contract documentation, contract documents not fully completed by the seller representative, ie dates missing or the identity of the parties not fully described or financial details not fully stated.
- Changes in the purchase price, adjustments to the purchase price, particularly in high percentage mortgage cases, or allowances off the purchase price, for example, for works to be carried out.
- Unusual transactions, transactions which do not follow their normal course or the usual pattern of events:
    (a) client with current mortgage on two or more properties;
    (b) client using alias;
    (c) client buying several properties from same person or two or more persons using same solicitor; and
    (d) client reselling property at a substantial profit, for which no explanation has been provided.

What steps can I take to minimise the risk of fraud?

Be vigilant: if you have any doubts about a transaction, consider whether any of the following steps could be taken to minimise the risk of fraud:

- Verify the identity and *bona fides* of your client and solicitors' firms you do not know, meet the clients where possible and get to know them a little. Check that the solicitor's firm and office address appear in the Directory of Solicitors and Barristers or contact the Law Society Regulation and Information Services (tel: 0870 606 2555).

- Question unusual instructions, if you receive unusual instructions from your client discuss them with your client fully.
- Discuss with your client any aspects of the transaction which worry you, if, for example, you have any suspicion that your client may have submitted a false mortgage application or references, or if the lender's valuation exceeds the actual price paid, discuss this with your client. If you believe that the client intends to proceed with a fraudulent application, you must refuse to continue to act for the buyer and the lender.
- Check that the true price is shown in all documentation, check that the actual price paid is stated in the contract, transfer and mortgage instructions. Where you are also acting for a lender, tell your client that you will have to cease acting unless the client permits you to report to the lender all allowances and incentives. See also the guidance printed in [1990] Gazette, 12 December, 16 [see Annex 25F, p500 in the Guide].
- Do not witness pre-signed documentation, no document should be witnessed by a solicitor or their staff unless the person signing does so in the presence of the witness. If the document is pre-signed, ensure that it is re-signed in the presence of a witness.
- Verify signatures, consider whether signatures on all documents connected with a transaction should be examined and compared with signatures on any other available documentation.
- Make a company search where a private company is the seller, or the seller has purchased from a private company in the recent past, and you suspect that the sale may not be on proper arm's-length terms, you should make a search in the Companies Register to ascertain the names and addresses of the officers and shareholders, which can then be compared with the names of those connected with the transaction and the seller and buyer.
- Remember that, even where investigations result in a solicitor ceasing to act for a client, the solicitor will still owe a duty of confidentiality which would prevent the solicitor passing on information to the lender. It is only where the solicitor is satisfied that there is a strong *prima facie* case that the client was using the solicitor to further a fraud or other criminal purpose that the duty of confidentiality would not apply.
- Any failure to observe these signs and to take the appropriate steps may be used in court as evidence against you if you and your client are prosecuted, or if you are sued for negligence.

Further guidance can be obtained from the Law Society's Practice Advice Service (tel: 0870 606 2522).

© The Law Society 2004. All rights reserved.

Appendix 12: Law Society Yellow Card – banking instrument fraud

THE LAW SOCIETY FRAUD INTELLIGENCE OFFICE
Warning Banking Instrument Fraud

Fraudulent investment schemes are on the increase. 'prime bank guarantees', 'prime bank letters of credit', and 'zero coupon letters of credit' are not issued by the legitimate banking community. The legitimacy of such investments must always be questioned.

Solicitors should exercise extreme caution if approached by individuals promoting such transactions.

Example of such schemes

Investors are often persuaded that these types of investment, 'can be bought and sold by investing say $8.8m to purchase a prime bank instrument with a face value of £10m, issued by a prime bank, which will mature in one year and one day or can be traded in a second tier bond market for an immediate 7% profit'. The fraudster will often claim that these instruments are so special that the banks are keeping them secret and therefore will not discuss them with the general public.

There is no trading of such instruments in the legitimate financial market

Clients anxious, perhaps desperate to obtain substantial loans, should be warned about the dangers of making advance payments to brokers or individuals offering these types of instruments.

Why involve you as a solicitor?

The fraudster wants to be associated with the legitimacy and respectability which you as a solicitor can provide.

(a) They want you to endorse the scheme by confirming that you will participate, and will act as their banker, solicitor etc.
(b) They may ask you to provide a communication to someone they will nominate.
(c) The fraudster may seek a letter from you, addressed to their company, or a third party.
(d) They would like you to open an account, awaiting receipt of funds.
(e) Fraudsters have frequently included, within the voluminous documentation accompanying such schemes, reference to the solicitor being insured with the Solicitors' Indemnity Fund.

Exercise caution in communicating with potential fraudsters

(a) Never send them anything – fax, letter, memo.
(b) Never even give them your visiting card.
(c) Never meet them on your own.
(d) Never assume that a 'bank's telephone number' given to you is actually that of a bank it's probably not.

Common characteristics of banking instrument fraud

(a) Large transactions (ranging from $1 million to $100 million and much more).
(b) Promises of further sizeable transactions (often huge sums $100 billion); there may be reference to secret markets.

Appendix 12

(c) Small first transaction with several subsequent trenches to follow.
(d) Unusual currencies (eg billions of new Kuwaiti dinars).
(e) Prime bank guarantees (PBGs) being offered or being the 'product' to be financed.
(f) Proposals received by fax.
(g) Letterheads of companies which could have been easily produced by laser printer.
(h) The issuing bank may not be identified, be geographically remote or licensed within a jurisdiction with little or no regulations. Letters, possibly forged, from respectable banks being used to support the documentation.
(i) Strange, weird, confusing and complex transactions, hazy descriptions.
(j) Overwhelming amount of transaction description along with supporting papers and even flowcharts of the transaction.
(k) Large commission, even large 'bonus' or large 'discount' or 'spread' being offered to the bank.
(l) Suggestions that the scheme is supported by, or operates under the auspices of a major international body (eg IMF, UN, Federal Reserve or Bank of England).
(m) Outlandish projects, difficult to verify, eg financing of an island resort on a far away (unknown) island. Retirement home village in a far away country or good causes such as United Nations development or third-world reconstruction.
(n) Documents will invariably be signed by 'the president' or 'the chairman of the board' or 'the chief executive officer'.
(o) A power of attorney document may be produced, duly authenticated by a bank and/ or lawyer.

Look for typical phrases some of them meaningless

Ready, willing and able.

Prime bank guarantees (PBGs).

Prime bank notes (PBNs).

Guaranteed by top-100 world prime bank.

Unconditional SWIFT wire transfer.

Freely negotiable, irrevocable, clear SWIFT wire transfers.

Callable conditional sight drafts.

Closing bank.

Issuing bank.

Fiduciary bank.

Bank menu.

International banking days.

ICC (International Chamber of Commerce) 400.

UCC (Uniform Commercial Code) form references.

Banking coordinates.

Fresh-cut paper.

Seasoned paper.

Collateral houses, collateral source, collateral supplier.

Collateral first transaction.

Grand master collateral commitment.

Validation of the MCC (Master Collateral Commitment).

Collateral purchase orders.

Appendix 12

Collateral provider.
Instruments delivered free of all liens and/or encumbrances.
Non circumvention and non-disclosure agreements.
Irrevocable pay order.
Irrevocable, irretractable commitment of funds to purchase instruments.
Lending bank, funding bank, closing bank.
Good, clear cleared funds of non-criminal origin.
With full corporate and legal responsibility.
Interest at 7.5%, payable annually in arrears.
5, 10, 20 years etc plus one week or one day.
Fully binding commercial letter contract.
Client company principals.
Transaction tranches.
Millions or billions or dollars with rolls and extensions.
Emissions, remission, commissions and fallout.
Transaction parameters.
There is to be no communication with our bank other than through the normal bank channels; no telephone call allowed.

Request for details of client account

Beware of any scheme which requires the depositing of any substantial sums of money to you for safe keeping at lucrative rates for doing very little. It may sound too good to be true and probably is.

Beware of any scheme which requires you to send details of your bank, client account or blank letterheads. Such information may be used to make unauthorised payments from your client account.

Do not give any form of undertaking to guarantee a financial obligation unless you have funds or equivalent security. The word of someone backed by 'an international bank' is not enough. If asked to provide money from client account on the security of another firm's undertaking, ask that firm for evidence of their ability to comply. NEVER send a client account cheque on the basis of a verbal confirmation that the money is on its way into your client account, check it's there.

If you require further information concerning investment schemes, especially those involving prime bank instrument or standby letters of credit you may contact the Fraud Intelligence Office on 0207320 5703 or Professional Ethics on 0870 606 2577.

REMEMBER if it sounds too good to be true it probably is!

Fraud Intelligence Unit telephone number is:

01926 439662

Professional Ethics:

0870 606 2577

Office for the Supervision of Solicitors:

Victoria Court,
8 Dormer Place,
Leamington Spa, Warwickshire,
CV32 5AE

© The Law Society 2004. All rights reserved.

APPENDIX 13: LAW SOCIETY MONEY LAUNDERING WARNING CARD

WARNING TO ALL SOLICITORS
MONEY LAUNDERING
Be on your guard

Your firm, whatever its size or nature of practice, could be a target for criminals wishing to launder the proceeds of their crime through legal transactions. You might commit a criminal offence if you help them by missing the warning signs.

The Proceeds of Crime Act 2002 means that if you fail to report to the National Criminal Intelligence Service you will be judged by the standard of whether a reasonable solicitor should have been suspicious in all the surrounding circumstances. Learning to spot warning signals is more important than ever before.

The criminal law and regulatory requirements are undergoing rapid change. Keep up to date by reading Law Society guidance and interim updates which can be found at www.lawsociety.org.uk.

What does this mean in practice?

You will need to ask your clients more questions. By June 2003 most solicitors will be legally required to establish the identity of most clients. Honest clients should be happy to assist. Make sure you and your colleagues receive some training about money laundering.

Know your client

- Check the identity of new clients and be wary of clients who are reluctant to provide such details.

- Where possible meet new clients in person. Be cautious about third parties introducing clients who you do not meet.

If anything about the circumstances, particularly these warning signals, give cause for concern then **ask more questions**. The answers may deal with your initial cause for concern. If they do not, then the answers may give foundation to a suspicion and you may have to consider whether or not to make a report under the legislation.

Causes for concern can include the following:

Unusual settlement requests

Anything that is unusual or unpredictable or otherwise gives cause for concern should lead you to **ask more questions** about the source of the funds. Remember, proceeds of crime can arrive through the banking system as well.

Think carefully if any of the following are proposed or occur:-

- Settlements by cash

- Surprise payments by way of third party cheque

- Money transfers where there is a variation between the account holder or the signatory

- Requests to make regular payments out of client account

- Settlements which are reached too easily

Appendix 13

Unusual instructions

- Why has the client chosen your firm? Could the client find the same service nearer their home?
- Are you being asked to do something that does not fit in with the normal pattern of your business?
- Be cautious if instructions change without a reasonable explanation
- Be cautious about transactions which take an unusual turn

Use of your client account

- Using solicitors' client accounts to transmit money is useful to money launderers
- Do not provide a banking facility if you do not undertake any related legal work
- Be cautious if you are instructed to do legal work, receive funds into your client account, but then the instructions are cancelled and you are asked to return the money either to your client or a third party

Remember you may still be assisting a money launderer even though the money does not pass through your firms bank accounts

Suspect territory

- If you are instructed in transactions with an international element you can refer to the Financial Action Task Force (www.oecd.org/fatf) who produce up to date information about different countries
- Be cautious if a client is introduced through an overseas bank or third party based in countries where the production of drugs, drug trafficking, or terrorism may be prevalent.
- Take care if funds are being routed into and out of the UK without a logical explanation

Loss making transactions

- Be alert to instructions which could lead to some financial loss to your client or a third party without a logical explanation, particularly where your client seems unconcerned
- Be cautious about confusing movements of funds between different accounts, institutions or jurisdictions without apparent reason

The better you know your client and the full details of and reasons for the transaction before accepting the retainer, and particularly before accepting funds, the less likely you are to become involved in money laundering.

What if you are suspicious?

In many situations, the law will require you to make an official disclosure to:

The National Criminal Intelligence Service
Spring Gardens
Vauxhall
London SE11 5EF
Tel: 020 7238 8282
Fax 020 7238 8286.

Appendix 13

Helpful guidance notes about money laundering are issued by:

The Joint Money Laundering Steering Group
Pinners Hall
105 –108 Old Broad Street
London,EC2N 1EX
Tel: 020 7216 8800
Fax 020 7216 8811.

Confidential advice can be obtained from:

The Professional Adviser
Professional Ethics
The Law Society
Ipsley Court
Berrington Close
Redditch, B98 OTD
DX 19114 Redditch
Tel: 0870 6062577
Fax 0207 320 5897.

Version 2 September 2002.

© The Law Society 2004. All rights reserved.

Appendix 14: The UK's Anti-Money Laundering Legislation and the Data Protection Act 1998 – Guidance Notes for the Financial Sector

GUIDANCE NOTES FOR THE FINANCIAL SECTOR
April 2002

Introduction

1 This guidance has been prepared by the Government departments that co-ordinate the UK's anti-money laundering legislation in response to concerns expressed by some banks and other financial institutions about the interaction between anti-money laundering laws and the Data Protection Act 1998 (DPA). It has been discussed with the Information Commissioner, who supports the approach taken.

2 In particular, this guidance addresses the relationship between the obligation not to 'tip off' an individual about whom a Suspicious Transaction Report (STR) has been made on the one hand, and the individual's right of access to his personal data and the corresponding obligations on financial institutions on the other.

3 Please note that this guidance has no legal status. If you are concerned about any aspect of compliance with money laundering legislation or the DPA you should seek independent legal advice.

The UK's anti-money laundering legislation

4 The UK has fulfilled its international obligations to create money laundering offences in several pieces of primary legislation – the Criminal Justice Act 1988 (as amended), the Drug Trafficking Act 1994 and the Terrorism Act 2000 (as amended). These create two different types of obligation to make STRs. In both cases, an STR can be made either to the law enforcement authorities or, where the individual works for an employer who has a Money Laundering Reporting Officer (MLRO), to the MLRO. Once a report is made to an MLRO the responsibility rests on him to decide whether to make a report to the law enforcement authorities.

5 The first obligation to make STRs is that each of the statutes listed above requires that a person must make an STR if he knows or suspects that **he or his organisation** is about to become involved in money laundering. For example, a solicitor who suspects that he is being asked to put funds into his client account in order to conceal their criminal origin would be obliged to make an STR and obtain the consent of the authorities before carrying out the transaction. If he does not make the STR and gain the consent, he will be guilty of a money laundering offence if he puts the funds into his client account. The solicitor can make the STR after putting the funds into his client account if he has a good reason for not making it before.

6 The second obligation to make STRs is that the Drug Trafficking Act and the Terrorism Act contain offences of 'failure to report'. These are committed where a person knows or suspects (or, in the case of the Terrorism Act, has reasonable grounds for knowing or suspecting) that **another person** is engaged in laundering either the proceeds of drug trafficking or terrorism related property but does not make a report to the law enforcement authorities.

Appendix 14

7 The Money Laundering Regulations 1993 oblige financial institutions to ensure that they have systems in place to make STRs to the National Criminal Intelligence Service (NCIS).

8 The Proceeds of Crime Bill will consolidate the provisions of the Drug Trafficking Act and the Criminal Justice Act so that the law on laundering the proceeds of drug trafficking and laundering the proceeds of other crime is contained in one piece of legislation. The obligation on people who become personally involved in money laundering to make STRs will not change significantly. However, the Bill extends the Drug Trafficking Act offence of failure to report another's involvement in money laundering in two respects. First, the provision is brought in line with the Terrorism Act so that a person must make an STR if he has 'reasonable grounds to believe' that another person is engaged in money laundering. Second, the obligation to make an STR will no longer be restricted to the situation where another person is laundering the proceeds of drug trafficking, but will be extended to the laundering of the proceeds of any crime. In order to take account of these extensions, the failure to report offence is now limited to people who come across the information about money laundering in the course of conducting business in the 'regulated sector'. 'Regulated sector' is defined in Schedule 6 to the Bill. Broadly, it currently encompasses every institution that is obliged to comply with the Money Laundering Regulations.

9 The Proceeds of Crime Bill will replace the money laundering provisions in the Criminal Justice Act and the Drug Trafficking Act. However, the Terrorism Act will continue to regulate the laundering of funds for terrorist purposes.

'Tipping Off'

10 In order to prevent individuals from warning those about whom they have made an STR, the money laundering legislation also criminalizes 'tipping off'. Where a person knows or suspects that an STR has been made to the law enforcement authorities, it is an offence for him to make any disclosure which is likely to prejudice any investigation which might be conducted following the making of the STR. The most obvious example of a disclosure likely to prejudice an investigation is letting an individual know that the authorities are interested in him so that he has time to destroy evidence.

11 No offence is committed where disclosure of an STR would not be likely to prejudice an investigation. For example, where the existence and contents of an STR have been revealed in the course of criminal proceedings, it is unlikely that any prejudice would be caused by the subsequent disclosure of the STR to the individual concerned. Similarly, in the case of an STR made many years ago and in relation to which the file has long since closed, it seems unlikely that any prejudice would be caused by disclosing the STR.

12 In cases where financial institutions are concerned about how to avoid arousing suspicion in a customer that one of their transactions is being investigated, they should contact NCIS for advice on how to deal with that customer.

The Data Protection Act

13 Under section 7 of the DPA, on making a request in writing to a data controller (ie any organisation which holds personal data), an individual is entitled:

- to be informed whether the data controller is processing (which includes merely holding) his personal data; and if so

- to be given a description of those data, the purposes for which they are being processed and to whom they are or may be disclosed; and

- to have communicated to him in an intelligible form all the information which constitutes his personal data and any information available to the data controller as to the source of those data.

14 Such a request is known as a Subject Access Request. Data controllers must respond to Subject Access Requests promptly, and in any case within 40 days. The 40 days begin from when the data controller has received the request, any further information he may need to identify the applicant and locate the personal data sought, and, if he charges one, the fee (of up to £10 maximum).

15 Data controllers may withhold information identifying another individual, for example information identifying a bank teller as the source of the data, unless that individual has

Appendix 14

consented to the disclosure or it is reasonable in all the circumstances to disclose the information without their consent (see sections 7(4) to 7(6) of the DPA).

16 The DPA provides certain exemptions to the right of subject access, of which section 29 is the most relevant in the present context. This provides that personal data are exempt from section 7 in any case to the extent to which the application of that provision would be likely to prejudice the prevention or detection of crime or the apprehension or prosecution of offenders.

17 Even when relying on an exemption data controllers should provide as much information as they can in response to a Subject Access Request.

Section 7 and Tipping Off

18 Concerns have been raised as to the interrelation of the tipping off provisions and section 7 of the DPA.

19 The starting point is the similar language used in the tipping off offence (disclosure would be likely to prejudice any investigation which might be conducted following the making of the STR) and the DPA section 29 exemption (disclosure would be likely to prejudice the prevention or detection of crime or the apprehension or prosecution of offenders). In summary, where disclosure of a particular STR would constitute a tipping off offence, the section 29 exemption will apply, and where disclosure of an STR would not constitute a tipping off offence, the section 29 exemption will not be available in respect of the money laundering element. However it must be emphasised that each request for information must be considered on its merits, as explained in more detail below.

How to deal with a Subject Access Request

20 To take an example, Mr X deposits £500,000 in cash into his bank account and immediately transfers it to an offshore account. The bank is suspicious that this may represent money laundering and so sends an STR to NCIS. NCIS pass the STR to a police force and await further information.

21 Mr X then makes a Subject Access Request to the bank under section 7 of the DPA. The bank is now caught in a seemingly difficult position – should they disclose the STR to Mr X and risk committing the tipping off offence, or should they withhold it, and risk breaching the DPA?

22 It is impossible to lay down any general rules as to how to deal with a subject access request, as the requirements of section 7 DPA and the application of section 29 DPA must be considered on a case-by-case basis. It should never be assumed that the section 29 exemption applies automatically to STRs. Each time a Subject Access Request is received, the institution concerned must carefully consider whether, in that particular case, disclosure of the STR would be likely to prejudice the prevention or detection of crime.

23 In determining whether the section 29 exemption applies, it is legitimate to take account of the particular way in which financial crime is investigated. The detection of money laundering often depends on fitting together a number of separate pieces of information. Thus even though a particular piece of information (eg an individual STR) does not show clear evidence of criminal conduct when viewed in isolation, it might ultimately form part of the jigsaw which enables law enforcement agencies to detect crime.

24 Where a financial institution is in doubt as to whether disclosure would be likely to prejudice an investigation or potential investigation, it should approach NCIS for guidance. Institutions should bear in mind the requirement to respond promptly to a Subject Access Request and in any event within 40 days and ensure that they approach NCIS in good time.

25 It should be noted that, where an institution withholds a piece of information in reliance on the DPA section 29 exemption, it is not obliged to tell the individual that any information has been withheld. It can simply leave out that piece of information and make no reference to it when responding to the individual who has made the request.

26 Data controllers may wish to keep a record of the steps they have taken in determining whether disclosure of an STR would involve 'tipping off' and/or the availability of the section 29 exemption. This might be useful in the event of the data controller having to respond to enquiries made subsequently by the Information Commissioner or the courts.

Appendix 14

Internal reports

27 When a bank clerk makes an STR to his Money Laundering Reporting Officer (MLRO) but the MLRO has not passed on an STR to NCIS, the principles outlined above also apply. While this particular STR may not have raised enough suspicion for the MLRO to deem it worth passing to NCIS, the internal STR may be the basis for establishing a pattern of future transactions that arouse suspicion. Therefore when dealing with a Subject Access Request the same considerations apply as set out above.

28 If the institution considers that disclosure of an STR made by a bank clerk would be likely to prejudice the prevention or detection of crime, even if the STR has not been passed to NCIS, then section 29 may be relied on to withhold that information.

Summary

29 Section 29 does not provide a blanket exemption to subject access obligations for STRs; each request for information must be considered on its merits. Institutions must consider whether, in the particular case, disclosure of the STR would be likely to prejudice the prevention or detection of crime.

- Where telling an individual that an STR relating to him has been made would constitute a 'tipping off' offence, that information can be withheld in reliance on section 29 of the DPA. This applies even where the STR has not been passed to NCIS.

- Where disclosure of an STR would not constitute a 'tipping off' offence the section 29 exemption will not be available in respect of the money laundering element.

Comments

30 The Government will review this guidance within the next three years.

If you have any questions or comments, please contact:

The Financial Crime Branch,
HM Treasury,
Allington Towers,
19 Allington Street,
London,
SW1E 5EB

NB from August 2002:

The Financial Crime Branch,
HM Treasury,
1 Horse Guards Road,
London,
SW1A 2HQ

© Crown Copyright 2002.

INDEX

Tables are denoted by page numbers appearing in italic print

Please note the following abbreviations:

DPA 1998	Data Protection Act 1998
FATF	Financial Action Task Force
MLR 2003	Money Laundering Regulations 2003
MLRO	money laundering reporting officer
NCIS	National Criminal Intelligence Service
PACE 1984	Police and Criminal Evidence Act 1984
POCA 2002	Proceeds of Crime Act 2002
TA 2000	Terrorism Act 2000

acquisition, use and possession offence
   POCA 2002 (s329)
      dangers to avoid   128
      knowledge   32
      and 'reasonable excuse' defence   30
      report completion   48
advance fee fraud
   West Africa   143-144
agents
   identification procedures   66
   instructions from
      as warning sign   99
Ainsworth, Bob   187
'all crimes' policy
   money laundering legislation   21, 32-33
ancillary relief proceedings
   other legal work contrasted   128
anti-money laundering framework (UK)
   background   11
   enforcement   15
   European Directives, and   13
   FATF
      40 recommendations   12-13
   future developments   15
   guidance   14-15
   international role of UK   11-12
   investigation   15
   legislation   14

Anti-terrorism, Crime and Security Act 2001
   substantive law   24
areas of suspicion
   conveyancing transactions   98
   holding money   99
   instruction changes   100
   instructions from nominees/agents   99
   litigation   99
      settlements   100
   mistaken transfers   100
   money transfers   99
   suspect territory   100
   transaction circumstances, changes   100
arrangements offence
   POCA 2002 (s328)
      dangers to avoid   128
      knowledge   32
      and 'reasonable excuse' defence   30
      report completion   48
***Assessment of Threat of Money Laundering in the UK* report**
   NCIS   15
Asset Recovery Agency
   confiscation proceedings   160-161
   tipping off offence   26
assistance offence
   description   18

Index

atypical instructions		identification	*see* **identification procedures**
as warning sign	98		
		individual	
back-to-back transactions		identification documents	68-69
mortgage fraud	100	information to	
Bank of England Sanctions Unit	140	and *P v P* case	111
banking instrument fraud		new	
case study	102-104	compliance measures	56
LS Guidance	19	identification procedures	64
banking services		overseas	138-139
listed	148	return of money by	
Bishopsgate bomb, London (1993)	32	claims for	153
		secretive	97
C v S & ors		Commission	*see* **European Commission**
case study	111-113	**communication**	
case studies		insurers and brokers	165-166
C v S & ors	111-113	risk-based approach	181-182
corporate offences	104-105	**Companies House**	3
Governor & Company of the Bank of		**Compensation Recovery Unit**	49
Scotland v A Ltd & Others	113-114	**compliance measures**	
international issues	137-138	client engagement process	57-58
mortgage fraud	101-102	failure to comply	
negligence claims	154-153	penalties	52
P v P		general considerations	53
client, informing	111	internal reporting procedures	58
decision	107-108	know your customer	54-56
LS Guidance	108-110	Law Society	
NCIS guidance	108, 109	'Golden Rules'	53, 54
personal injury litigation	120	LS Guidance	52-53
privilege/matrimonial	110-111,	monitoring	59-60
matters	118, 128	new clients	56
relevant business	37	partners	
terms of engagement	158	annual report to	61
tipping off	26, 109	'procedures of internal control'	52
prime bank instrument		record keeping	58
fraud	102-103	MLR 2003	1, 51, 52
privilege		risk-based approach	53-54, 183
facts	130-131	sampling	60
issues	131-132	systems and procedures	51-52
Tayeb v HSBC Bank Plc & anr	115-116	training	58
cash settlements		**concealing offence**	
as warning sign	97	POCA 2002 (s327)	
cash smuggling		dangers to avoid	128, 129
and PATRIOT Act (US)	142	knowledge	32
client accounts		and 'reasonable excuse'	
cash paid into		defence	30
as warning sign	97-98	report completion	48
clients		**confidentiality**	
disadvantaged	78	defined	122
engagement process	57-58	statutory provisions	149

263

Index

confiscation proceedings
  terms of engagement, restricting
    liability through   160-161
  tipping off offence   26
consent
  defence
    POCA 2003 (s338)   28-29, 43
    NCIS, obtained from   28, 49, 153, 153
consideration
  adequate
    POCA 2002 defence (s329)   31
constructive trusts   151-154
  and CHAPS transfers   116
  dishonest assistance   29, 153-154
  knowing receipt   152
  liability under
    disclosure   29
Consultative Committee of Accountancy Bodies
  client engagement process   57
  disclosure recommendations   48
conveyancing transactions
  areas of suspicion   98
corporate offences
  case study   104-105
  international issues   143
costs
  insurance   169
Council of Licensed Conveyancers
  guidance issued by   142
Council of Mortgage Lenders' Handbook
  identification evidence   67
  risk management   174
criminal conduct
  defined   27, 139
  UK, no offence in   32
criminal law   119
criminal property
  defined   27
  UK, no defence in   31
Crown Prosecution Service guidance
  adequate consideration defence   31
Customs returns
  guidance   33

Data Protection Act 1998   *see* **DPA 1998**
defences
  adequate consideration
    POCA 2003 (s329)   31

consent
  POCA 2003 (s338)   28-29, 43
  lack of knowledge/suspicion   28
  professional legal adviser   32
  'reasonable excuse'   30, 127, 184-185
  training, lack of
    POCA 2002 (s330)   31
  UK, no offence in
    POCA 2002 (s340)   31-32
definitions
  circumstances   162
  claim   162
  confidentiality   122
  criminal conduct   27, 139
  criminal property   27
  legal advice privilege   123
  litigation privilege   124
  money laundering   7
    and drug trafficking   11-12
  international   8-9
  new clients   64
  privilege   122-123
  relevant business   35, 147, 148
  satisfactory evidence of identity   66
  serious offences   13
delay
  loss of transactions caused by   153
Directives, European
  Banking Consolidation   148
  First Money Laundering (1991)   13
  Second Money Laundering (2001)   13
  Third Money Laundering
    (under discussion)   13
  relevant business   36
disclosures
  authorised   125-126
  completing report   48-49
  Economic Crime Unit   42-43
  importance   43-44
  MLRO, by   43, 44
  MLRO, to   82-83
  NCIS
    made to   29, 42
    role   41
    sending report to   49-50
  POCA 2002
    failure to disclose (s331)   31, 45
    form and manner of
      disclosure (s339)   45-46
    reporting offence disclosures (s331)   45

Index

prioritising by NCIS 42
protected 125
  MLR 2003 44
reporting forms
  limited intelligence value
    report 33, 46-47
  standard disclosure 47-48
  risk-based approach 181
solicitors, by
  authorised 125-126
  protected 125
dishonest assistance
  constructive trusts 29, 153-154
documents
  identification procedures 67-68
  risk management 175-177
  Source Registration 46, 48
    see also **reporting**
DPA (Data Protection Act) 1998
  and disclosures 85-86
drug trafficking
  legislation 11, 20
due diligence
  European Directives 13

ECBDutyDesk@ncis.co.uk
  disclosure guidance 48
Economic Crime Branch (NCIS)
  disclosure 42-43
  role 15
employees
  training requirements 92-94
enforcement
  risk-based approach 182-183
European Commission
  FATF membership 8
evidence (identification procedures)
  obtained when 66
  requirements 66-67

failure to report offence
  and failure to disclose 31, 45
  general description 19
  POCA 2002 (ss330-332) 25-26
  'reasonable excuse'
    defence 30, 127, 184-185
FATF (Financial Action Task Force)
  establishment 8, 12
  40 recommendations
    background 12-13

European Directives 13
  identification checks, international 140
  updating 14
membership 8
website 9, 179
Financial Action Task Force *see* **FATF**
financial loss, instructions leading to
  as warning sign 98
Financial Services Authority *see* **FSA**
Financial Services and
Markets Act 2000 *see* **FSMA 2000**
financial transaction
  legal services involving
    participation in 35-39
    Treasury view 37
  personal injury practitioners 36, 38-39
  relevant business 36
  risk-based approach 37
firm's practice, changes in 145-146
First Money Laundering Directive
(1991) 13
40 recommendations
(FATF) *see* **FATF: 40 recommendations**
419s
  international issues 143-144
fraud
  advance fee ('419') 143-144
  banking instrument 19
    and knowing receipt 152
  mortgage 100-102
  prime bank instrument 102-104
Fraud Advisory Panel
  on identity theft 3
FSA (Financial Services Authority)
  compliance measures 52
  Handbook 14
  identification documents 68
  regulation by 1
  risk-based approach 175
FSMA (Financial Services and Markets
Act) 2000
  identification evidence 76
funds, payment of
  terms of engagement, restricting liability
  through 159-160

G7 countries
  drug trafficking measures 11
  Paris summit
    FATF, establishment 8, 12

Index

Governor & Company of the Bank of Scotland v A Ltd & ors		personal attendance impossible	78-79
		PO Box numbers, use in checks	141
case law	113-114	record keeping	88
'Green Card'		regulated sector	
property fraud		instructions and referrals from	75-77
Law Society warnings	19, 101	MLR 2003	63
guidance		'satisfactory evidence of identity'	66
anti-money laundering		transitional provisions	
framework (UK)	14-15	existing clients	77-78
Joint Money Laundering		€15,000 limit	64-65, 177
Steering Group	14-15	**identity theft**	
Law Society	*see* **LS Guidance**	fraud, dangers of	3-4
and legislation records	17	**Income and Corporation Taxes**	
Guide to Professional Conduct		**Act 1988**	*see* **ICTA 1988**
Law Society	157	**instructions**	
Gulf Co-operation Council		changes in	
FATF membership	8	as warning sign	100
		insurance	
Hansard procedure		brokers, notification to	165
tax evasion cases	47	'circumstances'	
holding money		defined	162
areas of suspicion	99	'claim'	
		defined	162
ICTA (Income and Corporation		communication with insurers	
Taxes Act) 1988		and brokers	165-166
corporate offences	143	costs	169
identification procedures		insurers	
agents	66	cooperation with	168
clients		notification to	163-165
disadvantaged	78	requirements of	166-168
existing, transitional provisions	77-78	and risk-based approach	186
individual	68-69	notification to insurers	163-165
'new'	64	insurers' requirements	166-168
commercial providers of client		policies	
identification	79	'claims made' basis	163
documents	67-68	policy requirements	161-163
evidence		professional indemnity claims	163
documentary	67-68	**insurers**	
obtained when	66	co-operation with	168
requirements	66-67	notification to	163-165
exceptions		requirements of	166-168
regulated sector	75-77	and risk-based approach	186
transitional provisions,		**integration phase (money laundering)**	9
existing clients	77-78	example	10
individual clients	68-69	**international issues**	
international issues	139-142	case study	137-138
'new clients'		corporate offences	143
defined	64	domestic firms, relevance to	137
nominees	66	firms with overseas offices	142
one-off transactions	64-65	419s	143-144

foreign lawyers, instructions from	139	suspicious activities	97
identification checks	139-142	transactions	178-180
overseas clients	138-139	on personal injury work	39
POCA 2002	138	Professional Ethics Line	50
US PATRIOT Act	142-143	on relevant business	37

investigations
- confiscation   26
- money laundering regime (1993-Feb 2003)   17
- MLRO   17, 20

JMLSG (Joint Money Laundering Steering Group)
- changes in firm practice advice   146
- formation   14
- guidance notes   14-15, 19
- know your client (KYC) guidance   55-56
- risk-based approach   175
- solicitors with employers in regulated sector   149
- specimen certificate produced by   77

Know Your Client   *see* **KYC**

knowing receipt
- constructive trusts   152

knowledge
- actual   32
- constructive   32

knowledge or suspicion, lack of
- defence   28

KYC (know your client)
- compliance measures   54-56
- general ambit   2-3

large firms
- and MLROs   82

Law Society
- case studies
  - *P v P*   108-110
- on consent issues   29
- current money laundering regime   22-24
- England and Wales   4
- 'Golden Rules'   53, 54
- guidance issued by   *see* **LS Guidance**
- Guide to Professional Conduct   157
- Minimum Terms and Conditions   145, 161, 162, 169
- Money Laundering Warning Card   21
- 'new clients'   64

- on risk-based approach   65
- as supervisory authority   52-53

layering phase (money laundering)   9
- example   10

legal advice privilege
- definition and case study   123-124

legal profession
- ancillary work   128
- changes in   3-5
- criminal work   119
- matrimonial law   118-119
- money laundering regime (2003-2004)   21-22
- personal injury law and similar litigation   120
- property law   117-118

    see also **solicitors**

legal professional privilege
- case law   110, 131
- erosion
  - case studies   4
- 'items subject to'   122-123
- risk-based approach   186

    see also **privilege**

Legal Risk
- training survey   92

Legal Services Commission
- compliance, auditing for   183

legislation, money laundering
- aim   10
- 'all crimes' policy   21, 32-33
- definition of money laundering   7
- money laundering regime (1993-Feb 2003)   17-19
- new   1

    see also **MLR 2003; POCA 2002; TA 2000**

liability
- civil
  - know your client   54-55
  - constructive trusts   151-154
    - dishonest assistance   153-154
    - knowing receipt   152
  - limiting through terms of engagement   156-161
  - confiscation proceedings   160-161

Index

funds, payment of	159-160
mediations	160
practical issues	158-159
professional conduct rules, restrictions imposed by	157
right to cease acting	160
Solicitors Act 1974 (s60)	157-158
Unfair Contract Terms Act 1977	157
negligence claims	
case studies	154-153
potential	
key areas	151
return of money by clients	
claims for	153
risk-based approach	156
limited intelligence value report	
disclosures	46-47
NCIS guidance note	33
litigation	
areas of suspicion	99
settlements	100
litigation privilege	
definition	124
flowchart	*133-134*
LLPs (limited liability partnerships)	
and identification procedures	77
status 3, 78	
London, Bishopsgate bomb in (1993)	32
LS Guidance (Money Laundering Guidance (Pilot - January 2004))	
advance fee fraud	144
availability	4
banking instrument fraud	19
compliance measures	52-53
risk-based approach	53-54
and consent defence	29
constructive trusteeship	151
costs 169	
criminal work	119
disclosures	181
report completion	48-49
dishonest assistance	153
feedback on	23
foreign lawyers	
instructions from	139
identification evidence	66, 67, 68, 77, 79
international issues	139, 141
table	*70-74*
insurers and brokers	
communication with	165

and JMLSG guidance	15
legal services	
involving participation in financial transaction	36
matrimonial law	119
MLRO	
choice of person	81
disclosures to	83
money laundering regime (1993-Feb 2003)	18, 19, 20
money laundering regime (Feb 2003-2004)	21
NCIS, report sent to	49
offences	25
'reasonable excuse' defence	30, 127, 184-185
P v P case	109
phases of money laundering	10
prime bank instrument fraud	102
privilege	129
property fraud	19
'reasonable excuse' defence	184-185
record keeping	88
relevant business	36
risk management	172
solicitors with employers in regulated sector	149
suspicious activities	97
training requirement	91, 92
method	94
relevant employees	93
see also **Law Society**	
matrimonial law	118-119
P v P case study	110-111, 118
mediations	
terms of engagement, restricting liability through	160
mistaken transfers	
areas of suspicion	100
MLR (Money Laundering Regulations) 1993	
and MLR 2003	19
guidance (1993-Feb 2003)	18
MLRO, requirement to appoint	19
MLR (Money Laundering Regulations) 2003	
and 1993 Regulations	19
compliance requirements	36, 51, 52

Index

current money laundering regime	22	solicitor's employer	
definition of money laundering	7	nominating	149
disclosures	44	suspicious transaction reports	
effect on anti-money laundering		duty to send to NCIS	43
strategy	17	**money laundering**	
effective from	2	drug trafficking, and	11-12
general requirements	1, 51	general definition	7
identification procedures	63, 66	international definitions	8-9
internal reporting procedures	58	legislative definition	7
legislation, backing up	14	phases	9
MLRO		examples	10

Money Laundering Guidance
(Pilot – January 2004)   *see* **LS Guidance**

appointment	81	**money laundering regime**	
disclosures to	83	**(1993-Feb 2003)**	
internal reporting framework	83	development of legislation	18-19
one-off transactions	65	guidance	17
penalties for failure to comply with	52, 87	investigations	17
personal injury work	38	offences	18-19
records	58, 87	records of legislation	17
regulated sector, widening of scope	14	regulations	19
substantive law	24-25	**money laundering regime (2003-2004)**	
training requirements	58, 91	LS Guidance	21

see also **LS Guidance**

MLRO (money laundering
reporting officer)

appointment of nominated officer as	81	legal profession, position	21-22
choice of person	81-82	POCA 2002	20-21

see also **POCA 2002**

Money Laundering
Regulations 2003   *see* **MLR 2003**

compliance monitoring	59-60		
consent given by	28		
disclosures by	43, 44	**money laundering reporting**	
disclosures to	82-83	**officer**	*see* **MLRO**
and documentation	175	**Money Laundering Warning Card**	
DPA 1998	85-86	**(Law Society)**	21
identity	182	'new clients'	64
internal reporting		suspicious activities	97
framework for	83-85	**money transfers**	
investigation powers	17, 20	areas of suspicion	99
large firms	82	**monitoring**	
and negligence claims		compliance measures	59-60
case studies	154	**mortgage fraud**	
privilege and confidentiality		case study	100-102
issues	121-122		
production orders	20		
record keeping by	17	**National Criminal Intelligence**	
reports, disclosure		**Service**	*see* **NCIS**
completing	48	**NCCTs (non-co-operative countries**	
requirement to appoint	19	**and territories)**	
risk assessment	172	FATF list	140
risk-based approach	182	**NCIS (National Criminal Intelligence**	
role	1-2, 19-20	**Service)**	
seniority	182		
sole practitioners, and	82	on advance fee fraud	144

269

Index

Assessment of Threat of Money Laundering in the UK report	15
as clearing house	42
consent obtained from	28, 49, 153, 153
disclosures made to	29, 42
reports	49-50, 84
Economic Crime Branch	15, 42-43
establishment, purpose of	41
funding	15
on identity theft	3
limited intelligence value reports guidance note	33
and negligence claims case studies	154
P v P case guidance	108, 109
role	7-8, 15
disclosure	41
United Kingdom Threat Assessment of Serious and Organised Crime 2003 report	8, 41
website	45-46
negligence claims	
case studies	154-153
'Nelsonian blindness'	
and knowing receipt	152
nominated officer	*see* **MLRO**
nominees	
identification procedures	66
instructions from as warning sign	99
non-co-operative countries and territories	*see* **NCCTs**
Northern Ireland	
Law Society of	4-5
OECD (Organisation for Economic Co-operation and Development)	
FATF, secretariat housed by	8
offences, money laundering	
assistance	18
corporate	104-105
international issues	143
failure to report description	19
POCA 2002 (ss330-332)	25-26
LS Guidance	25
POCA 2002 acquisition, use and possession (s329)	30, 32, 128

arrangements (s328)	30, 32, 48, 128
concealing (s327)	30, 32, 48, 128, 129
failing to report (ss330-332)	25-26
principal (ss327-329)	25, 117
tipping off (ss333 and 342)	26-27
principal	
POCA 2002 (ss327-329)	25
property law	117
TA 2000 (ss15-18)	25
tipping off	
description	18
P v P case	26, 109-110
POCA 2002 (ss333 and 342)	26-27
widening of scope (POCA 2002)	21, 24
one-off transactions	
identification procedures	64-65
Organisation for Economic Co-operation and Development	*see* **OECD**
***P v P* case study**	
client, informing	111
decision	107-108
LS Guidance	108-110
NCIS guidance	108, 109
personal injury litigation	120
privilege/matrimonial matters	110-111, 118, 128
relevant business	37
terms of engagement	158
tipping off	26, 109-110
PACE (Police and Criminal Evidence Act) 1984	
case law	112
legal advice privilege	123
privilege defined	122-123
legal advice	123
litigation	124
Paris summit	
FATF, establishment	8, 12
partners	
annual report to	61
PATRIOT Act	
United States	142-143
pdf (Portable Document Format)	48
penalties	
POCA 2002 stated in (s334)	28

270

Index

tipping off 26
regulations, failure to comply with 52, 87
PEPs (politically exposed persons) 140
personal injury
  Compensation Recovery Unit,
    on claims 49
  financial transactions' 36, 38-39
  law 120
placement phase (money laundering) 9
  example 10
PO Box numbers
  use in identity checks 141
POCA (Proceeds of Crime Act) 2002
  assets, seizure of
    funding for NCIS 15
  confidentiality override provisions 149
  consent to act required by 28-29, 43
  constructive trusts 151
  criminal conduct
    defined 27
  criminal property
    defined 27
  defences
    adequate consideration (s329) 31
    consent (s338) 28-29, 43
    professional legal adviser 32
    training, lack of (s330) 31
    UK, no offence in (s340) 31-32
  definition of money laundering
    (s340) 7
  disclosures
    authorised 125
    failure to disclose (s331) 31, 45
    form and manner (s339) 45-46
    importance (ss327-329) 43
    protected 125
    reporting offence
      disclosures (s331) 45
  effect on anti-money laundering
    strategy 17
  effective from 2, 20
  general requirements 1
  international case 138
  knowledge (ss327-329) 32
  money laundering regime
    (Feb 2003-2004) 20-21
  offences
    acquisition, use and
      possession (s329) 30, 32, 128
    arrangements (s328) 30, 32, 48, 128

    concealing (s327) 30, 32, 48, 128, 129
    failing to report
      (ss330-332) 25-26, 30, 31
    limited intelligence value
      report form, and 46
    LS Guidance 25
    principal (ss327-329) 25, 117
    tipping off (ss333 and 342) 26-27
    widening of scope 21, 24
  penalties (s334) 28
  relevant business
    defined 35
  risk assessment 173
  Royal Assent 20
  substantive law
    money laundering offences 22, 24
Police and Criminal Evidence
Act 1984 *see* **PACE 1984**
politically exposed persons *see* **PEPs**
privilege
  and dangers to avoid 128-129
  definition 122-123
  legal advice 123-124
  legal professional
    erosion (case studies) 4
  litigation 124
  MLRO, areas of concern for 121-122
  non-existent 124-125
  P v P case 110-111
  risk-based approach 185-186
  rules
    definition 122-123
    legal advice 123-124
    litigation 124
    non-existent privilege 124-125
'procedures of internal control'
  compliance measures 52
Proceeds of Crime Act
2002 *see* **POCA 2002**
professional conduct rules
  restrictions imposed by 157
Professional Ethics Line
  Law Society 50
professional indemnity claims 163
professional legal adviser
  defence 32
property fraud
  Green Card 19, 101
  LS Guidance 19
property law 117-118

Index

record keeping
  compliance measures 58
  identification procedures 88
  MLRO, by 17
  Regulations 58, 87
  retention of records 88-89
  risk-based approach 184
regulated sector
  employers of solicitors in 149
  instructions and referrals from 75-77
  nominated officers
    failure to disclose offence
      (POCA 2002, s331) 45
  relevant business
    defined 35, 147-148
  widening of scope 14, 21, 36
relevant business
  categorisation difficulties 37-38
  compliance measures 183
  definition 35, 147, 148
  failure to comply 52
  financial transaction
    legal services involving
      participation in 35-39
  widening scope of
    Regulations 2003 24
reporting
  forms
    limited intelligence value
      report 33, 46-47
    standard disclosure report 47-48
  internal procedures 58
  partners
    annual report to 61
  risk-based approach 186-187
    see also **documents;**
    suspicious transaction reports
risk-based approach
  communication 181-182
  compliance measures 53-54, 183
  decision making 187
  disclosures 181
  documentation 175-177
  enforcement 182-183
  general points 171-172
  identification procedures 65
  insurers, involvement of 186
  know your client (KYC) 54
  limitation of risk 156
  MLRO

    identity/seniority 182
  personal attendance impossible, where 78
  policies 173-175
  privilege 185-186
  'reasonable excuse'
    defence 30, 127, 184-185
  record keeping 184
  regulations, compliance with 36
  relevant business
    Law Society recommendations 37
  reporting obligations 186-187
  risk assessment 172-173
  systems 173-175
    application 177-178
  training 181
  transactions 178-180
sampling
  compliance measures 60
Sarbanes-Oxley Act
  reporting obligations 187
Scotland
  Law Society of 4-5
Second Money Laundering
  Directive (2001) 13
secretive client
  as warning sign 97
'serious offences'
  definition 13
settlement requests
  unusual, as warning sign 97
sole traders
  and MLROs 82
solicitors
  changes affecting client
    need for knowledge of 2-3
  dangers to avoid 128
  disclosures by
    authorised 125-126
    protected 125
  disclosures not made by
    protection 126-128
  employed outside private practice
    application 147
    confidentiality issues 149
    employees in regulated sector 148
    MLROs 148
    regulated sector 147-149
  foreign
    instructions from 139

Index

MLRO
   requirement to appoint   19
   non-relevant business   36
         see also **criminal law;**
      legal profession; matrimonial law;
      personal injury law; property law
Solicitors Act 1974
   terms of engagement
      limiting liability through (s60)   157-158
Solicitors Indemnity Fund
   insurance claims   164
Solicitors' Indemnity Insurance Rules
   professional conduct, restrictions
      imposed by   157
Source Registration Document   46, 48
   standard disclosure report form
      contents   47-48
sub-sale
   mortgage fraud   100
surprise payments
   as warning sign   98
suspicious transaction reports
   Economic Crime Branch (NCIS)
      analysis by   15, 42
   MLRO, responsibility to send
      to NCIS   43
systems
   compliance measures   51-52
   training   95

TA (Terrorism Act) 2000
   confidentiality override provisions   149
   definition of money laundering, and   7
   and limited intelligence value report   46
   principal offences   2, 25
   and solicitors employed outside
      private practice   147
   substantive law   24
tax evasion cases
   standard reports   47
Tayeb v HSBC Bank Plc & anr
   case study   115-116
terms of engagement
   client engagement process   57
   limiting liability through   156-161
      confiscation proceedings   160-161
      funds, payment of   159-160
      mediations   160
      professional conduct rules,
         restrictions imposed by   157

      right to cease acting   160
      Solicitors' Act 1974 (s60)   157-158
      Unfair Contract Terms Act 1977   157
   other   161
territory
   suspect
      areas of suspicion   100
Terrorism Act 2000   *see* **TA 2000**
Third Money Laundering Directive
   (under discussion)   13
third parties
   and warning signs   98
tipping off offence
   case studies   26, 109-110, 114
   general description   18
   POCA 2002 (ss333 and 342)   26-27
training
   compliance measures   58
   lack of
      as defence   31
   method   94
   MLRO, reporting to   84
   proof   94-95
   regulations   58, 91
   relevant employees   92-94
   requirement for   91-92
   risk-based approach   181
   systems   95
transactions
   back to back
      mortgage fraud   100
   circumstances, changes in
      areas of suspicion   100
   financial
      legal services involving
         participation in   35-39
      meaning   36
   loss of
      delay resulting in   153
   one-off
      identification procedures   64-65
   risk-based approach   178-180
   sub-sale
      mortgage fraud   100

Unfair Contract Terms Act 1977
   terms of engagement   58
      limiting liability through   157
United Kingdom
   all crimes policy

Index

money laundering legislation	32
no offence in	
criminal property, defined	31-32

United Kingdom Threat Assessment of Serious and Organised Crime 2003 (NCIS report)

general contents	8
property law	117
risk assessment	172
and role of NCIS	41

United States

PATRIOT Act	142-143

VAT returns

guidance	33

Vienna Convention (1988)

drug trafficking regulation	11

warning signs

areas of suspicion	98-100
case studies	
corporate offences	104-105
mortgage fraud	100-102
prime bank instrument fraud	102-104
guidance	97-98
mortgage fraud	100-102
prime bank instrument fraud	102-104

West Africa

organised crime in	143-144

Whittaker, Andrew M. 176

Zurich Professional

insurance policy wording	162